COMPANION INTO BERKSHIRE

By R. P. BECKINSALE, D.Phil.

WITH TWENTY-TWO PLATES
AND ENDPAPER MAP

SPURBOOKS LIMITED

First published by Methuen & Co. Ltd.

This edition, with revised photographs and endpaper map, by
SPURBOOKS LIMITED,
88 Blind Lane, Bourne End, Bucks,
1972.

Reprinted offset litho by
Biddles Ltd., Guildford, Surrey.

INES

COMPANION INTO BERKSHIRE

The Companion Books

BUCKINGHAMSHIRE	LAKELAND
DERBYSHIRE	OXFORDSHIRE
DORSET	SOMERSET
DURHAM	SUFFOLK
ESSEX	SURREY
GLOUCESTERSHIRE	SUSSEX
HAMPSHIRE	TWEED
KENT	WORCESTERSHIRE

The White Horse, Uffington Castle and the Manger

TO

MONICA, ROBERT DOVER, *and*
MARY ANN,

WHOSE GUSTO AND TOLERANCE
ARE UNLIMITED

PREFACE

THE chronicles of Berkshire, as Vincent says, 'are not small beer but good and delicate wine of many vintages', and those who know the county become connoisseurs of little things and of subtle shades of difference. In the north the variety of landscapes ranges from the narrow ridge of sands and coral limestone near Oxford to the wide flat Vale of White Horse and the rolling chalk hills of the Lambourn Downs. Southward the Kennet valley and chalk bastions of Inkpen Beacon are distinct enough, but over a vast tract of wooded country the patchwork of gravels, sands and clays causes bewildering and fascinating local variations in life and landscape. On its eastern edge Berkshire ends in a blaze of glory where, sharing the Thames with many neighbours, it keeps Windsor as its own.

The county, however, may be divided by means other than scenery. There is a rural Berkshire and an urban Berkshire distinct in word, thought and deed; although the strong rural independence which I knew in my youth—the contentment with *the* village and the pursuit of village crafts—has weakened before the call of the town. But the loss of local craftsmen is partly offset by the presence of those town-workers who seek country homes, bringing with them new brooms which sweep pleasantly clean.

This condition, common enough elsewhere in Britain, should not hide the existence of a deeper problem. Modern Berkshire seems to be falling fast into two halves—that which bows down and worships the metropolis, and that which retains its old allegiance to the upper Thames. The tentacles of the great wen reach out farther yearly but still weaken beyond the Thames' gap at Streatley and Pangbourne. Reading, the county capital, sits astride the danger zone and does not forget that while London encroaches on the south, Oxford expands on to the north where those once-delightful hills overlook the mob-encumbered streets of the university city.

In the following chapters no more is attempted than to portray those parts of Berkshire which we, as a family, have long found of interest. The book, in fact, describes where we like to go and what we tell the friends who tolerate us. In addition to the usual topographical matter, we have especially endeavoured to recall the literary connexions of the county, and to discuss, in a simple way, the site and growth of towns. In this matter, although ourselves preferring to see the sunset against a skyline of trees and fields we feel that each citizen should know the site and shape of his city as clearly as the shepherd knows the undulations of his hills. Surely a knowledge of the evolution of his town is essential to a citizen's appreciation of his birthright?

It would, of course, be idle to pretend that all is perfect in Berkshire. It has changed much—and not always for the better—since for Sunday School treats we went by wagonette to the White Horse and having fought for a seat on that quadruped's eye, filled ourselves with tea and bun and slid like avalanches down the Manger. Much of the change is understandable and universal but what cannot be forgiven is indifference to natural and architectural beauty. Many villages in Berkshire—even to their churchyards—are a delight to the eye, but a few have yet to learn that if each man swept before his doorstep the street would be clean. We, rightly or wrongly, must confess to an especial liking for buildings and villages garnished with a pride of ownership.

It is a pleasure to thank the following authors, executors and publishers for permission to quote extracts from their printed works: two quotations (pp. 1 and 100) from the *Poetical Works* of Robert Bridges by permission of the Clarendon Press, Oxford; two extracts (pp. 164 and 165) from Sir W. M. Child's *Making a University* by kind permission of J. M. Dent & Sons Ltd.; two verses (p. 59) from 'Puck's Song' in Kipling's *Puck of Pook's Hill* (published by Macmillan & Co. Ltd.) by kind permission of Mrs. Bambridge, daughter of the late Rudyard Kipling; three quotations (pp. 101, 114 and 115) from the late Kenneth Grahame's *The Wind in the Willows* by kind permission of his executors and Methuen & Co. Ltd., publishers of *The Kenneth Grahame Book*; four lines (p. 65) from G. K. Chesterton's *Ballad of the White Horse* by kind permission of Miss Dorothy Collins and Methuen & Co. Ltd., publishers of his *Collected Poems*.

I, if I may now stand unaided, would also like to express gratitude for assistance to Stanley H. Horrocks, borough librarian of Reading; to Mrs. C. S. Orwin for much help with the Blewbury district; and to several of my colleagues who have allowed me to share their excursions into Berkshire geography.

Like most husbands, I am deeply indebted to my wife who has contributed much to all parts of the volume, while she, in her turn, wishes to thank the London Library for its never-failing assistance.

R. P. B.

CONTENTS

ILLUSTRATIONS

**Photographs by 'The Times'.*
†Photographs by A. F. Kersting, F.R.PS.
‡Photographs by Raymond Lea.

CHAPTER I: Matthew Arnold's Country

Sweet Thames! run softly till I end my song.
EDMUND SPENSER, *Prothalamion* (1596)

OF all riparian counties Berkshire has the largest share of the Thames for it includes 100 miles of water meadow stretching from Lechlade to Old Windsor. Where it enters the county the 'stripling Thames' is already navigable, a broad stream thickly fringed with reeds and rushes, the familiar haunt of water fowl, and from here all the way to Oxford the utter loneliness and quiet of the river is its most memorable quality. 'For me', says one writer, 'all that Cotswold valley of the Thames above Oxford holds a perpetual and abiding charm. There is nothing striking about it. It is just a willowy landscape of meadows and copses and the Thames running through it between beds of reeds, and water flowers. But the sun shines and the wind blows in the willows, and turns them to silver; and in the spring the copses are full of primroses; and if you stand up in your canoe . . . you will see the dikes golden with marsh-marigolds and all the meadows scattered with oases of cowslips; and the mornings are full of larks and the evenings of the chime of village bells . . . and the whole valley is England in excelsis.' Away from the river's bank the white and purple fritillary crowns a flora of unusual interest while on or near the watercourse the common heron is frequently disturbed. But the heavy commercial traffic has gone and only a poet sees the

'laden barges float
By banks of myosote
And scented flag and golden flower-de-lys
Delay the loitering boat'.

The charm of the upper Thames increases downstream of Newbridge whence it winds in a great loop round Boars Hill, Cumnor and Wytham. The ancient bridge at Newbridge with its pretty inn, the well-known ferry at Bablock Hythe, the graceful stone-structure spanning the river at Eynsham and near it the Oxford waterworks—a dream of perfection come true—are precursors to Godstow and 'The Trout' and the vast flatness of Port Meadow.

But it is the hills which catch the eye and none more than Wytham Hill, a wooded bastion thrust into the heart of Oxfordshire. This isolated limestone hillock, which rises 300 feet above the Thames at Oxford, is approached only by by-roads and its greater part is kept in grand seclusion as Wytham Park. Wytham itself, the most northerly village of Berkshire, stands between the wooded flanks of the hill and the shallow Seacourt stream. Unusually picturesque and tidily built in stone with roofs of either Stonesfield slates or thatch, as becomes a situation amid the limestones and cornlands, it is wonderfully well cared for. In recent years the University of Oxford has acquired, subject to certain life rights, the Abbey with its large park, and the whole of Wytham. The chief architectural feature is the church of All Saints. The original structure, said to have been built by monks from Abingdon Abbey in about 1480, was rebuilt in 1811 by the third Earl of Abingdon who demolished Cumnor Place to add portions of the stonework to Wytham church in much the same way that he dismantled Rycote Place to erect his house in Wytham Park. The handsome gateway of the church with the inscription *Janua vitae verbum domini* and some beautiful traceried, or late-Decorated, windows came from Cumnor, the east window being traditionally that from Amy Robsart's room. The corbels supporting the roof include one of a man playing the bag-pipes while the windows contain some seventeenth-century glass, probably Flemish. The porch, too, is delightful, and another small window in the east end, sadly encumbered with malignant ivy.

From Wytham a narrow road leads southward past the oaks and elms of the park to Botley which has in late years undergone a transformation sad and strange. This is a story of road traffic and of suburban expansion all too typical of modern England. Up to about the mid-eighteenth century Botley was a delightful collection of stone-built, stone-tiled houses and farmsteads situated athwart the main bridle track from South Wales to Witney and London and at a distance of over one mile from the outermost houses of the city of Oxford. At that time the main road for wheeled traffic from Gloucester and South Wales to London, after leaving Witney kept well north of the Thames loop to Hanborough and so ran north of Oxford. About 1760 the Thames marshes at Eynsham were drained, the fine toll-bridge constructed and a new coach road created from Witney through Botley to Carfax, Oxford. Botley was too close to Oxford to benefit and in modern times this road has encouraged Oxford to engulf the Berkshire bank of the Seacourt stream and has, by widenings, diversions and new by-passes, played havoc with the few seventeenth-century cottages still standing. Botley today is looking for a soul while Oxford, like a leech, sucks the life blood of its community giving it in return cinemas and cigarettes.

What Oxford is doing to and on the twin hills south of Botley is likewise a matter of speculation. The roadside parts of Cumnor hill and the flanks and sandy summits of Boars Hill are sprinkled with 'desirable' residences; the Hinksey villages are narrowly missed by a vast new by-pass but as yet there are open spaces and footpaths enough and the views of Oxford lose little of their interest. As one topographer so cunningly puts it, 'In a sweet summer evening these villages and paths are very pleasant and during many a ramble has the old, old story that is ever new been gently whispered in their pretty meandering ways; and many a troth has been plighted which has been followed by a happy wedding.' Yet others will remember that this is Matthew Arnold's country and 'In the two Hinkseys nothing keeps the same.'

Many find pleasure in retracing the two Oxford poems *Thyrsis*, and *The Scholar Gipsy* back to the scenes Arnold loved so well—to Chilswell Farm, 'the fir-topped Hurst', and Bablock Hythe. But the charm of poetry can be soured by too trifling an analysis and the essential quality of Arnold's poems too often evades his followers, who do not always strike

> 'the sweet spring days,
> With whitening hedges and uncrumpling fern,
> And bluebells trembling by the forest-ways,
> And scent of hay new-mown'.

Yet the Hinkseys, despite modern encroachments, have much in their unpretentious way to please the rambler. Both villages appear very early in history as part of the gift of Ceadwalla, King of the West Saxons, to the abbey of Abingdon about 686. Nearly three centuries later all the land in the great loop of the Thames between Kennington and Bablock Hythe was granted to the abbey in whose hands it remained until 1546 when George Owen, the royal physician, gave Henry VIII two closes in St. Thomas's parish, Oxford, together with the site of Rewley Abbey and £301 in exchange for the Hinksey-Cumnor territory. North Hinksey was linked to Osney by ferry path before this time, for the historian Anthony Wood mentions an agreement between the Abbot and the ferryman of 'Hinksey Hith' for making a foot and horse-way from near Osney Bridge to the village. Today the path is shaded by pollard willows and comes out close to the church and 'The Fishes'. The church stands on a small grassy knoll and has some early

Norman work, including a window and arch, now both blocked, and a fine south doorway. Nearby stands one of the old tithe barns of Abingdon Abbey, a welcome survival in a part of Berkshire not well blessed with such buildings. Yet parts of the village are sadly neglected and several ruinous thatched cottages seem incredible after the pride taken in immaculate Wytham.

Beyond the Green at North Hinksey the road proper dwindles into a deeply-rutted lane and here Ruskin and his students attempted a mutual improvement by toiling and moiling. With creditable wisdom Ruskin directed operations mainly from Genoa, and asked Dr. Acland to get Mr. Harcourt's consent. He wanted his Oxford drawing class to see what a country road should be, and the alteration was to be done with delicate touching to preserve 'all loveliness it has', the chief object, however, was 'to let my pupils feel the pleasure of useful muscular work, and especially of the various and amusing work involved in getting a human pathway, rightly made, through a lovely country, and rightly adorned.' From Italy, Ruskin sent clear instructions. 'When after crossing the ferry, you turn to the left in the lane under the hills, you come presently to a place where the road is depressed, in front of a cottage which has beautiful old steps going up to its door; and this depression . . . is usually full of stagnant water . . . I want this to be first filled up and levelled, and the road made good over it, with a drain beneath to carry the hill drainage clear. In doing this I should like you to pet those cottage steps, and if possible run a little bit of garden ground, with a daisy or two, . . . along the front of the cottage as far as they project. You must appoint . . . a general guardian of innocent weeds and moss. What shall we call him? You will find out some pretty Latin and dignified name for him if you debate this point. I can't stop to think today, and besides am always doubtful of my crazy Latin. But this office should be charged with the care of the moss on those steps, and the recommendation of them also to the care of the cottage inhabitant. Minute prizes, offered to the children of any family, for well-kept doorsteps, would I think be a legitimate use of bribes.

'This part of the road being set to rights, when you go a little farther you come to a much larger depression; in a space of land about as large as the square before the Duomo of Torcello, but triangular, not square, and with cottages on all sides of it. This space I want filled and turfed over. Which being done, a pretty little piece of grazing ground will be obtained for the geese and the donkeys of the neighbourhood. Without being desirous of expressing too strong a fellow-feeling for those animals, it seems to me wholly desirable that the village green should be kept clean and sweet for them.

'Proceeding further, the length of the lane will be found traversed by ruts of depths, which, it seems to me, only the cart wheels of centuries could have cut. Supposing that, when our work is once begun, it should enlist wider sympathizers, and our little company become larger, any force of men might be put, this term, upon the road work required here; making the surface even, the breadth definite, the substance secure, and planting with any transportable common flowers, the banks developed by the levelling.'

The students, mostly Balliol men, had seven months' digging and levelling before Ruskin came home to take a hand, and expose himself to the vulgar gaze of the rude and scoffing multitude. What Oscar Wilde said to the onlookers has unfortunately remained unrecorded but Ruskin took the ridicule good-naturedly and admitted that the road was the worst in the three Kingdoms and gave the credit for any level patches to his own gardener. On the completion of the project the surveyor sent by the owner was able to report that 'the young men have done no harm to speak of'.

At South Hinksey a sense of pride of ownership returns

and modern Ruskins have found many a stone-built cottage worth preserving. Students of Arnold will recall the inn once kept by Sybilla Kerr, while ecclesiologists will notice the small church of St. Lawrence, with its early fourteenth-century windows, and an exquisite miniature double piscina in the wall near the pulpit.

The sandy, fir-clad summit of Cumnor Hurst provides the widest views of the upper Thames near Oxford but the flanks of Cumnor Hill and Boars Hill near the two Hinkseys afford by far the best view of the city. The hill-slopes near Hinksey Hill Farm are 'sufficiently elevated to command the whole city; the beautiful series of buildings fall into a most picturesque composition, the foreground being in a fertile and richly wooded tract, with the silvery Thames winding through it, while the line of softly swelling uplands make an admirable background to the spires and towers, and completes a picture which once seen is never forgotten'. Today a new note is added by New Hinksey and above all by the gasworks, modern mathematical leviathans which break a scene that reached its greatest beauty in the early-nineteenth century before the coming of the railway and of the red suburban rash. The latest threat, a new and bigger gasometer, has united town and gown in an endeavour to remove the whole monstrosity, on which accomplishment nostalgic dons will need no poetic licence to exclaim:

> 'And that sweet City with her dreaming spires
> She needs not June for beauty's heightening,
> Lovely all times she lies, lovely to-night.'

From these same viewpoints footpaths run

> 'Up past the wood, to where the elm-tree crowns
> The hill behind whose ridge the sunset flames'

Southward tracks lead to Jarn Mound, an artificial hillock raised by Sir Arthur Evans, complete with a view indicator;

and to Bagley Wood, a paradise of wild flowers, of daffodil, anemone and lily-of-the-valley, except where modern conifers discourage luxuriant undergrowth. Beyond Bagley is Sandford and the deepest lock on the Thames, or if you keep more to the south, the woods near Radley which in their turn give place to the spacious park surrounding St. Peter's College, one of the three well-known public schools in Berkshire. The school stands upon a wide plateau among huge trees so that the mixture of old and new buildings that forms the college, and the playing fields with their woodland setting and Thames-side fringe must make for Arcadian memories for any ex-Radleian.

Founded in 1847 by Dr. William Sewell, who leased the red-brick Queen Anne mansion that still forms the nucleus of the buildings, it was a highly individual venture. Of Tractarian principles and keen artistic sensibilities, he was firmly convinced of the value of beautiful surroundings and, with utter disregard for expense, proceeded to make a collection of fine pictures and rich furniture. He adorned the chapel with a priceless carved reredos, rich stained glass and the famous Tibet carpet, which normally hangs on the wall and is only laid on very special occasions.

The honeymoon period of the school under this notable man lasted for thirteen years by which time Dr. Sewell's debts amounted to £40,000. By great good fortune the largest creditor was J. G. Hubbard, M.P., later Lord Addington, who shouldered the burden of the debts and sold a good many of the treasures but put the school upon a sound financial basis. Whatever remains to Radley College of Sewell's inspiration it owes to Lord Addington's more practical abilities.

Today, the school is noted, among other things, for its rowing, and the Radley reach of the Thames is a joyous sight on a fine summer's afternoon. The river is alive with craft—single skulls being urged in courses reminiscent of dogs after rabbits, and eights impelled with a grim gusto as if afraid of being rammed by the coach's motor-boat. Here former 'blues' yell at future 'blues' all the invective learnt a mile or two upstream, and never a gleam of pleasure enlivens the dismal task. Heaven help the eight which grins with joy or sings with happiness as it rows!

Just outside one corner of the Park, close beside a delightful timber-framed house and a new red-brick vicarage, stands the parish church. Built of stone mainly in the fifteenth century, it still retains its square-headed Tudor windows and its original tower. There is, however, in the transept a little Decorated work which has since been restored. The interior is lofty and dim by reason of the stained-glass windows which contain a collection of brightly-coloured heraldic panels unequalled in any parish church in Berkshire. This late fifteenth- and sixteenth-century glass, which was given to the church about 1840, includes, in the west window, a half-length portrait reputed to be of Henry VII. The chancel holds some beautiful seventeenth-century stalls, backed with panelling and surmounted by canopies. The medieval oak canopy over the pulpit is said to have come from above the speaker's chair in the House of Commons, having been given by William Lenthall who was Speaker in the Long Parliament. Radley church has other riches, which it bears with easy grace; among them the altar-tomb to William Stonehouse (*ob.* 1631) who once owned the manor.

If from North Hinksey and Hinksey Hill Farm the tracks leading westward up the hillside are followed they come out at Cumnor, once a residence of the abbots of Abingdon, and after that abbey's dissolution in 1538, the home of Thomas Pentecost the last abbot. After many changes of ownership —for the lands of Berkshire are skittish and apt to cast their owners—the estate was leased in 1560 to Anthony Forster, agent and intimate friend of Sir Robert Dudley. On the eighth day of September in this same year Amy Robsart,

Dudley's wife, happened to be staying here with other ladies. In the morning she sent her servants to the fair at Abingdon but when they returned in the evening they found her body at the foot of the hall-staircase with neck broken and head much bruised without disarrangement of her cap. At Dudley's request Sir Thomas Blount went to Cumnor and made inquiries which led nowhere. Some of the public 'were disposed to saie well and some evill' for to so close a favourite of Queen Elizabeth a wife was evidently an embarrassment but at the inquest, in spite of dislike of Dudley, the death was declared accidental, whereupon Dudley gave his wife a magnificent funeral and callously refrained from attending it. The event was gradually slipping further into oblivion when Sir Walter Scott wrote *Kenilworth*. Scott, who was a frequent visitor to the house of the vicar of Uffington, Dr. Hughes, no doubt heard the stories of this part of Berkshire from the vicar or his parishioners, after seeing Cumnor Hurst from the White Horse. A thoroughly unreliable account of Amy Robsart's death taken from Ashmole's *Antiquities of Berkshire* formed the basis of Scott's story and he heightened its inaccuracies. The kindly, honest Forster became a deep-dyed villain while Sir Richard Varney actually had nothing at all to do with the tragedy.

Cumnor estate had been for over two centuries in the hands of the ancestors of the Earls of Abingdon; Amy's ghost had been laid in a nearby pond by nine parsons from Oxford, and the third Earl of Abingdon had in 1810 finally demolished the ruinous house in order to rebuild Wytham church, when Scott's *Kenilworth* re-created a national interest in the spot. So great was the sympathy excited that even the Earl of Abingdon, in a forgetful moment, was induced to drive some visitors from Wytham to view the ruins which he himself had had removed.

Although Cumnor Hall has gone, the church is well worth a visit for its many Transitional or late-twelfth-century features, more especially the tower with its fine arch and graceful west doorway. Early English alterations may be seen particularly in the north aisle arcade while before 1400 other changes in detail but not in plan were made. The sixteenth and seventeenth centuries brought a curious collection of interior treasures. The graceful stone statue of Queen Elizabeth probably came from Cumnor Park and has found the same resting-place as copies of some letters of Amy Robsart. Here too is a beautiful marble tomb to Anthony Forster (*ob.* 10 Nov. 1572), with a Latin inscription describing his many accomplishments—eloquence, charity, justness, learning in the classics, in literature, music, architecture and botany—an odd confounding of virtue and worldly wisdom. Most of the stall-ends in the chancel are carved into poppy heads, decorated fore and aft. On the front of one are the five stigmata, and upon the reverses the symbols of the Passion. Other notable woodwork includes a Jacobean pulpit and pew, and a remarkably fine circular oak staircase built in 1685 to ascend to the belfry. A chained bible of 1611 also survives and a letter which makes the whole survival more remarkable. It was written in February 1644 by a Mrs. Peacock who describes how the troopers up to five hundred strong, came from Abingdon to Cumnor. 'The chieftains view the church, goe up the steeple to overlook the country, as if they meant to garrison there, but finding it not answerable to their hopes and desires, they descend, but are loath to depart without leaving a mark of their iniquitie and impiety behind them.

'Some they employ to take down the weathercock . . . , others to take down a Cross from off an aisle of the church . . . , others to plunder the countrymen's houses of bread, beere, bacon and whatsoever was fit for sustenation.' The corbels in the church escaped molestation for they are humorous enough to please all comers.

Cumnor, as befits its connexions with the Earl of Leicester, has its 'Bear and Ragged Staff', a gabled stone-built inn which once formed with the church and ill-fated hall the essential trilogy of the ancient village. Southward on the way to Appleton is Cut's end, another old and attractive domestic building. This road gives pleasant views of Boars Hill and of the Thames valley, for unlike the main thoroughfare it crosses open country. At Appleton the residential needs of Oxford are losing their influence, but a few old cottages have, in fact, been 'petted' by Oxford dons and from rustic dwellings may emerge here ploughman, there philosopher.

The limestone used for building gives sizeable blocks and mellows attractively while the road traffic is neither continuous nor merciless. The most unusual architectural structure is the moated manor, parts of which date back to the reign of King John. They consist of three round-headed arches; the one forming the main doorway of the hall has stiff-stalk foliage and deeply-cut mouldings; the other two, although also of about 1200, are plainer but have the same monstrous head between them. Later additions include an Elizabethan porch and panelling and some Jacobean woodwork.

The church barely antedates the manor, as its main feature, a row of Transitional pillars and arches, was built presumably about 1180. The remainder is mainly restoration or rebuilding after a disastrous fire. In the chancel is a richly-decorated monument to Sir John Fettiplace (*ob.* 1593), who is shown in his armour as are half a dozen John and Edmund Fettiplaces in the church at Swinbrook in Oxfordshire. The Fettiplaces resided mainly at Childrey and East Shifford in the fifteenth century, and thereafter expanded or removed to Appleton and Swinbrook, the former estate being sold by them in 1600. The parishioners have ingeniously packed ten bells into the belfry and think nothing of ringing a 'Bob Major' on their days of rest.

Appleton has other attributes: a cottage porch with

seventeenth-century plasterwork; a picturesque barn, part timber and part mellowed brick with an upper story at one end unobtrusively adorning the pond near the centre of the village; the views of the Cotswolds from the rough trackways leading westward to the sharp drop to the Thames; and the fine woods surrounding the village except on the river side. What was written (in *Jackson's Journal*, 21 March 1778) of a single house here might well be applied to all Appleton. 'On a delightful dry hill, not far from the banks of the river Isis . . . in the midst of lawns and groves, where all the beauties of Nature are drawn, as it were, to a centre; the violet, the daffodil, the primrose, and the blue-bell deck the fields, please and delight the eye: the nightingale and the thrush, the lark and the cuckoo, charm and captivate the senses; is situated Walter Furze, a house opened for the purpose of inoculation.'

A rural road out of Appleton makes for Tubney Wood and Bessels Leigh and crosses on the way a river with no official name but locally always called the Os. Bessels Leigh formerly belonged to the Besils family of Provence, whose English branch gave rise to the Sir Peter Besils (*ob.* 1434) who gave the stone for the building of bridges at Abingdon. He also left money for repairing these bridges and for making fresh roads, and altogether was the kind of man who would enjoy working as a county councillor in Berkshire today. Eventually the estate was sold to William Lenthall, the Speaker of the Long Parliament, 'the weak tool' as Ashmole calls him.

In 1644 when the Parliamentarians were holding Abingdon, a party of Royalists occupied the manor house at Bessels Leigh, concerning which Major General Browne wrote from Abingdon: 'The house is very strong, and they will be ill neighbours to us. I am preparing a party to go thither this night to remove them, but the issue we must refer to the Almighty.' Browne's company succeeded in dislodging the enemy but as he could not spare troops to garrison the house he rendered it useless to others by having the walls and doors broken down.

Fifty years later there was quadrilling here of another sort when Wood wrote of 'a solemn ball at Besell's Lee in the house of Sir John Lenthall, performed by 50 or 60 maidens, virgins of quality, that are sojourners there'. It is hard to believe that it was so stern an occasion since Hearne dryly notices that this forerunner of St. Hugh's 'occasioned a more than ordinary resort thither of young Oxford scholars' so that the ear of fancy catches a faint titter from among 'the virgins of quality'.

The old manor house was destroyed in 1784 and, except for a few fragments and two fine gateposts near the church, has disappeared completely. Today the little parish church stands in grand isolation beside the busy main road. It is a charming little building, of the fifteenth century, all of stone, even to tiles and bell-cote. The porch, however, is wooden and obviously Jacobean while the entrance door still retains some admirable Decorated ironwork. The interior is a pleasant simple harmony of unpretentious fitments, mostly of the seventeenth century and including a singers' gallery and a double-decker pulpit. It looks as if it might be easy to pray in the box pews although they have been somewhat modernized and especially in the family one privileged to be in the chancel. The stencilled walls rise to a seventeenth-century roof which keeps its angels and so adds to the interest of a church that escaped modern restoration because the population of its parish did not grow.

Beyond Bessels Leigh, on the Faringdon side, the motor route passes through the wide expanses of treegrowth and shrub known as Tubney Wood and within two miles approaches Fyfield, the outermost edge of Matthew Arnold's country but now shorn of the ancient 'elm'. Here is a characteristic assembly of limestone cottages, manor and church.

The manor house was originally built about 1325 by the Golafre family, who also at various times altered and enlarged the late-Transitional church. The most attractive parts of both buildings belong to the Decorated period and have ball-flower ornament. The church was gutted by fire in 1893 but most of the stonework survived, including the two contrasting effigies of Sir John Golafre junior (*ob.* 1442), the upper as armoured knight and the lower as shrouded skeleton. A richly ornamented canopied tomb in the chancel is said to be that of Lady Catherine Gordon (*ob.* 1537) 'The White Rose of Scotland' and wife of Perkin Warbeck. After Warbeck was hanged, Henry VII treated his widow like a sister, allowing her—under her maiden name—a high position at court, a pension and wardrobe expenses. Henry VIII gave her lands in Berkshire and in his reign she married three times, her fourth husband being Christopher Ashton who lived with her at Fyfield. The tomb is still known as 'Lady Gordon's monument' and strange to say an even finer memorial with effigies of herself and her third husband, rests in Swansea church. She was generally acclaimed as outstandingly beautiful and intelligent, which could not be gainsaid of a woman who continually pleased both Henrys, charmed four husbands and lived to acquire twice the normal number of tombstones.

CHAPTER II: The Corallian Ridge

Shepherds had met him on the Hurst in spring;
At some lone alehouse in the Berkshire moors,
On the warm ingle-bench, the smock-frock'd boors
Had found him seated at their entering.

MATTHEW ARNOLD, *The Scholar Gipsy*

THE hills that dominate Oxford are the most majestic parts of a ridge which stretches to the Berkshire boundary near Coleshill. West of Fyfield this ridge narrows appreciably but its higher summits are still capped with Greensands which encourage conifers and give in places warm soils for market gardening. Fortunately in most localities beds of limestone also occur and yield a good building stone and here and there fossil corals which cause the strata to be called Corallian. This Corallian ridge is better developed in Berkshire than in any other county and is peculiarly a land of private parks and pleasant villages, of stately mansions and stone-built cottages.

At Longworth the rose gardens claim much attention, and the view from the churchyard—in the foreground is Harrowdown Hill, an isolated elm-capped hillock about 120 feet high, with the winding Thames near Newbridge, and beyond it the Windrush valley and the flat outlines of the eastern Cotswolds.

At Buckland the charm lies in village and manor alike. The limestone cottages are less reflective than at Wytham for the building stone is smaller and greyer but the same preservation and harmony prevails. A good deal of the church is Norman and Early English and has suffered many alterations, including the obtrusive Victorian mosaics in the south transept. A triangular aumbry contains the dried heart of William Holcot a religious reformer who combined prudence with zeal in the reigns of Edward VI, Mary and Elizabeth, while on a slab in the floor of the church is a quaint inscription, of about 1300, in Old French asking passers-by to pray for 'Dame Felice la Blonde'.

The church stands close to the old manor house which came into the hands of the Throckmortons in 1690. About 1757 this house was put to more menial uses and adorned elaborately, and a grander mansion was constructed farther in the park to the designs of J. Wood junior of Bath. In the twentieth century this mansion was greatly enlarged, a rare event in the bigger houses of modern Berkshire. The park itself takes full advantage of the steep slope overlooking the Thames and to its fine beeches have been added grottoes, temples and a tree-lined lake. The Throckmorton family still possess the famous coat that was made for a wager in 1811 from wool which was growing on the sheeps' backs in the early morning and thirteen hours twenty minutes later had been sheared, spun, woven, tailored and put on for dinner. The animated process is shown in several prints, one of which may be seen in Newbury museum.

Whereas Buckland and other settlements of the Corallian ridge have barely grown into villages, Faringdon is in all senses a town. Yet it seems peculiarly compact, and clings so desperately to the highway that it lacks the spaciousness usually associated with market towns. The road is in fact the key to Faringdon's growth and when in recent years a by-pass was suggested the townsfolk whole-heartedly rejected the idea. The arms of Faringdon might well be two tradesmen couchant impaled on an omnibus rampant with the motto 'La route, c'est la vie'.

Nature cunningly designed the town as a meeting-place of routes, for here the ridge narrows and lowers so that a gap is formed between the Folly and Ring Clumps hill. Upon this gap routes converge from the Vales of White

Horse and upper Thames and create a nodality which early embroiled the town in civil wars. In Saxon times it was the site of a royal palace and Alfred the Great is thought to have lived here, and here his son Edward the Elder died in 924. On so strategic a spot Robert of Gloucester, in 1140, built a castle which Stephen in his turn had razed to the ground. During the thirteenth century the manor passed from King John to Beaulieu Abbey and shortly afterwards Henry III granted a market to the abbots. The royal household actually stayed one night at Faringdon and the cost of the visit is known: for the King 100*s.* 6*d.*; for the Queen 75*s.*; for Prince Edward 50*s.* 6*d.* and for Roger de Mortimer 4*s.* The most exciting local event of the next century was the battle of Radcot Bridge in 1387 when Robert de Vere was defeated and fled in exile to Louvain. Of more lasting effect was the building in the reign of Henry V of the stone bridge over the Thames at Abingdon as traffic from Gloucester and Cirencester now began to pass through the town.

The manor of Faringdon after the Reformation changed hands many times and eventually came by purchase to the Untons who dwelt at Wadley House, one mile east of the town. Sir Thomas Unton, who was knighted at the coronation of Anne Boleyn, died in 1553, and his monument and that of Elizabeth his wife is the most handsome in Faringdon church. Sir Alexander Unton, who succeeded, has a canopied altar tomb to the left of his father's. Sir Edward, the next in line, travelled widely and entertained Queen Elizabeth at Wadley when he presented her with 'one jewel of gold garnished with diamonds and rubies, and five pearls pendant, one bigger than the rest'. His monument too is in the Unton chapel. Colonel Edward Unton, who next held the manor, was caught up in the wars with Spain and died fighting in Portugal with Sir John Norris and Francis Drake. His successor, Sir Henry, was the last and most famous of the Untons. He took part in the siege of Zutphen when Sir

Philip Sydney was slain, and was knighted by the Earl of Leicester. In 1592, when ambassador to France, he sent the following spirited challenge to Henri, Duc de Guize in resentment of slighting words spoken 'impudently, indiscreetly and overboldly' of Queen Elizabeth: 'I say you have wickedly lyed in speaking so basely of my Sovereign: and you shall do nothing else but lie, whensoever you shall tax her honour. Moreover that her sacred person ought not to be evil-spoken of by tongue of such a perfidious traitor to her Law and Country as you are. And here upon I do defy you, and challenge your person to mine, be it either on horseback or on foot, I being issued of as great a race and noble house as yourself. So I will maintain the lie I gave you. If you consent not to meet me hereupon I will hold you and cause you to be generally held, for the arrantest coward and most slanderous slave that lives in all France. I expect your answer.' The Duke saw fit to refuse the challenge and Sir Henry died in Paris of the 'purple fever'.

In 1622 the manor of Faringdon was bought by Sir Robert Pye and it was his son who held a commission in the Cromwellian army. In 1644 Faringdon House was stoutly garrisoned for the King and during the following year Cromwell himself failed to take it. Whereupon Sir Robert Pye the younger had the unusual duty of assaulting his father's house and although presumably he knew every cranny of it and blasted down the church spire and much of the town in the operation he too failed abjectly. Nor was it until June 1646 that the garrison surrendered and then only at the King's orders. The town was by now in such a deplorable condition that the people petitioned Parliament for much money to rebuild it but the spireless church probably indicates the ill-success of the venture.

The present Faringdon House which stands close to the church was built in about 1780 by Henry James Pye the most feeble of the poets laureate. The mansion is modest, graceful and charmingly complete—in all ways the reverse of Pye's poetry. He was described by Sir Walter Scott as 'eminently respectable in everything but his poetry', yet he has left his mark in English literature as well as in Berkshire. His first ode on the birthday of George III was so crammed with allusions to feathered songsters that it provoked the well-known epigram:

> 'And when the pie was opened
> The birds began to sing;
> And wasn't that a dainty dish
> To set before a king?'

In Byron's *The Vision of Judgement* is another scathing reference:

> 'The Monarch, mute till then, exclaim'd, 'What, what!
> Pye come again? No more—no more of that!'

It was during Pye's tenure as poet laureate that the traditional dole of a tierce (about 35 gallons) of canary wine was compounded for a fixed salary of £27 a year. He, too, it is said, planted Faringdon Folly with pines, most of which have already or are rapidly reaching the end of their days. The Folly is a hillock of Greensand whose flat summit has escaped the encroachments of the plough. As a viewpoint it stands unrivalled hereabouts. Northward the eye travels over the flat vale of Thames, with here and there a spire or tower, to the Cotswolds; southward lies the Vale of White Horse and beyond it the steep face of the chalk downs and, in the glint of the sun, the White Horse itself. The tall, ornamental structure amid the pine trees—built in 1936 for the fourteenth Lord Berners to the designs of the seventh Duke of Wellington—was a kindly addition intended solely to act as an observation tower, and which, unfortunately, has had to be closed.

The view westward includes Faringdon itself which

appears within the gap with tentacles of houses stretching along its southern exits. The main part of the town lies athwart the Gloucester–Abingdon road, which, as we have seen, early helped to increase the town's prosperity. Yet few of the existing houses precede the eighteenth century and the architecture is that of local tradesmen rather than of wealthy merchants and prosperous manufacturers. The seventeenth-century Town Hall with pillared undercroft is symbolical of Faringdon's great local significance but only Pye's mansion and the church are outstanding architecturally.

The latter building is large, spacious and cruciform in plan. Mainly erected about 1200 in Transitional-Norman and Early English styles, it retains much good stone-carving and its harmony has not been spoilt by additions, particularly of windows, during the next three centuries. Inside, the numerous monuments recall especially the Untons and Pyes. One of the finest was the alabaster altar tomb erected to the last Sir Henry Unton (1596) by his wife Dorothy, whose effigy used to kneel at his feet. This tomb was so badly damaged during the Civil War that it had later to be rebuilt and the kneeling figure was banished to the north transept, nearer the marble monuments to the Pyes. The gracious lady might well exclaim with Browning:

> 'Yet still my niche is not so cramped but thence
> One sees the pulpit o' the epistle side,
> And somewhat of the choir, those silent seats,
> And up into the aery dome where live
> The angels, and a sunbeam's sure to lurk:'

The change of taste between the sixteenth-century monuments to the Untons and the eighteenth-century memorials to the Pyes may be a controversial battleground but in Faringdon the Untons' challenge is ensured of a favourable reply.

From Faringdon a pleasant road continues along the ridge to Badbury camp whence a by-way winds to Great Coxwell, a manor which before the Reformation also belonged to Beaulieu Abbey. Here the abbots kept a grange and enriched it with a tithe barn of gigantic proportions. It measures 152 feet by 40 feet, has walls 4 feet thick and a Stonesfield slate roof rising at its apex over 50 feet above the ground. The walls are strengthened by nicely-judged buttresses while the great weight of the roof is supported by large towering timbers, based on stone pedestals and carefully tied by flying beams. The east and west doors are original and over the latter is a delightful porch and a sleeping-place for monks during harvest. The state of preservation is amazing and the whole structure so impressive that William Morris used to declare it one of the finest buildings in the world. With the coming of mechanical transport an adequate water-pump ought to be at hand although the ingenious stone pedestals almost obviate the risk of fire.

Footpaths and a shaded by-road lead westward from Great Coxwell to Coleshill, a charming, well-kept village abounding in attractive cottages some of which were erected about eighty years ago. Coleshill House adorns the nearby park but is well seen from the main road. Built between 1650 and 1660, it was always thought to be the best work of Inigo Jones, and the earliest road-books had no hesitation in saying that 'having since undergone no alteration or addition, it is remarkable for being the most (if not the only) complete work now remaining of that great architect'. Its builder was Sir Roger Pratt and today it is believed that he too was the architect although the old and enfeebled Inigo Jones may have approved or improved the plans. The house is square and surmounted by a stone parapet and central lantern. Its appearance has a great elegance and perfection, all the ordinary architectural requirements of a dwelling being raised to so dignified a level that all other decoration is dispensed with. The interior is equally fine, especially the double staircase to the gallery with balustrades of unusual form and wreaths of fruit and flowers.

The last village in this angle of Berkshire is Buscot which stands in the flatter part of the Vale leaving the upland to Buscot House and Park. The seventeenth-century rectory and the little aisleless church stands within a short distance of the second lock on the Thames. The church contains Transitional and Early English work but has been much altered, the more pleasing additions being glass by Burne-Jones and a pulpit composed of an old Flemish triptych with paintings of the Annunciation and Adoration. The main part of Buscot village dates from the end of last century when it was planned as a model settlement and being nicely built in stone rewarded the effort. The parish hall might well be envied by less-fortunate Berkshire hamlets, Wytham included.

The fervour of building at Buscot about 1897 involved the great house which up to then retained the Classic character of its original construction in 1780. Additions were made in an Italian style but these were removed about twenty years ago and the former harmony restored. The house contains the famous Briar Rose series of Burne-Jones's paintings illustrating the story of the Sleeping Beauty, the canvas panels being fitted into large decorated gilt frames or pilasters which occupy a whole room. The influence of Burne-Jones in this part of Berkshire arises partly from its proximity to Kelmscot, the home of William Morris.

Buscot, however, has its roots deep in the soil and has long been a cradle of Berkshire agriculture. Mr. Loveden, who built Buscot house, wrought many improvements in implements and stock, and improved the cheese trade by building warehouses and letting them to London cheesemongers. From Buscot wharves on the Thames were despatched by barge each year between two thousand and three thousand cheeses, of which about half came from the Berkshire end of the Vale of White Horse. Varieties akin to single Gloucester predominated but specialities were indulged in. At Snowswick Farm in Buscot parish, cheeses of a peculiar richness and delicacy of flavour were made in the shape of pineapples, just as at Stanford-in-the-Vale the favourite shape was a hare crouching in her form, which was sometimes coloured green with sage. At Buscot, Sir Alexander Henderson, later Lord Faringdon, raised a noted breed of shire horses and Buscot Harold, winner of the first prize at the London Shire Horse Show, was the finest shire ever foaled and by all accounts is the village's best remembered inhabitant. Pigs too there must have been but the palm for this race probably goes to Pangbourne where in 1797 at Tidmarsh Farm a hog was killed weighing well over 40 score and with eleven inches of fat on the shoulder. The owners of Buscot maintain the spacious deer-park and the great agricultural tradition. Nor have all the traditional sports died out beyond recall. As late as 1903 a genuine black Berkshire pig with his tail well greased was pursued by maids and matrons in a paddock and (to quote from Vincent) 'with snout tip-tilted like the petals of a flower' remained at last in the grip of a woman possessed of many children.

CHAPTER III: *The Vale of White Horse*

The ayre is temperate, sweet and delightful, and prospect for pleasure inferior to none. The soile is plenteous of corne.

JOHN SPEED, 1611

THE Vale of White Horse begins somewhere near Shrivenham and ends at the Thames near Abingdon. It is for all purposes the lands draining to the Ock, which has numerous headsprings, including a slow seepage near Little Coxwell, a sturdier spring at Compton Beauchamp and several strong upwellings in the woods above Woolstone. The unity comes as much from the hills to north and south as from the damp, floodable pastures along the watercourses, for the former attracted the thoroughfares and settlers while the latter could rarely be built upon and are crossed by routes as expeditiously as possible. Only by-roads follow the Ock and seldom approaching within half a mile of it, leave mile after mile of its willow-lined banks undisturbed even by footpaths.

Shrivenham stands at the head of the Vale on the water-divide between the Ock and the Cole, where the influence of Swindon weakens allegiance to Berkshire. A pleasing village, with wide streets and a good deal of stone and thatch, its architectural high-lights are Elm Tree House, the church and the new university. The first is a late-seventeenth-century house which would fit gracefully into Chipping Campden or any Cotswold village. The church was mainly rebuilt just before the Civil War; it has a fine tower (Perpendicular) resting on four somewhat unusual arches in that each has rows of plain mouldings which continue right to the floor without capitals. Around this about 1635 were built aisles which appear to mark the transition from English Gothic to early Renaissance, as the tapering pillars would indicate. The church has a certain dignity and pleasant balance, and within contains, among other features, several eighteenth-century monuments to local celebrities.

Beckett Park adjoins Shrivenham village and has brought it wide fame. The Bower Brook waters the park and feeds an ornamental lake, overlooking which is a gabled mansion rebuilt about 1830. However, the manor was mentioned in Domesday Survey and King John is said to have stayed here for a while. By the time of Edward III the de Becotes held it by the service of coming before the King whenever he should pass Fowyeare's Mill in Shrivenham showing him at the same time two white capons and saying 'Ecce Domine, istos duos capones quos alias habebitis sed non nunc'. The King, presumably was not given either bird.

Sir John Wildman the Anabaptist lived here in the late seventeenth century. An alderman of London and Post-master-General, he spent much of Charles II's reign in prison but was restored to his home and knighted by William III. John Wildman, his son, who also suffered imprisonments, is chiefly interesting for his adoption of John Shute, later the first Lord Barrington with his seat at Beckett House. The two Wildmans and Shute as well as some of his family have ornate monuments of marble in the church. Swift referred to this Shute as 'a notable young Presbyterian gentleman' and, in truth, few Berkshire men could have had a more successful family. The eldest, William Wildman Barrington, the second viscount, made the grand tour and shortly after his return in 1738 entered Parliament as a member for Berwick-on-Tweed. He served in Parliament for 39 years holding many offices of state, including treasurer of the navy, secretary of state and secretary for war by the King's express desire, and on his retirement was awarded a pension of £2,000 a year. The monument in the chancel of Shrivenham church was erected 'to his memory by his three surviving brothers to whom he was the best of fathers and of friends'.

The second son, Daines Barrington was a bencher of the Inner Temple and apart from gaining fame on his own account is referred to by Charles Lamb in his *Old Benchers of the Inner Temple* as 'another oddity—he walked burly and square—in imitation, I think, of Coventry—he did pretty well, upon the strength of being a tolerable antiquarian, and having a brother a bishop. When the account of his year's treasurership came to be audited, the following singular charge was unanimously disallowed by the bench: 'Item, disbursed Mr. Allen, the gardener, twenty shillings for stuff to poison the sparrows, by my orders'.

He was as Bentham described him 'an English polyglot lawyer . . . not intentionally a bad judge though he often was a bad one'. The fact was that Daines Barrington had a versatile brain of wide rather than accurate learning;

> 'About old pots his head forever puzzling
> And boring earth, like pigs for trifles muzzling.
> Who likewise from old urns to crotchets leaps,
> Delights in music, and at concerts sleeps.'

To his credit it cannot too often be said that it was with his warm encouragement that Gilbert White wrote *The Natural History of Selborne*.

Shute Barrington, the third son, became Bishop of Durham and in 1791 made a public entry into his see with speeches and interchanges of courtesy and other addresses. Unfortunately another Barrington of different family and criminal learnings with a great deal of publicity got himself at the same time transported to Botany Bay and the coincidence was too good an opportunity for the wits to miss.

> 'Two namesakes of late, in a different way
> With spirit and zeal did bestir them
> The one was transported to Botany Bay,
> The other translated to Durham.'

The last of the brothers to gain fame was Admiral Samuel who at the ripe age of eleven was entered on board the *Lark* (44 guns) and by the year 1747 when he was just 18 years old had command of the sloop *Weazel*. Later transferred to the frigate *Bellona* and to the *Romney* (50 guns), he saw practically continuous active service until he struck his flag in 1783. His most renowned action was in 1757 when cruising in the *Achilles* off Cape Finisterre he fell in with the *Comte de Ste. Florentine* a French privateer. After two hours' engagement the French ship was dismasted, had lost her captain and suffered 116 men killed and wounded while the casualties aboard the *Achilles* were 2 killed and 22 wounded. The flag won from the French ship on this occasion still hangs in Shrivenham church beside a memorial to the gallant admiral, whose talents and energy, kindness and consideration for his crew, deserved a better epitaph than the tedious thoughts of Hannah More.

Beckett Park had a new fame thrust upon it about 1940 when the government built upon part of it a large military college, which grew into the shape and size of a residential university. Here was the first American University in Europe and hither within a few months, at a time of incredible difficulties, fifty thousand volumes were collected. Many thousands of soldiers, now living in hamlets in the Middle West or in towns of New England, will recall the landscape of the whole Vale of White Horse as seen from the air—the whitish face of the downs, the straight line of the railway, the winding course of the derelict canal and the strip of riverine meadow traversed by the tiny Ock.

They may recall the nearby village of Uffington and the writings of Thomas Hughes. 'I pity people who weren't born in a Vale. I don't mean a flat country but a vale; that is, a flat country bounded by hills. The having your hill *always* in view if you choose to turn towards him, that's the essence of a vale.' So wrote Hughes in his story of *Tom Brown's*

School Days, and his description of the Vale of White Horse, one of the two English neighbourhoods he knew thoroughly, can hardly be bettered. 'It is a land of large rich pastures, bounded by ox-fences, and covered with fine hedgerow timber, with here and there a nice little gorse or spinney, . . . There being little ploughland, and few woods, the Vale is only an average sporting country, except for hunting. The villages are straggling, queer, old-fashioned places, the houses being dropped down without the least regularity, in nooks and out-of-the-way corners, by the sides of shadowy lanes and footpaths, each with its patch of garden. They are built chiefly of good gray stone and thatched; though I see that within the last year or two the red-brick cottages are multiplying . . . There are lots of waste ground by the side of the roads in every village, amounting often to village greens, where feed the pigs and ganders of the people; and these roads are old-fashioned, homely roads, . . .'

The Vale has changed much since 1856 and has undergone extensive ploughings during the two last continental wars, yet the same spirit is there and Uffington is at heart the same village that welcomed the infant Hughes on October 19th, 1822. Thomas lived at the vicarage here until he was eight when his family moved to Donnington Priory near Newbury and he went to Rugby School. Among their visitors at Uffington were Barham, author of the *Ingoldsby Legends*, and Sir Walter Scott who used much of the local settings and legends in his *Kenilworth*. Before his death in 1896 Thomas Hughes wrote several other books but none so popular as *Tom Brown's School Days*. He was a member of Parliament for nine years and was much devoted to the bettering of his fellows, and led so busy a practical life that his writings on historical and archaeological matters are little more authentic than Scott's novels.

There is a memorial tablet to Hughes in the church where his grandfather so often preached as vicar. The building is the noblest church in the Vale and consists, apart from one reticulated window and the higher parts of the tower, of Early English work. The central octagonal tower is supported by fine piers and arches and on or sometime previous to December 2nd, 1740, or 1743, itself supported a steeple which was then 'beat down by a tempas, wind, thunder and liten'. Most of the windows in the church are finely-recessed under well-moulded arches but those in the nave suffered from the zeal of Richard Saunders and Thomas Lockey, churchwardens, in 1678, who built a flat leaden roof—now changed—and were, it is said, wisely excommunicated by the vicar before they could effect further 'repairs'. The fine doorways on the south side deserve minute attention and for those who like ironwork the door in the porch and the old clock, made presumably by the local blacksmith, have much to commend them. The architectural qualities of the church remind us that its founder was probably Faritius, one of the greatest of Abingdon's abbots (1100–17). He was a great builder and rebuilt almost all the abbey and church at Abingdon, partly from payments received for his work as a physician to Henry I and other important persons. When Queen Matilda was expecting her first child the King sent her to stay near Abingdon under the care of Faritius and another Italian physician. The church at Uffington alone remains of the architectural works of the saintly yet scientific abbot, and no man could wish a more inspiring memorial.

Many of the older cottages in Uffington have chalk-block walls and thatched roofs, and are content to be unobtrusive, but readers of Tom Brown will remember that 'Our village was blessed among other things with a well endowed school . . . an old gray building with a steep roof and mullioned windows.' Here it still stands beneath its finial crosses, a small chalk building, erected in 1617 by John Saunders whose painted recumbent effigy rests in the nearby church.

On the vale side the nearest sizeable neighbour to Uffington is Stanford, where the chalk is quite replaced as building material by stone and brick, and tiled roofs are common. Stanford-in-the-Vale, to give it its full name, is probably an old settlement, for Roman coins and signs of a contemporary village occur on Chinham Farm. The later growth seems to have been much influenced by access to two large commons or greens, which, together with sandy sites above the floodable Ock, have combined to form a straggle of irregularly-spaced houses stretching for well over a mile. Between the cottages with their garden patches rise here and there a larger house with more extensive grounds, and interspersed at remarkably regular intervals are inns with stabling yards. There was an intriguing completeness and independence about Stanford forty years ago. The green on the Bow side had its own mill, while another grist mill stood a mile away on the Ock; the local brickworks was still capable of building and tiling the village; local shops made the collars and harnessings of the cart-horses as well as the great farm wagons for harvest; the local barber cut the hair—or the ear!—in a fashion quite his own; and if journeys must be made a five-mile walk each way never daunted a parishioner. The motor car and other machinery have brought inevitable changes, some good, some bad, but the topographer may at least put in one plea—when grist mills fall idle and their mill-ponds fill with mud, may not the dam be removed so that the stream resumes its ancient velocity and thereby clears its upper course of stagnant weed and bed-encumbering sediment?

Stanford, however, as a whole, has kept well clear of the Ock and is grouped about—if such a scatter can have a centre—the ancient church. Here the doorway in the south porch is Norman while the porch itself with corner vaulting-shafts is Perpendicular. Much of the building retains its late Early English and Decorated characteristics, some of the tracery on the chancel windows being unique in Berkshire to this church. Other interesting features include a most unusual piscina surmounted by a tabernacle of open stone-work, and an old brass to Roger Campdene dated 1398.

In summer pleasant footpaths can be followed southward from Stanford-in-the-Vale to Goosey which exceeds its neighbour only in one thing—its common or green. From one side of this vast expanse of greenery, the distant inn barely appears above the horizon, and upon its face the cattle roam as in pre-enclosure days. The cottages and houses and church are grouped around the common irregularly and haphazardly but with an undeniable charm. The tiny rectangular church has a Norman window with old glass in the nave but consists for the most part of much-restored Early English work. By no means least is the thirteenth-century door-key.

An elm-lined road from Goosey winds across the flat vale to Charney Bassett, which unlike its neighbours stands close to the watercourse and possesses a village green only of insignificant proportions but which redeems itself by encircling the remains of an old stone cross. The little church standing beside the Ock attracts attention chiefly by reason of its Norman stonework, particularly that of the south doorway showing a row of heads with ornamented protruding tongues, and that of a tympanum re-set in the chancel depicting an upright figure grasping two dragons by the neck with remarkable self-confidence.

Charney Bassett, like Goosey and Uffington, early came under the control of the abbots of Abingdon, who in the late thirteenth century had a grange erected just north of the church. Part of this building remains unaltered and includes a small chapel, a cellar with arched fireplace, and above in the solar a fine timber roof. The old name Charney Wick seems to denote the 'wick' or dairy farm of the manor.

A short stretch of country road through fields of wheat

and beans leads to the tiny hamlet of Lyford. Here better provision is made for the aged than in any other English village, for the Ashcombe almshouses have twenty separate dwellings while there are not above forty families in the parish. Founded in 1611, these almshouses were rebuilt about a century later in brick on three sides of a quadrangle. The simple chapel complete with clock stands at the west end and makes a pretty picture between the two rows of gables. A church largely of Early English much restored, a few rustic stone cottages, and the early seventeenth-century Manor Farm, with some mullioned windows and old chimney-stacks, would not themselves have given Lyford its claim to fame. This arises from the very isolation of Lyford Grange, a moated mansion (now much changed) standing in fields two furlongs away and belonging in 1581 to a certain Mr. Yates. Here on the 16th of July the Jesuit Edmund Campion was betrayed to the authorities.

Campion was born in London in 1540, the son of a book-seller, and having a 'sharp and pregnant wit' was sent when ten years old to Christ's Hospital by the London Company of Grocers. When Sir Thomas White founded St. John's College, Oxford, he willingly admitted Campion and the Company gave an exhibition to maintain him. At Oxford he was greatly admired for the grace of his eloquence and was chosen to deliver the funeral oration at Amy Robsart's funeral. In 1566 he welcomed Queen Elizabeth in the name of the university and she herself recommended him to the Earl of Leicester's patronage. Campion was already junior proctor when in 1569 his conscience led him to Ireland and eventually to Douai and a priesthood. Within a few years he returned to England and his preaching in the secret assemblies of the Catholics was producing such an effect that the government did their best to entrap him. He was safe in hiding at Stonor when he was induced to visit Mr. Yates at Lyford. On the fatal Sunday he said mass before about fifty people among whom was a spy who returned shortly afterwards with a number of constables. Campion was hidden in a secret hiding-place but was discovered next morning, and went from Lyford to a gruesome death at Tyburn.

Strangely enough the road from Lyford Grange to West Hanney crosses the Childrey Brook at Gallows Bridge and hereabouts, in an otherwise somewhat orthodox atmosphere the Nazarenes hold their annual gathering. There is nothing unorthodox about West Hanney itself, it duly belonged to Abingdon Abbey and acquired a church which now retains one late-Norman doorway and a good deal of other early stonework, including a rather unusual Transitional font. The six brasses spread over two centuries, from a priest of the fourteenth century down to Oliver Ayshcombe (1611) who presumably founded the almshouses at Lyford.

The rest of the village is, as at Stanford-in-Vale, a varied collection of country cottages with several larger houses, the gabled priory being probably the oldest, and West Hanney House, once the rectory, almost certainly the most imposing by reason of its tall façades of different-coloured bricks. The whole scene is typical of the individualism of the Vale of White Horse—no vast mansion with its large park, no uniform arrangement of houses and house-types, no centralized control or direction. The lack of uniformity makes the charm evasive and what is variety may often be mistaken for untidiness. The truth is that the Vale takes much knowing and improves with acquaintance. It is known only by footpaths which fortunately traverse it in great numbers. By pathway should be visited Cherbury Camp, a great oval earthwork, built on an island of harder ground above marsh and damp meadow. Only on foot are seen the kingfishers of the Ock, the hornets' nests in the bullrushes of the large water-filled sandpits, the isolated ponds abounding in efts and aquatic flora, and the honey-filled combs of the wild bees in the mossy banks below the hedgerows. The Vale,

Wallingford's Market Hall and St. Mary's Church

The former Town Hall in Wantage Market Place

Christ's Hospital and the Spire of St. Helen's

The Abbey Gateway, Abingdon

too, does many little things on a surprisingly big scale; the colonies of moles are not equalled in Berkshire, while whole fields may be set aglow with cowslips or tinged purple with the common orchid.

Buckland makes a good starting-point for a pedestrian crossing of the Vale. One footpath goes by way of Mount Pleasant Farm to Pusey, where the estate is said to have been given by Canute on cornage, or the tenure of a horn (p. 51). Thence paths and trackways lead to Charney Bassett and so to West Hanney. Another by-way from Buckland begins at the south end of the park and goes past the Home Farm, on through the pines and firs with here and there an araucaria and rhododendron and an occasional sweet chestnut. The open spaces of secondary growth glow with broom and gorse and along the verges the harebell abounds. Where the path finally leaves the woods it bridges a small stream so laden with lime that objects placed in it are petrified in less than a fortnight. On past Hatford and the mill-stream, with its fern-lipped plunge-hole, the way continues through Stanford to the mill on the Ock, whence flat, well-hedged country is crossed to the vast common at Balking. And so again to Uffington, where as Thomas Hughes wrote 'within a circle of five miles, there is enough of interest and beauty to last any reasonable man his life'.

CHAPTER IV: Abingdon

And thanne shall the Abbot of Abyngdoun,
And al his issue for evere,
Have a knok of a kynge,
And incurable the wounde.

'*Piers the Plowman*'

THE junction of Ock and Thames, fended on one side by the main river, and rich in water-meadow and fish was destined by nature to nurture a town. The gravel and sand patches south of the river-junction were the first to be occupied and from at least the Bronze Age have been inhabited by man. This site became well-populated in Anglo-Saxon times when a large cemetery existed at the present-day Saxton Road. Recently, much of this cemetery has been excavated and objects from over two hundred burials are now exhibited in the museum at Abingdon and the Ashmolean at Oxford.

The north side of the Ock-Thames junction came to the fore after the seventh century, when Cissa, an under-king of Wessex granted Hean, a Saxon nobleman, some land on which to found a religious house. Hean chose a site on the north bank of the Thames but as the river was then often a highway for marauders the life of his abbey for its first three hundred years was constantly broken and disrupted. Moreover, as the building stood in the debatable ground of the middle Thames, which for long formed a boundary between Mercia and Wessex, it fell alternately under the protection of one or other of their respective rulers. It was in 777, after one of these ding-dong battles in which Offa, King of Mercia defeated the West Saxons that he built himself a palace on Andersey Island in mid-Thames opposite the abbey, giving the monks in exchange the manor of Goosey. But the royal falconers and huntsmen became such a nuisance that on Offa's death the Abbey exchanged Sutton Courtenay for Andersey. In 871, the Danes left only the walls standing.

In the early years of Athelstan's reign the abbey appears as St. Mary's Stow and the 'town' of Uffington was bequeathed to it, and during this reign and the succeeding one there was a royal residence nearby. In 939, according to the *Abingdon Chronicle*, King Athelstan kept Easter at Abingdon with his full court and to him there came an embassy from Hugh Capet, King of France, which, like the three wise kings from the East, arrived with magnificent presents for the King, among which were spices, gems, emeralds, an onyx vase and coursers with gold bits and bosses.

The abbey continued as a small monastery on a royal estate until put under the authority of St. Ethelwold who was an outstanding figure in English monastic life during the tenth century. From then on the unbroken life of the community begins and it rises out of insignificance into an important school of monks. Ethelwold, born 908, the intelligent son of well-to-do citizens of Winchester, was early an inmate of the royal household. He was ordained with St. Dunstan and entered the monastery of Glastonbury where he was dean, and showed himself humble, studious, interested in poetry, grammar and theology, and constant in fasting and prayer. In 954, King Eadred gave him charge of the Abbey of Abingdon, bequeathing to it all the royal lands there, made him generous gifts of money and raised buildings for him. The King's mother was, if possible, even more generous. During one of the royal visits to the abbey at this time, it is said that Ethelwold invited the King and his Northumbrian theyns to dinner, and the doors being shut that the nobles might not 'shirk their drink', it was seen that the abbot's cask of mead 'failed not nor wasted more than a hand's breadth' so that the Northumbrians went back 'as drunk as hogs'.

Ethelwold's own gifts to the abbey were more in keeping

with his divine office, for he is said to have given for the use of the church a golden chalice, three crosses of gold and silver, and an organ. He also enriched it with the work of his own hands for like many monks he was a craftsman, and made two bells which hung alongside those made by St. Dunstan, and a machine called the 'golden wheel' overlaid with gold and hung with many little bells, a tintinnabula for ceremonial uses. Having firmly established the abbey he now set about improving its function, and sent one of his monks to Fleury to learn the Benedictine rule, and, on his return, introduced it into Abingdon, whence it spread to Glastonbury and throughout the country.

In 963, Ethelwold was transferred to Winchester and on leaving he composed a prayer for the safety of the house which may still be read in the *Abingdon Chronicle*. His career diverges at this point from that of the abbey but it remains to be said that he was one of the three greatest clerics of his day, all of whom were made saints.

After Ethelwold's tenure the abbey had a continuous history and although at the Norman Conquest it suffered some depredations, *Domesday Survey* shows it as one of the largest landowners and possessed of forty manors.

The abbey precincts formed an enclosed triangle of land stretching, according to present landmarks, on the one side along the Thames from the lock to Abingdon Bridge, on the second along Bridge Street to Stert Street and so to the railway station, and on the third, thence back to the river with a loop northward to include the home farm. In addition, there lay beyond the farm to the north-west the abbey vineyard, and to this day the street overlying the site is known as the 'Vineyard'.

The buildings that remain today are fragmentary, as after the dissolution, the great abbey church was pulled down in a matter of weeks, and most of the other structures disappeared in the next fifty years.

The abbey gateway built in the mid-fifteenth century still stands off the market place, and is approached by a recess formed by St. Nicholas' church to the north and the Hospital of St. John (now the Borough Council Chambers and Courts) to the south. The central arch is for wheeled or horse traffic and a doorway at the side for foot passengers; the archway next to the Council Chambers is modern and replaced a porter's lodge of which traces may be seen. Both the ancient arches are contained in square frames surmounted by the arms of king and abbot, while above the main arch is a richly canopied niche containing a stone figure of St. Mary the Virgin, the patron saint of the abbey. The figure is contemporary with the building except for the head which was replaced in Victorian times by a mayor of the town. Worth noticing too are miniature corbels on either side of the arch which are said to represent Edward IV and his queen. The archway is crowned by a plain stone parapet; and through it passed the visitors, episcopal, royal, official—

> 'An abbot on an ambling pad
> A long haired page in crimson clad'—

and all the pageantry and colour of a medieval civilization. For instance, in the spring of 1518 Henry VIII established himself at Abingdon to escape the sweating sickness, and maintained a seven-hours post between himself and Wolsey in London, which communications he is said to have studied avidly. Later he amused himself with conferences held between the best learned scholar of the University, and Privy Councillors such as Sir Thomas More—forerunners maybe of Union debates.

To the right of the gateway was the old Hospital of St. John for sick and needy travellers, with its small chapel at the east end. In the sixteenth century the hospital seems to have become an infirmary for aged employees of the abbey. Shortly after the dissolution, it was, with the abbey gateway, sold to the Corporation, who at one time used it as a prison and ensured it the dubious honour of being condemned by John Howard. Today, restored and well cared for, it is used as Court Rooms below and Council Chambers above. A wing of this Hospital was sold by the Corporation to John Roysse, a native of Abingdon and citizen and mercer of London, who wished to found a free grammar school here. The school with small additions lived in this room for 307 years from 1563 until 1870. There had, it should be noticed, been an earlier free school at Abingdon attached to the abbey and mentioned as early as 1372 which numbered among its pupils the Sir John Mason who saved the Oxford colleges that were monastic foundations from losing their revenues during the general confiscation of ecclesiastical property. Roysse's foundation, however, is always known as Abingdon School. It followed the old tradition but his instructions to the Mayor and Burgesses on the choice of a schoolmaster are interesting. They were 'to chuse an honest sadde and discrete man, vertuous in livynge, honest in his behaviour, and charitable in his doyinges, as nere as they may, a learned man a priest or a wedded man, such as to them shall seeme most mete, to be the scholemaster of the said free schole and that he hath no cure or benefice'.

This was the beginning of a notable line of headmasters and scholars among whom Thomas Tesdale is perhaps the best known as the co-founder in 1624 of Pembroke College, Oxford, upon an ancient Abingdon foundation. It is less well known that he was a clothier, with three teazles proper in his coat of arms, and was a sower and manufacturer of woad for dyeing and 'the greatest dealer therein . . . in the whole realm'. Roysse's room is now linked up with the rest of the Borough buildings as just before 1870 the school occupied their present premises at Albert Park.

The other side of the abbey gateway is bordered by St. Nicholas' church built right over the little river Stert in the late twelfth century for the use of the lay servants of the abbey. The Norman west door and the remains of Early English lancets may still be seen, but it is full of old and curious treasures in stone, including a rare lantern holder. The tombs of John and Jane Blacknall, dated 1625, stand in a shallow recess on which doles of bread are placed for distribution among the poor. John Blacknall came into possession of the abbey and its Account Rolls at the dissolution. His daughter Jane married a Verney, at whose seat in Buckinghamshire the Account Rolls were discovered in a great wainscoted room in the roof. They contain the accounts, rarely extant, of the kitchener, sacristan, refectorer and gardener, and are, of course, of great historical interest.

The church of the abbey stood on the site of the gardens of the present Abbey House, where a few pieces of original construction have been confounded by the addition of several reconstructed oddments of masonry. It is as if pieces of a skeleton were strewn at odd angles over a tomb for the benefit of anatomists. The great church deserves a better fate and it is a sad reflexion on Abingdon that more has not been done to enhance the architectural and historical interest of the lay-out. St. Ethelwold's church, itself built over Hean's seventh-century monastery, was 370 feet long by 170 feet wide and culminated, in much the same manner as that at Wells, in twin towers and a fine central tower. So it stood until the Conquest when successive abbots extended and altered the structure which at its destruction was indeed 'a great and goodly thing'.

Traces of a cloister and chapter house have been discovered south of the church, and a building which in all probability was the abbot's lodging. Yet even today the outlines of the various buildings round the cloister have not been traced and it is the humbler, domestic side of the community which is best preserved architecturally. Most of these face the millstream and a mill which occupies a site first used for grist by

St. Ethelwold. Most have been acquired by the Friends of Abingdon who are cherishing and restoring what is left after four centuries of use as cottages and commercial premises.

Already part of the abbey granary, after serving as a bridewell or house of correction, has been re-conditioned and serves as the custodian's office but the jewel of the collection is the Checker (or Chequer), a thirteenth-century building with tall massive buttresses and a magnificent chimneystack. It is square in plan with two stories surmounting a vaulted crypt, which was probably the wine cellar. The two most unusual architectural features are a fireplace with a stone canopy (now sadly mutilated) and the tall chimney which with its lancet-filled gables is by far the finest of its date in the country.

The Long Gallery which adjoins the eastern end of the Checker dates from the fifteenth or early sixteenth century and may have been built for the accommodation of the clerks who dealt with the accounts and records kept in the Checker. The gallery consists of ten bays, originally twelve, of which the central six formed two large rooms and the three bays at each end were three smaller rooms. A gallery or passage, lighted by unglazed windows, served all the rooms, which were partitioned off from it. After the dissolution of the abbey the Long Gallery was much abused and at one time became part of a brewery. Since 1945 the Friends of Abingdon have begun to wipe out the sins of their forefathers and under their care,—to quote from their own useful pamphlet—if public support is forthcoming 'it should in a few years time be possible to view in quiet and dignified surroundings this small but unique fragment of the former great Abbey of Abingdon'.

The small lay community which grew up outside the abbey walls at first found the abbot a beneficial neighbour. In the twelfth century, Abbot Vincent—the same who set a little meadow aside to provide 'hay under the feet of the monks at the baths'—obtained the rights of a full market at Abingdon, the judgement of the crown being assisted by three hundred marks of silver, but the grant so angered the men of Oxford and Wallingford that they marched over and tried to expel the stall-holders who 'taking courage I know not whence' drove them off. Later, as the townsfolk increased in numbers, they became restless of the abbey's tutelage and from 1327 onwards riots and disputes were common. In 1538 the friction ended for in the February of that year Thomas Pentecost handed over the abbey to the king, and was given Cumnor manor-house and an annual pension of £200 while the twenty-four monks received sums corresponding to their status.

It must be admitted, however, that before the dissolution the citizens themselves had already acquired a prime essential to civic growth in the form of a national highway. The river Ock was easily fordable except in flood and even then, long before the year 1110, it could be crossed by a bridge at the entrance to the town. The Thames proved a far greater obstacle, and seriously hindered access from London and the east, as the fords and ferries over it were inconvenient, expensive and dangerous. Travellers from the Oxfordshire side had to cross a backwater at Culhamford and then traverse the marshes of Andersey Island before being ferried over the main stream. The credit of overcoming this barrier goes to the Brotherhood of the Holy Cross, an old fraternity of merchants and townsfolk around which the civic life centred. In 1416 the Brotherhood undertook the building of two bridges and a connecting causeway. Sir Peter Besils furnished stone from his quarries at Sandford and Bessels Leigh while Geoffrey Barbour, once bailiff of Bristol, gave one thousand marks in money and, shortly afterwards, William Hales, later sheriff of London, built at his own expense three new stone arches at the south end of the bridge nearest Abingdon to carry off flood-water. Much of this, however, is described in a long poem written about 1458 by a local ironmonger, who over-patriotically ascribes the foundation to the king.

'King Harry the fyft, in his fourthe yere
He hath i- founde for his folke a brige in Berkshire,
For cartis with cariage may goo and come clere,
That many wynters afore were marred in the myre.

'Many moo myscheves there weren I say.
Culham hithe hath causid many a curse,
I blyssed be our helpers we have a better waye,
Without any peny for cart and for horse.'

Of the commercial effects of the bridge a great deal could be said, for a main road from London to Gloucester and the West now passed through Abingdon and the older Thames-crossing at Wallingford lost much of its importance. Strangely enough the Brotherhood became an incorporated guild in 1441 through the good offices of Sir John Golafre (p. 15) who 'built at his own charges the great stone bridge, called New Bridge in Oxfordshire'.

The Guild of the Holy Cross met in the Exchequer, a small room over the second north-porch of St. Helen's church. On or near this site when Hean was founding the abbey, his sister Cilla founded a nunnery in honour of St. Helen. The present church contains three stories of an Early English tower but dates for the most part from the mid-fifteenth to the early-sixteenth century, being essentially Perpendicular. Its tall spire soars above five aisles which have, as it were, grown outwards until the building is broader than it is long. At least one of the outer aisles was erected in 1539 and appears to be an addition intended to recompense for the destruction of the abbey church—or to make use of masonry from it.

St. Helen's shelters many memorials to the merchants who

made their fortunes here, especially in the cloth trade. A fine brass, once in the abbey, commemorates Geoffrey Barbour, the bridge builder, while a tomb marks the resting-place of John Roysse, the founder of the Grammar School. A different type of monument in St. Catherine's aisle recalls the good fortune of William Lee, who married three times, had seventeen children, seventy-eight grandchildren and one hundred and two great-grandchildren, all of whom are named. The churchwardens' accounts, still extant, also remind us of the 'good old days': 1612, 'pd. to Bartholomew for his yeres wages for whipping doggs out of the church XIId;' 1638, 'for looking unto the unruelye boys 8*s*. 8*d*.'

A manuscript history of the Guild of the Holy Cross down to 1627, written by Francis Little, is preserved in Christ's Hospital, which the Guild founded as almshouses in 1553. Facing the church this pleasant building has a long wooden gallery into which open the doors of the living rooms; on the other side facing the garden, the walls are of stone with tall brick chimneys nicely spaced each side of a quaint lantern and a fine mullioned oriel window; on the river side the appearance is equally charming if only for the four foliated windows. The hall of the Hospital has panelled walls round which hang portraits, for the most part of the early seventeenth century, of many of Abingdon's benefactors—Geoffrey Barbour, Sir Peter Besils, Sir John Mason and others—and of a later date of the Rev. Walter Harte and his beloved Elizabeth Hawkins, who lies beneath a grand marble monument in St. Helen's. Christ's Hospital was extended in brick in 1797 and so completes with the church and Twitty's almshouses (1707) a quite remarkable square of charity and godliness. Some distance away in Ock Street are more almshouses, founded and well endowed in 1733 by Benjamin Tomkins a wealthy maltster.

These charitable bequests may be taken as signs of the prosperity of post-Reformation Abingdon which became a borough in 1555. Trade and traffic and local industries, apart perhaps from cloth, steadily increased. Of the Civil War the less said the better for here in a bloody encounter at Culham Bridge, Sir Henry Gage was slain; here King Charles parted for the last time from Queen Henrietta just two months before the birth of their daughter; here, in St. Helen's church lies a rabid Roundhead, Thomas Trapham, who, as chirurgeon to the general of the parliament army, embalmed the King's body after the execution and afterwards remarked that 'he had sewed on the head of a goose'. Yet about this time the town lost and gained at least one notable feature. In the market-place stood a tall, ornate cross erected by the guild in the reign of Henry VI but its elaborate decoration displeased Waller who, in 1644, had it removed as 'a superstitious edifice'. Nearby was an old market house, itself a reconstruction of Elizabeth's time, which in 1678 was replaced by the present graceful structure. The architect is not known but the master-mason was Christopher Kempster who worked under Wren on St. Paul's and later built himself a pleasant house at Kitt's Quarries, near Burford in Oxfordshire.

The corporation treasures kept in the hall include one of great appeal to geographers. It is a mid-fifteenth-century map, brightly coloured in oils, of the Thames valley from Radley to Abingdon, measuring in all about 9 feet by 18 inches. The two-storied building with a tower shown at the west of the map is probably St. Edmund's Chapel which may have stood near the Saint's birthplace on a site near the present Old Vicarage. Saint Edmund Rich (1170–1240) was undeniably Abingdon's greatest son and as Archbishop of Canterbury for six years wielded a sobering influence on an unruly court.

Of the charms of eighteenth- and nineteenth-century Abingdon much has recently been written, but the difficulty is sometimes the seeing—for to step out into the street is to test that second dividing the quick from the dead. Yet East and West St. Helens Street may be safely and agreeably followed as also may Stert Street which runs on arches built over the stream of that name. And always there are the riverine meadows, with the spire of St. Helen's dominating the Thames. The truth is that Abingdon has never been fossilized; it has remained through the centuries a living organism, which has acquired the accretions of each age and been overwhelmed by none.

CHAPTER V: *The Villages at the Foot of the Downs*

Unnumber'd cottages and farms
That have for musing minds unnumber'd charms.

GEORGE CRABBE

THE transition from the clay soils of the Vale of White Horse to the porous wind-swept downs occurs at a steep scarp or slope where a remarkable string of villages is threaded together by the Icknield Way. Here the wide unsettled spaces of the Vale give way to a rapid succession of hamlets, and the re-appearance of fine parks and stately mansions denotes the existence of lords of the manor rather than village yeomen.

The Icknield Way dates at least from the Iron Age and, entering Berkshire from Wiltshire in the parish of Ashbury, follows a perfectly clear course to Wantage. Unlike the Ridge Way it is a hill-side route which hugs the foot of the downs though subtly avoiding the damper meadows and cunningly keeping above the powerful springs issuing from the base of the chalk. At Wantage, the road forks, the northern branch being known in the eleventh century as the Port Way. This section has been in use throughout Christian times and early seems to have quite replaced the southern fork which, although retaining the name of Icknield Way, has fallen into disuse and dwindled into a discontinuous track.

East Hendred is one of the prettiest and certainly the largest village lying near the Port Way. Here the Ginge Brook drove several mill-wheels, and fulling mills were at work in Tudor times and one piece of ground used to be called 'Fulling Mill Mere'. Some traces of terraces said to be connected with cloth-drying may be seen near the church, in which are memorials to former merchants, including Henry and Roger Eldysley (1439) and William Whitwey, *pannarius et lanarius*, (1479): a trackway, still known as the Golden Mile, leads up to the downs at Scutchamer Knob and a fair was held along it in the old days. The wealth acquired from trade helps to account for the many dignified houses although much of the charm of the village derives from the fold in the downs which shelters the growth of numerous elms.

At the very entrance to East Hendred, where two roads converge, is the small Champs Chapel, dedicated to Jesus of Bethlehem and built originally by the Carthusian monks of Sheen in Surrey who once owned the manor. The diminutive Perpendicular structure stands beside a timber-framed house with barge-boards which seems to have been the residence of the monks serving the chapel.

At the foot of the hill is the gabled manor house, belonging to Mr. Thomas More Eyston, one of the old Berkshire families, and descended by marriage from Sir Thomas More through his only son John and Ann Cresacre his wife. Sir Thomas More needs no description. He is today remembered more for his scholarship and integrity than for his Lord Chancellorship. His stature has increased with the centuries and it is now generally agreed, as his latest biographer says, 'that More has had to wait four hundred years for his real importance to be fully discerned, that his ideals still lie before striving mankind, and will make him more and more important as the years pass on'. Today his descendants still carry on his name and possess his drinking mug and a copy —one of three or four in existence—of Holbein's famous group of the More Family. The manor house of the Eystons, part ancient, part Georgian, contains a thirteenth-century chapel to St. Amand, in which mass has been said regularly for several centuries.

The parish church has a quiet dignity as its various styles from 1200 onwards have been skilfully blended. Within, it contains in a chapel, separated off by a fine Perpendicular arcade, many monuments to the Eystons. Among other notable features are a clock made in 1528 and still working; a curious reading desk (thirteenth-century), the stand of which is carved into a mailed fist with three dragon's heads, and a Jacobean pulpit with a carved head of Charles I. The church was drastically restored in the 'sixties and some graves were disturbed, which so enraged the villagers that one old man used to sit at his cottage door with a loaded gun ready to shoot the vicar at sight.

The Port Way serves no more interesting village than East Hendred, for its timber-framed and cob cottages, mostly thatched, and its raised stone causeways have such a natural air. Some may prefer the smaller West Hendred where the church stands bravely between the Ginge Brook and the bare bastion of Goldbury hill; others may be charmed with the planned ensemblage of half-timber and thatch at Ardington where the dog-tooth of the north doorway of the church disarms all criticism; yet others may like the downright honest planning of Lockinge, but only East Hendred has, like Sir Thomas More, grown in quality throughout the centuries.

Even the most ardent admirer has never dared to say this of Wantage, the principal market-town in the Vale of White Horse. Famed as the birthplace in 849 of King Alfred, the name might well lead the unwary to expect a storehouse of treasures. In truth, not a trace of the royal palace held by Ethelwulf, father of Alfred remains, nor for that matter did a statue of the great king adorn the wide market place until 1877 when Lord Wantage presented the present memorial carved by Count Gleichen. Of all English kings Wantage has surely chosen the finest, for the astonishing thing about Alfred is the manner he soars above all his contemporaries. 'He is', to quote the *Dictionary of National Biography*, 'the one great character of our early history whose name still lives in popular memory and round whose well-known historical career a vast mass of legend has gathered'. On to Alfred have been foisted the deeds and foundations of a long stretch of time, yet his merits needed no fictitious embellishment. At once general, lawgiver, saint and scholar he devoted himself single-mindedly to the welfare of his people and with medieval completeness excelled in peace as much as in war. He died on the 28th October 901 in his fifty-third year and was buried at Winchester, the heart of the Wessex he knew so well.

It seems doubtful if the people of Wantage took much interest in Alfred until the stone-figure with its battle-axe constantly reminded them of him. In 1849 on the millenary of Alfred's birth the celebrations projected by Martin Tupper almost died of apathy. As the Berkshire gentry were not keen, Tupper tried unsuccessfully to obtain the Guildhall in London. Finally, Mr. Charles Eyston of East Hendred came to the rescue and with the help of Mr. Pusey the local M.P. ensured that the celebration was held at Wantage. Mr. Pusey brought the famous horn to drink from and the whole affair went so well that it was repeated on the millenary of Alfred's death and will, presumably, be repeated on the 28th day of October each centenary thereafter. There was a sequel to the first great celebration, for Martin Tupper having roused the nation with his Anglo-Saxonism, now kept an ambitious eye on the poet laureateship. When Queen Victoria was struck on the head by a retired officer—to wit Henry Pate—Tupper consoled the Queen with his poetry.

> 'O dastard! Thus to strike that brow
> Anointed and so fair;
> O brave young Queen! that bruise is now
> The brightest jewel there!'

The gallant inspiration was 'appreciated and much

admired' at the Palace—and Tennyson was appointed Poet Laureate!

In his will Alfred left the royal manor of Wantage to his wife Ealswith, but by 1246 it had come into the hands of the Fitzwarrens who held it for many centuries. Within the church a noble alabaster altar tomb of 1361, with effigies, commemorates Sir William Fitzwarren and his wife Amice. Here too is a brass to their son Sir Ives whose daughter Alice became the wife of Richard Whittington, thrice Lord Mayor of London.

Indeed, the seeker after antiquity in Wantage would be sadly disappointed were it not for the church which dates partly from the second half of the thirteenth century. The mixture of Perpendicular and later work seen from the outside hardly prepares one for the interesting interior. The lovely Early English font is well worth a visit, not to mention much wood-carving and some fine roof-timbering.

Next in age is the Grammar School, known since 1849 as King Alfred's School, which was founded in 1597 and stood near the church on the site of a Norman chapel. When the school moved to its present palatial home near the Port Way, a fine Norman doorway was incorporated into the building. Of Wantage between the death of Elizabeth and coming of the Georges even the most ardent enthusiasts can find little remarkable to say. In 1692, Bishop Joseph Butler, author of *The Analogy of Religion*, was born here and is remembered by a good portrait in the church. But Wantage really came to life with the agrarian revolution and most of the town consists of comfortable brick houses of Georgian and Victorian times. The manufacture of hemp and hats and a large tanning industry—the paths of the courtyard of Stiles's almshouses are paved with the knucklebones of sheep—were partly replaced by the making of agricultural implements and today a foundry still flourishes at East Challow.

The mid-nineteenth century brought changes of many

kinds. 'Black Wantage', as the town had long been known from its gambling sports frequented by vagrants and gipsies, was purified by the zeal of the Rev. W. J. Butler, a tractarian, who in thirty-seven years with the help of top-hatted curates (a foible of his) wiped out the demoralization. The south chapel of the church was restored in his honour and he is also remembered by the existence of the many pleasant buildings of the Sisterhood of St. Mary which he founded here in 1850.

This moral improvement of Wantage coincided with the coming of cheap coal by canal, and of quick transport by railway. The town had to be linked to the main line by a steam tramway which was taken up in 1948. The veteran engine, 'The Shannon', built in 1857, was then working well and has since been placed in honoured preservation in a shelter on the platform of Wantage Road Station. Even in its younger days it was sure rather than swift and had evoked the following ribald comment:

> 'A curious race has come to pass
> Between an engine and an ass
> The Wantage Tram, all steam and smoke
> Was beat by Arthur Hitchcock's moke.'

The outstanding benefactors of Wantage since Alfred have been Lord and Lady Wantage of Lockinge Park. P. H. Ditchfield in his *Byways in Berkshire and the Cotswolds* described how Lord Wantage, who won the Victoria Cross in the Crimean War and later became the local M.P., revived Berkshire agriculture, farmed on a colossal scale, built model cottages and villages, and 'was never tired of conferring benefits upon the town of Wantage. In all this work Lady Wantage was his faithful coadjutor . . .'. Today the Victoria Cross Gallery in the town houses a larger number of oil paintings of people winning the Victoria Cross than is to be found in any other room in the world.

The Icknield Way out of Wantage climbs steadily up to the downs with on the left-hand a wide, rolling expanse of chalk, part grass, part arable, having many a sharp depression and corresponding hill, and a general level of about 400 feet. As Gilbert White says 'there is something peculiarly sweet and amusing in the shapely figured aspect of chalk hills, in preference to those of stone, which are rugged, broken, abrupt and shapeless'. At the first cross-roads a beech hangar marks the steep descent into Childrey, a village at the head of a sheltered combe where a perennial stream issues from the junction of greensand and chalk. Here a pocket of fertile soil, known locally as the 'blacklands', supports a pleasant mixture of houses that are grouped about a long narrow green with a pond in its midst. The manor house may be recognized by a walk of clipped yews leading up to a Perpendicular door and window above it. This was the original seat of the Fettiplaces who held estates in Berkshire for five centuries and grew rich in comfortable obscurity. The house has been much altered but retains a room in which Charles I slept. It was Sir George Fettiplace who, in 1732, built the red-brick schoolhouse in the village, bearing his coat-of-arms. This school, however, was probably founded by William Fettiplace (*c.* 1526) who established a chantry under the care of Queen's College, Oxford. The chantry chaplain had also to teach in a free school in his house and neither this nor the chantry as it was connected with the college, was suppressed at the Reformation.

The church at Childrey stands at the north of the village and makes a pretty picture with the dark yews. A large cruciform building, its interior is spacious and shelters eleven monumental brasses, of which seven are in the chancel. The earliest, a brass to William Fynderne and wife (1444), is the largest in the county being 9 feet 6 inches by 3 feet 8 inches. There are also two shroud brasses, one of the year 1516 and another, somewhat earlier, to Jone Strangbone. The chancel was rebuilt about 1280 but most of the rest of the church is Perpendicular, and includes some excellent bench-ends, and a remarkable leaden font probably of the twelfth century.

One mile west of Childrey in an almost identical situation below the Icknield Way, lies Sparsholt a village of elms, and half-timbered cottages and farms, among which Hall Place stands out because of its mullioned windows and barge-boarded gables. The church as at Childrey contains interesting brasses but its chief treasures are the wooden effigies representing Sir Richard Achard and his two successive wives. Probably fewer than one hundred such effigies exist in the country. Once richly coloured, they are of considerable artistic merit. Each was probably carved out of the single trunk of an oak and the flowing lines of the drapery seems almost to be realized out of the inherent quality of the timber. The veiling falls in soft delicate folds and the faces wear a gentle withdrawn smile as if they were listening to the music of the angels about their heads.

The country west of Sparsholt is shaded by two fine parks, where in the woods and warrens on the greensands squirrels and foxes abound. Foxes used regularly to be imported from Scotland and Germany and at one period when they caught mange it was found that the local badgers occupied their earths and thoroughly cleansed them. These foxes prowl for miles over the hedged-lands of the Vale of White Horse and leave the open chalk downs to the less-cunning hare.

At the cross-roads on the edge of Kingston Lisle park, a little towards the hills, is a small stone house, once an inn, where an oak shades a sarsen stone of irregular shape and sponge-like perforations. By blowing into the topmost hole some gifted persons can produce a noise unknown to musicians. But Tom Hughes' description of this Blowing Stone can hardly be bettered:

'This here is the Blowing Stwun his self', putting his hand on a square lump of stone, some three feet and a half high, perforated with two or three queer rat holes, like petrified antediluvian rat-holes, which lies there close under the oak, under our very nose. We are more than ever puzzled, and drink our second glass of ale, wondering what will come next. 'Like to hear un, sir?' says mine host, setting down Toby Philpot on the tray, and resting both hands on the 'stwun'. We are ready for anything; and he, without waiting for a reply, applies his mouth to one of the rat-holes. Something must come of it, if he doesn't burst. Good heavens! I hope he has no apoplectic tendencies. Yes, here it comes, sure enough, a grewsome sound between a moan and a roar and spreads itself away over the valley, and up the hill-side and into the woods at the back of the house, a ghost-like, awful voice 'Um do say, sir,' says mine host, rising purple-faced, while the moan is still coming out of the stwun, 'as they used to warn the countryside by blowing the Stwun when the enemy was a-coming.'

The visitor who fails to blow the stone may take heart from the beauty of the Icknield Way which now undergoes a subtle change. Hereabouts the sandy beds which to the east have formed a platform at the foot of the chalk almost disappear and the road is forced higher up the hillside. For the same reason the springs now break out right against the road which winds tortuously round the deep combes and divides the lush plant-life of the watercourses from the bald wiry turf of the dry hollows above. The two finest combes eat into White Horse Hill, and one of them, the Manger (p. 65) rises serenely from above the Icknield Way near one of the strongest sources of the Ock.

The villages of this district are small and consist mostly of small thatched cottages of chalk or half-timber or brick. Woolstone is charming and at its inn shows almost every kind of building material from sarsen stones to flint and tiles. Compton Beauchamp sits more prettily higher up the hills and has a greater antiquity for from a pit on Knighton Hill early Iron Age pottery and a Saxon cooking pot have been unearthed.

Ashbury, which distinguishes itself by sitting athwart the Icknield Way, yields nothing in charm to its neighbours. Behind it the chalk slopes rise abruptly and on each side a steep ravine sinks down to springs of fresh water and water-cress beds. The manor house here has much fifteenth-century work, including chimneys that root down to the foundations. The front has mullioned and foliated windows and a gabled porch, the upper story of which was added in 1697, while at the rear deeply-recessed windows are spaced unsymmetrically in the face of the wall. The parish church shows the usual mixture of styles from Transitional to Perpendicular but it bases its claim to fame more on the Rev. Thomas Stock who, in 1777 started in it the first Sunday School ever held in England.

Ashbury may lead for sobriety but Compton Beauchamp takes pride of place for individuality. Its little church is tucked away up a rustic lane rich in country smells, and sits at ease in a pleasant churchyard. It contains a few fragments of fourteenth-century glass and such a wealth of things more modern that it should on no account be missed. Its utter tidiness, although almost beyond a male's comprehension, will, like the memorial eulogy to Rachel Richards, greatly impress—or depress—all housewives. The churchyard adjoins the terraced lawns and sloping, topiaried gardens of the manor house, a lovely moated building partly of brick of Tudor age.

In this village in the eighteenth century dwelt a woman charmingly different from the bulk of her sex. Devoted to sports and in particular coursing, she was wealthy and personable with good blood but although courted continuously preferred a life of single blessedness. At Compton the remains of Wig Avenue still exist, where the gallants changed from their small riding wigs to flowing perukes in which they hoped to lay siege to the lady. But all to no purpose, wet or fine, fair or foul, she was dragged in her coach at six over the downs to the 'meet' and then on foot with her dogs sometimes for twenty miles would spend the day coursing. She managed her estate with shrewdness and was quixotically generous to all callers and neighbours, yet her love of dogs exceeded all other passions. Their place in her house was 'wherever they think fit to go' and in every room an ottoman was provided for their exclusive comfort. At her death in 1771 her dogs and estate were bequeathed to an adopted child and to the world she left:

An Epitaph of Miss Ann Richards, of Compton Beauchamp
Written by Herself.

Reader, if ever sport to thee was dear,
Drop on Ann Richards' tomb a tear,
Who when alive with piercing eye,
Did many a timid hare descry:
Tattle and tea! she was above it,
And but for form appeared to love it,
At books she laugh'd, at Pope and Clarke,
And all her joy was Ashdown Park.
But Ann at length was spy'd by death
Who cours'd and ran her out of breath:
No shifting, winding turn, could save
Her active life from gaping grave:
As greyhound with superior force
Seizes poor puss and stops her course,
So stopped the fates our heroines view,
And bade her take a long adieu,
Of shrill so-so! and loud haloo.

CHAPTER VI: The Lambourn Downs

And see you, after rain, the trace
Of mound and ditch and wall?
O that was a Legion's camping-place
When Caesar sailed from Gaul.

And see you marks that show and fade,
Like shadows on the Downs?
O they are the lines the Flint Men made,
To guard their wondrous towns.

RUDYARD KIPLING

THE world of chalk has looked kindly on Berkshire as its smooth bald slopes occupy space enough to add variety and yet insufficient to oppress with vast uniformity. These downs are 'full of life and sunshine', and have since early times formed a natural routeway free of floods and all water hazards. The ancient Ridge Way, as it was called in Anglo-Saxon charters, keeps to the summit of the hills and in Berkshire stretches from above Ashbury to the Thames gap near Streatley. It is bounded on either side for most of its length by a low green bank erected probably in the eighteenth century to preserve the right of way and the width of the road which had been fixed at one chain. At places where these banks were not constructed the track has been greatly widened by the trampling of cattle. As it approaches the Thames valley and the hill-crest lowers, the Ridge Way loses its strength and splits into various tracks leading towards Moulsford, Streatley, Pangbourne and even farther south.

On the downs it is paved with incomparable springy turf sweet with the scent of wild thyme and tinged with harebells, bedstraw and trefoil and topped here and there along its length with beech and fir follies, and although it seldom rises above 750 feet here you can have 'all the world to yourself, shared only by sheep, an occasional shepherd and hundreds of hares all the way to Marlborough'. And yet out on that frozen sea of downland the Ridge Way is almost companionable in that in its purposeful way it seems to lead to human faces and voices once more and to link the solitary traveller with his fellows. 'There is', says S. P. B. Mais in his *England's Pleasaunce*, 'no way I know of regaining happiness more surely than of wandering along the Berkshire Downs.'

The Ridge Way is easily accessible for alone in complete competency it serves the lengthwise communications of the hills and all paths and roads hereabouts end at or cross it. From Gorse Hill near West Ilsley to Furzewick Down above Wantage it traverses a landscape much tamed by man who in his ploughings and reapings merely emphasizes the sweeping undulations of the chalk. West of Furzewick the Ridge Way climbs to its greatest heights and, with the chalk scarp, becomes truly majestic. No springs or dew-ponds, no farmsteads or dwellings break the dominance of the chalk but here and there a barn may brave the wind and lower down on the south, where great corrugations begin, a lonely farmhouse may find shelter in a deepening combe.

The route west of Wantage from Furzewick Down past the circular ramparts of Letcombe Castle or Segsbury Camp circumvents some remarkable combes, including the Devil's Punchbowl. In former years not everyone turned aside to descend to Letcombe Bassett, for once on the Ridge Way it is folly—and exhausting—to clamber up and down the escarpment in order to see hamlets which are properly reached from the Icknield Way. Yet Letcombe Bassett has fallen between two roads; it is far from the Icknield Way and 350 feet below the nearby Ridge Way. This very isolation has recently brought the village much into the public eye, for it has been suggested by a 'planning official' that most of its population should be re-housed in a larger neighbouring village where they could enjoy many modern amenities so patently lacking in their own. This threatened destruction of a village mentioned in *Domesday Survey* has raised floods of protests: 'it is equivalent to destroying a national treasure', its buildings have become overnight 'historic', 'old and humbly beautiful'. It is soon recalled that Letcombe was the Cresscombe of *Jude the Obscure* and here set prettily above the watercress beds is the thatched cottage in which the seductive Arabella lived. In the rectory near the church Swift spent the high summer of 1714 just before his final retreat to Ireland. From Letcombe Bassett he wrote farewell to the Earl of Oxford—'I have said enough; and, like one at your levee, having made my bow, I shrink back into the crowd'. Here too he heard from Lord Bolingbroke that 'The Earl of Oxford was removed on Tuesday; the Queen died on Sunday. What a world is this, and how does Fortune banter us!' Pope and Parnell and even Vanessa found their way hither to the ironical Dean.

The present visitor finds a hamlet of about two score dwellings, for the most part timber-framed and thatched and well-cared for but occasionally marred, as so often happens in rural Berkshire, by an indifference to tidiness and comeliness. It does not need a critical eye to detect the abominable use of corrugated iron for repairs, the incompatibility of new cottages, the over-restoration of the church and the conversion of the old rectory into 'a large untidy structure of no merit . . . In short, except for a pleasant eighteenth-century farmhouse, there are no buildings of historical or architectural importance in Letcombe Bassett, and the unique charm of the place lies in its lovely setting in deep narrow combes at the foot of the downs, where rise the chalk streams watering the cress beds in the valley below'.

Yet the threatened destruction of the village arises not from its architectural blunders but from its smallness, isolation and relative stagnation. It lacks a resident vicar, a school and most other amenities, mental and material, which moderns have every right to expect. There can be no question of letting Letcombe stagnate and its younger inhabitants suffer increasingly for the omissions of their forefathers. Nor can the parishioners solve the problem which is quite beyond their resources, not least because of the lack of a local magnate—as at Buckland and Ardington—to transform the scene. The solution therefore seems to lie negatively in mass migration or positively either in the acquisition of amenities at an exorbitant cost to the general public or in the enlargement of the village to a workable size. The issue has aroused the almost opposite feelings of sentimentality and common sense nor has the sight of the scaffold done the parishioners any harm. At this eleventh hour of reckoning one thing seems clear: had all the inhabitants beautified their holdings, cleared away shacks and galvanized iron, 'petted' grass verges and offset walls with delphinium and hollihock, had all shown more pride of ownership and love of community, the threat of destruction would hardly dared have been whispered. For at soul England is still artistic and the charity of county councils still elastic where new life springs on old roots.

Except in time of thaw when the chalk sticks like glue, the Ridge Way should be followed from above Letcombe Bassett right into Wiltshire. A short stretch of breezy downland leads to the place where Jude the Obscure after climbing the road from Lambourne (Marygreen) gazed longingly north to distant Oxford (Christminster). 'There are cold spots up and down Wessex in autumn and winter: but the coldest of all when a north or east wind is blowing is the crest of the down by the Brown House where the road to Alfredston (Wantage) crosses the old Ridgeway. Here the first winter sleets and snows fall and lie, and here the spring frost lingers last unthawed.'

Unless in the grip of the north-east wind and rain, the

traveller is well advised to proceed three miles farther westward to White Horse Hill (856 feet), the summit of the downs where the White Horse, wild and free, gallops in scoured chalk. The horse is by far the oldest of the seventeen chalk-cut horses in England and is one of the few that cannot be dated for certain with any precision. First mentioned in the eleventh century when a cartulary of Abingdon Abbey records the 'mons Albi Equi', it had then long been formed by cutting away the earth to the solid chalk over the whole body except the head which is in outline only, with an eye just over four feet across. Its present dimensions—365 feet in length and 130 feet in height—are somewhat less than originally as depressions in the turf show. In shape, it is a highly artistic conception, attenuated and disjointed, and remarkable, with its beak-like jaws and staring eye, for its general lack of resemblance to a plump, well-fed horse. It does, however, bear a distinct likeness to a horse imprinted on some early British coins, which in its turn may have descended from the coinage of Philip of Macedon; and the fact that early traditions name it as a horse leaves little room to speculate on what it might otherwise be.

The neighbouring archaeological remains, such as Uffington Castle, the 'pillow mound', and the lynchets, although provocative of ideas, have no irrefutable connexion with the figure. It is faintly possible that the horse was some sort of deity which may explain why it is so skilfully placed on the hillside as to be easily visible from the Vale, but all that can be said with certainty is that it was cut at the end of the Iron Age, probably in the first century B.C. Needless to say it has given rise to numerous copies whose corpulent figures lack the sinewy lines of the genuine thoroughbred. Perhaps we should add that the theory that it was cut as a memorial to Alfred's great victory at Ashdown in 871 was first advanced by Dr. Wise in 1738 and is quite unsupported by any archaeological evidence.

The White Horse has survived through the ancient custom of scouring and it may well be that lands in the vicinity were once held on terms of keeping it clear. Thomas Hughes's book on the scouring has recently been re-printed and makes pleasant reading even if his archaeology is highly fanciful. *Jackson's Oxford Journal* usually reported the event and gave the attendance in that good old-fashioned method of a lot of people equals twenty, or thirty, or even forty thousand. On April 29th, 1780, 'We hear from good authority that the usual ceremony of scouring the White Horse upon Uffington Hill, with a greater variety of rural sports than were ever exhibited upon that occasion, will be performed in Whitsun week, when it is expected that a greater concourse of all ranks of people will be assembled than were present the last time; although the numbers then present were supposed to exceed forty thousand.' On May 6th, the *Journal* describes the meeting: 'The sports included a silver cup to be run for by ponies the best of three two-mile heats: A thill harness will be run for by cart horses etc. in their harness and bells; the carters to ride in smock frocks without saddles. Crossing and jostling, but no whipping allowed. A flitch of bacon to be run for by asses. A good hat to be run for by men in sacks; every man to bring his own sack. A waistcoat; 10*s*. 6*d*. value will be given to the person who shall take a bullet out of a tub of flour with his mouth in the shortest time. Several cheeses will be run for down the White Horse Manger. Smocks to be run for by ladies; the second-best of each prize to be entitled to a silk-hat. Cudgel playing for a gold-laced hat and a pair of buckskin breeches, and wrestling for a pair of silver buckles and a pair of pumps. A jingling match by eleven blindfolded men and one unmasked with bells, for a pair of buckskin breeches. And sundry other rural amusements. A grinning match through a horses's collar for five shillings. An apple to be taken out of a tub of water for five shillings. Riding down the hill upon a horse's jawbones for

2s. 6d.' It is with stern reason therefore that the modern poet has warned his readers and:

> 'bade them heed
> Those peasants of the Berkshire breed,
> Who plucked the old Horse of the weed
> As they pluck it to this hour.'

At the very top of the hill is Uffington Castle, among the most splendid of the prehistoric earthworks on the downs. It has a defended entrance on the west and a strong ditch and rampart which in parts may have been double. The view of the Vale from the camp holds the memory; the shaven turf at one's feet slipping recklessly down to the wooded civilized Vale, 'spread out as the garden of the Lord', and bounded by no hill nearer than Faringdon Folly or the fir-topped Cumnor Hurst.

The defensive qualities of this Iron Age camp are greatly enhanced by the steep drop on the north side to the Manger, a large combe with many a rib and hollow. Here in remote time rose the copious springs which now break forth below the Icknield Way but the solvent action of water on chalk was probably also helped by the slow melting of patches of snow which lingered here for most of the summer in the last Ice Age. In places near the base of the Manger, flat, horizontal benches break the regularity of the slopes and these so-called lynchets have attracted much attention. It is generally assumed that they were formed either by ploughing in a certain manner, or, more probably, by terracing the hillside and that they date from Anglo-Saxon times. Being long and strip-like they contrast sharply with the older Celtic fields which have a square plan as may be seen so well near Ashdown Park and half a dozen other spots on the downs.

Another interesting earth-feature near the Manger is the small Dragon Hill, a rounded, semi-isolated hillock of quite natural formation. Yet rumour has cleverly seized upon it as the place where St. George slew a dragon and the bald patch on the summit marks the spot where the brute's blood killed the turf. This is the setting of Kenneth Grahame's *The Reluctant Dragon*, 'the most modest and retiring dragon in the world' who 'lolled on the turf', 'enjoyed the sunsets, told antediluvian anecdotes to the Boy, and polished his old verses while meditating on fresh ones'.

The prehistoric delights of White Horse Hill are increased by Wayland's Smithy, a tumulus or long barrow beside the Ridge Way twelve furlongs from Uffington Camp. In 955 in a charter of King Eadred it was known as Welandes Smidthan so that it would appear to have been exposed and its contents rifled before that date. The tradition of Wayland the Smith was incorporated in Scott's *Kenilworth* who heard the legend when staying at Uffington. It was believed that a wayfarer who had lost a shoe of his horse had but to tie the animal to the upright stone, leave a groat on the flat stone, whistle three times and go away for ten minutes and on returning would find the money gone and the horse shod. Oddly enough although the tumulus was so well known it was not explored scientifically until 1919 and consequently the finds were small. Inside, fragments of eight skeletons were found and outside a crouched burial, obviously of a much later date than the mound. The stones seen today are the remnants of several chambers which were originally hidden beneath the earth of the barrow. The tumulus is of Neolithic age—or about 2000 B.C.—and many finer examples exist in Gloucestershire, notably at Belas Knap above Winchcomb.

Of the many dry valleys near Wayland's Smithy the most pleasant is that winding away due south between Weathercock Hill and the woods of Ashdown Park. The house of Ashdown was probably built by John Webb, a pupil of Inigo Jones, who chose a site foursquare to the winds of heaven. The identical, tall faces of white chalk with stone-dressings are surmounted by a balustraded lantern which itself rises

The Ridge Way and Segsbury Camp

Aldworth Giant; Lord Nicholas

Pangbourne's Village Sign

cupola-like to a golden ball. The mansion was built for William, the first Earl of Craven who, born in 1606, lived through most of the troublous times of the House of Stuart and lavished much of his personal fortune on their cause. Lord Craven showed wide generosity also to sufferers during the Great Plague and Great Fire but on the abdication of James II he went into retirement and gratified his taste for building and laying out parks and gardens. He still loved to help in putting out fires and it is said that his horse on smelling a fire was in the habit of immediately galloping off to it.

The country around Ashdown Park abounds in traces of early man, although the Grey Wethers that litter the slopes near the mansion have no archaeological significance, being sarsen stones or the hard remnants of a rock stratum which once covered the chalk. The name comes from their likeness to sheep grazing on the downs. Just west of Ashdown woods is Alfred's Castle, an ancient circular earthwork quite unconnected with Alfred and which was used as late as Roman times. On the Lambourn side many tumuli and occasional Celtic fields and strip lynchets tell of a long occupation by man but the early settlement is felt most keenly about Seven Barrows Farm on the pleasant open road from Lambourn to the Blowing Stone. On inspection, the Seven Barrows prove to be twenty or more, most of them clearly visible. Some lie on the plateau and have been levelled by cultivation almost out of existence; others are on the valley slopes while quite a number nestle in the narrow combe, today a dry headward extension of the Lambourn stream but in prehistoric times rich in good springs and watering-places, where no doubt the herders gathered with their flocks from all the adjacent downland. A few of the barrows are long or Neolithic but most are round and belong to the Bronze Age and have, on excavation, yielded among other remains a bronze awl, an incense cup and various daggers.

Almost all the larger dry valleys that furrow the southern slopes of the downs hereabouts wind southwards, deepening and gathering up smaller dry combes, till they reach the river Lambourn. This stream is a mere trunk, the only surviving active section of a vast system of valleys that have been drying up for the last ten thousand years. Today the stream begins just above Lambourn town in a series of deep translucent pools that flow copiously except in the longer droughts, when its bed is quite dry as far as East Garston. In normal years the watercourse flows south-eastward for twelve miles to Newbury, forming a ribbon of perennial green and a string of habitations in an otherwise empty sea of chalk, for whereas prehistoric man preferred the open downland, his Anglo-Saxon successors, favoured with a drier landscape, have gone down to the shelter of the river-valleys.

Lambourn is the present metropolis of the downs yet it is little more than an overgrown village. As early as 1227 Fulk Fitzwarren was granted a fair at Chipping Lambourn, a name which suggests the existence also of a market. The fair survives but the market died out about 1874 having for some time previously 'dwindled to a weekly meeting of two old farmers at the George'.

The dwellings of the town centre upon the church and market place and are for the most part built of brick with some structures of sarsens, and flints. Since none has any visible claims to antiquity, the architectural attraction of Lambourn depends mainly upon its church, a grand structure which adequately bears its heavy responsibilities. Cruciform in shape, the building has expanded about a Transitional nave and tower, the remainder of it, apart from modern rebuilding and pseudo-Norman additions, being good Decorated and Perpendicular work. Among the interesting details are a rood-loft piscina and a fine archway from the transept to St. Mary's Chapel, which on one side is carved with ball-flower, winged heads, fishes and a couple of hounds chasing a hare accompanied by men blowing horns. The alabaster monuments of Sir Thomas Essex and Margaret his wife have a quiet charm, but the most visited tomb is that of John Estbury (*ob.* 1508), where the inhabitants of the nearby almshouses gather daily to say a special prayer for their founder. Even on Estbury's brass the local love of sport finds place as the words of the inscription are interspaced with a dog with a bone, a bird with a worm, an eagle, a fish, a dragon and a hare chased by two dogs.

Lambourn underwent a great revival in the nineteenth century and much building went on. The market cross and church were restored; the Place almshouses were built in a humble style; the Estbury almshouses, founded in 1501, were rebuilt on a grandiose scale in diamond-chequered red-brick with an embattled entrance tower and a small cloistered courtyard; Lambourn Place was turned into the 'Elizabethan' mansion which was recently pulled down. Finally at the very close of the century the railway came and together with the increase in horse-training ensured Lambourn's future prosperity. Today travelling horse-boxes are made and all the activities and oddities connected with the turf go on at expected and most unexpected hours. The town has taken on a cheerful prosperous look and dispenses tips with a liberality and authority quite its own. What Lambourn knows today England knows tomorrow.

At certain weeks of the year the horses and men and armour of Lambourn descend on Newbury, for only the bedridden —under nine months and over ninety!—do not follow the magic flute. On all but these days the Lambourn valley may be followed with undisturbed delight. At Eastbury, the first hamlet southward, the river still flows over flints and the thatched timber-framed cottages come down to the watercourse which is bridged by many a footpath. The elongated hamlet is dominated at one end by the chimney stacks of the gabled, stone-mullioned manor, once the home of the

Fitzwarrens and at the other by an octagonal dovecote of about 1620, constructed partly of flint with stone cornerings.

East Garston, apart from its latest additions, repeats the same pattern on a somewhat larger scale. The thatched cottages dotted alongside a winding tree-shaded street; the narrow valley hemmed in by chalk downs; the houses huddled close to the clear sparkling stream; the handsome brick manor house—this time some centuries later yet also with panelled rooms; and the small church severely restored in the nineteenth century, with the inevitable coloured glass.

The Shefford villages, two miles farther downstream, closely resemble their neighbours. Great or West Shefford seems the more flourishing and can boast of a panelled room where Charles I slept in November 1644 but East Shefford is certainly the older as an Anglo-Saxon cemetery has been discovered here. East Shefford has the unenviable distinction of having two disused churches. The one, standing knee-deep in weeds on the willow-lined fringe of the Lambourn stream, has windows ranging in age from Transitional through Perpendicular to eighteenth-century brick. All the interior wooden fittings have gone and the pew-less space adds grandeur to two splendid monuments to the Fettiplaces. The other church stands on drier ground near the main road and has redeemed its mid-Victorian ancestry by borrowing from its neighbour a few fragments of fifteenth-century glass showing a mitred bishop and the Annunciation.

At Welford, the typical 'Lambourn' pattern begins to weaken although the valley is still constricted. The heart of the village—a manor-house and church set at the foot of a wooded park—recalls the hamlets of North Berkshire, except for the constant use of flint and brick. Yet the views from the bridges have a sparkle and charm known only to chalk and the round, flint-tower bespeaks none other than chalkland deposits. The church at Welford has been largely rebuilt in the original style using much of the old material, only the nave and its aisles being quite new. The round lower stories of the tower represent a careful re-building of the twelfth-century structure while some original stonework is incorporated in the octagonal spire, although it must be admitted that the sudden tapering at its apex was apparently a mistake on the part of the Victorian masons. The interior, and especially the tall, vaulted chancel, has an agreeable richness which is supported by minor details, such as Early English sedilia, a delightful arcaded Transitional font and a kneeling alabaster figure of Lady Anna Parry, the mother of seven sons and twelve daughters all of whom are skilfully outlined in marble.

The parish of Welford stretches southward right to the Kennet and embraces the riverine hamlets of Weston and Easton and the upland hamlet of Wickham, which is perched near a Roman road upon the Lambourn watershed. This ridge, however, is not true downland as the chalk away from the steep valley-slopes is covered with sandy and clayey deposits on which the diminutive hangars of beech and follies of fir expand into sizeable woods, still sharply defined but rich in undergrowth and spreading as it were to the upper lip of the valley and threatening to overspill on to the exposed chalk below. In such a country Wickham arose as a hill station around a church tower which stands on the highest ground close to the ancient line of a Roman road. The tower's thick massive walls of mortared flint were broken only by tiny windows and an entrance (now blocked) about eight feet above the ground. On to this Saxon tower in later times was appended the chapel of St. Swithun which just before 1850 was replaced by the present building at the expense of the same Rev. William Nicholson who rebuilt the church at Welford. The small church at Wickham is fascinatingly Victorian. Without, it appears a perfection of squared split flints in good Norfolk style, and within a collection of pseudo-Decorated features dimmed by a patterned profusion of coloured glass. Large angels of papier-mâché adorn the nave roof while the roof-beams of the north aisle, amid a generous sprinkling of false ball-flowers, bear eight huge elephants' heads, also of papier-mâché, gilded and painted as became their original use in the Great Exhibition at Paris in 1862. An elaborate wooden font cover—carved by Maoris—a flamboyant chandelier and a touch of red plush do much to complete a very remarkable picture, the effect of which is heightened by the trim lawns and fine cedars of a most magnificent vicarage.

South of Wickham and Welford the Lambourn valley is losing its entity. Before Boxford is reached the valley-floor has widened and the stream is traversing a wide belt of peaty alluvium although gravelly shallows often yield good catches of trout and more rarely of grayling. Boxford possesses a pleasant situation beneath the tree-clad Hoar Hill and has improved on nature by a commendable tidiness and a profusion of flower-filled gardens. Although inhabited since at least Roman times no parishioner seems to have achieved any notable fame or notoriety except perhaps Oliver Sanson, a Quaker, who in the seventeenth century lived in the farmhouse near the church whence he kept up a constant feud with the vicar. About 1677 when the church tower collapsed into Sanson's garden he is said to have kept the debris as a gift from above. The vicar eventually had him gaoled for non-attendance at church.

Below Boxford the Lambourn stream passes into well-wooded scenery and at Snelsmore Common the presence of heaths and sphagnum bogs tells that the chalk is now deeply masked with sandy gravels and clays. And when wiry turf, the buckthorn and beech, and the purple-blue flowers of milkwort and gentian give way to pines, bracken, heaths and sundews then the Kennet country has already been entered.

CHAPTER VII: The Neighbourhood of Blewbury

Mine be a cot beside the hill;
A bee-hive's hum shall soothe my ear;
A willowy brook, that turns a mill,
With many a fall, shall linger near.

SAMUEL ROGERS

THE most animated countryside in Berkshire occurs on the greensands between Wantage and Wallingford. This is not because of the recent efflorescence of Harwell or the century-old industrialization of Didcot but because of the richness of the soil and quality of the farming. From Steventon to Blewbury the warm greensands have since the reign of Queen Anne encouraged an ever-increasing acreage of orchards which today have turned into a wide sea of cherry and apple. When fruit trees cease cereals take over and continue up the chalk slope until cold weather and poor crops frustrate further ascent of the plough.

With native cunning the villages where possible keep to the junction of sands and chalk for here springs arise and farmers could take advantage of chalk soils for grazing and sand for arable. The villages too lie close to the ancient Icknield Way and Port Way which join near Upton and continue thence through Blewbury to the Thames at Streatley. Yet only Blewbury has pandered to the highway and built a string of goodly houses and a substantial inn alongside it.

The rural seclusion is strongest at the Hagbournes, two of the most charming little places in Berkshire. Situated on a tongue of greensand, they lie amid well-kept orchards and rich ploughland where turnips were grown as early as 1717 and hops flourished to within living memory. The streams drove two grist mills at the time of Domesday Survey and some centuries later watered a paper mill that survived until 1860.

East or Church Hagbourne is a typical picture-postcard English village with quaint old cottages, some half-timbered and others with tile-hung half-fronts, dotted about in a haphazard way at the sharp corners of a twisting street. Some houses have bricks set zig-zag fashion, others have gables and thatched roofs and gardens partly enclosed by walls of cob and thatch. Near the church are a few cottages with carved wooden corbels supporting projecting upper-stories and here and elsewhere some of the windows show bottle-green glass in small leaded panes. The most charming groupings overlook the restored old market cross which with its five massive stone steps and tapering pillar ends today in a Jacobean sundial, the original stone crucifix having been lost. The bases of two other mediaeval crosses survive, one in the centre of the village and another at Coscote which have given rise to the tradition that Hagbourne within the limits of its three crosses was a place of sanctuary and that the ancient knocker on the church door served the same purpose.

The church of St. Andrew is mainly of the fourteenth century with a south arcade of a century earlier and a clerestory and south chapel of a century later. Inside, the chancel arch rests on grotesquely carved corbels and gives with the nearby rood stairs and piscinae an air of great antiquity. The lancets and stonework in the chancel are mainly Early English but many will equally admire the fine woodwork which includes the pulpit—a reconstruction of fifteenth-century material, the two porches, which rest on stone bases, and above all the late-fifteenth-century roofs of the chancel and nave. The latter is almost flat and has several carvings of hunting topics: one shows a deerhound pulling down a stag, and another—the eternal theme of the chalk downs—a greyhound chasing a hare. The west tower, built of a greenish stone, rises to a crocketed cote for a sanctus bell and holds a set of bells which are said locally to ring the truest peal in Berkshire.

These same bells summon the people of West Hagbourne, a village only one mile to the west which has no church presumably because it was too good to need one rather than too bad to desire one. A picturesque collection of half-timber and thatch, set on winding lanes and beside a village pond, West Hagbourne repeats on a smaller scale the cottage types and attractive tones—the mellowed russets and reds—of its more godly neighbour.

Upton also conforms to the pattern of cottages set in ones or twos on orchard-shaded lanes but clings more to the foot of the hills which here send out a small spur to hide the village from its railway station. The miniature church has much early Norman work and may in parts just fall into the Saxon age. There has been, it is true, the usual re-building and restoration yet the rude north door remains Saxon and the south door early Norman while, inside, the chancel arch has rude, massive masonry which could well be of either date. The nave retains one original round-headed window and the chancel three more, two of them narrow and deeply-splayed. In recent years the hamlet of Upton has not grown much and it is to be hoped that neither it nor West Hagbourne will be caught so firmly in the grip of Harwell that their agricultural calm is shattered.

The main road near Upton Lodge gives a pleasant prospect of Blewbury, which with its church and scattered houses and orchards rises boldly from above the sweeping cornlands. The village is carefully weather-fended with fruit trees for the smooth slopes, 'clean of officious fence or hedge', favour westerly winds which although refreshing enough in summer may in winter recall the feelings of John Wesley who on coming here in January 1746 found his 'hands and feet so cold he could scarce feel'. The dwellings are for the most part set actually on chalk subsoil and yet have an abundance of water as springs burst forth in several gardens and feed watercress beds while the water-table is high enough to keep orchards green in time of drought.

'That village hoary with age and mellow with the works of time', or as the *Abingdon Chronicle* said 'loco venerabilis, antiquitus, et adhuc cognomine noto Blewbury appelato', is recorded as a royal manor under Edward the Confessor and in the mid-twelfth century was granted to Reading Abbey. Agriculture formed its mainstay but not agriculture alone as merchants and hostlers appear later in its history. The Wantage–Reading road brought profits in coaching days and left among others an inn called the 'Load of Mischief', —the inn-sign being a copy of Hogarth's picture of a man carrying his wife on his back. Of merchants the most charming reminder is the school house founded by William Malthus, merchant, in 1709, which retains its Queen Anne façade with casement windows.

Blewbury has long been liked by artists and was the scene of 'The Village Wedding' by Luke Fildes, R.A., and the home of the late Sir William Nicholson. Many of the larger seventeenth- and eighteenth-century houses seem to have belonged to yeomen and tradesmen; typical are Boham's with its mellow brick and cluster of wooden barns, and the restored old malt house, which combine comfort and charm in a way satisfying alike to onlooker and inhabitant. And everywhere the large paddocks and gardens give such a sense of freedom and fertility that of a score of parishioners Dickens might have written: 'He lived in a pretty house, with a lawn in front, a bright flower garden at the side, and a well-stocked orchard and kitchen-garden in the rear, . . . But, indeed, everything about the place wore an aspect of maturity and abundance. The old lime tree-walk was like green clusters, the very shadows of the cherry-trees and apple-trees were heavy with fruit, the gooseberry-bushes were so laden that their branches arched and rested on the earth, the strawberries and raspberries grew in like profusion and the peaches basked by the hundred on the wall. Tumbled about among the spread nets and the glass frames sparkling and winking in the sun, there were such heaps of drooping pods, and marrows and cucumbers, that every foot of ground appeared a vegetable treasury.'

The church stands central amid the wide scatter of houses Originally early Norman, its subsequent changes baffle any but experts. In the twelfth century, a central tower was begun and a larger chancel was erected, on to which was added during the next two centuries an aisle to north and south and a small south-eastern chapel. About 1450, as the central tower had never been completed, the present tower with its pierced parapet of quatrefoils and vane-crowned crocketed pinnacles, was built at the western end. The craftsmen had also added two porches, of which that on the south is by far the finer example of carpentry.

Inside, the massive pillars and vaulted ceiling and an upper room of the old central tower remain as also do the roodloft stairs and roodloft piscina. The chancel retains a ring for the Lenten veil and some chained books, including Erasmus' *Paraphrase of the New Testament*, dated 1548. In the south chapel is a brass to Dame Alice Daunce (*ob.* 1527) and her husband, Sir John, who was surveyor-general to Henry VIII and was knighted by the King at Tournai in France on the day that the town surrendered.

Neither Daunce nor the many distinguished retired residents today can hope to equal the fame of the 'Blewbury miser'. The Revd. Morgan Jones, as he should be known, came to the village about 1781 as curate-in-charge for the Revd. John Keble, father of the great Keble. When Jones died here forty-three years later, his meanness had become a national by-word; his death was recorded under 'miser' in the *Annual Register* and forty years later Dickens introduced him into *Our Mutual Friend* as the miser known to Bella Wilfer as 'Blackberry Jones'.

Dickens may well have read William Hone's *Table Book of Daily Recreation and Information* from which the following details of the Revd. Morgan Jones have been taken. 'In his youthful days he made free with the good things in this life; and when he first came to Blewbury, he for some time boarded with a person by the week, and during that time was quite corpulent; but as soon as he boarded and lived by himself, his parsimony overcame his appetite, so that at last he became reduced almost to a living skeleton. He was always an early riser . . . and enjoyed an excellent state of health; so that for the long space of 43 years he omitted preaching only two Sundays . . . the whole expenses of his house did not amount to 2/6*d* a week for the last 20 years; as the fees exceeded that sum, he always saved the whole of his yearly salary—£50 per annum. By constantly placing this sum in the funds, and the interest, with about £30 per annum more (the rent of two small estates left by some relations) he amassed many thousands of pounds, as his bankers can testify.

'His industry was such, that he composed with his own hand upwards of 1000 sermons; but for the last few years . . . he only made alterations and additions to his former discourses, and this generally on the back of old marriage licenses, or across old letters, as it would have been nearly death to him to have purchased paper. His sermons were usually plain and practical, and his funeral discourses were generally admired, but the fear of being noticed, and the dread of expense, was an absolute prohibition to his sending anything to the press, although he was fully capable . . . The expense of a penny on the postage of a letter has been known to deprive him of a night's rest! And yet, at times, pounds did not grieve him. He was a regular and liberal subscriber to (various) societies . . . and more than once he was generous enough to give a pound or two to assist a distressed fellow creature.

'Although very fond of ale, he spent only sixpence on that liquor during the 43 years he was curate at Blewbury: but it must be confessed he used to partake of it too freely when he could have it without cost, until about ten years ago, when at a neighbour's wedding . . . it was noticed and talked of by some of the persons present. Being hurt by this, he made a vow never more to taste a drop of any strong liquor: and his promise he scrupulously and honestly kept.

'He cooked his pot only once a week—always on Sunday: bread, bacon and tea'. On the day he ordered his bacon he would visit the farmer and stay to tea and supper; a day or so later he would fetch the bacon and again stay to tea and supper, and a few days later would return to pay for it and partake of the same hospitality.

During his whole tenure at Blewbury he is said to have worn the same hat and coat. His hat was at one time falling to pieces but when crossing the fields from Upton he noticed one on a scarecrow which he gleefully carried home and stitched the brim of it to his own. His coat, a miracle of mendings and tackings and patchings, is still carefully preserved in a glass case with a bundle of love-letters at Blewbury.

He seldom lit a fire even in the depths of winter, preferring to go to bed if the cold became acute or if darkness came on, as he was 'generally without a candle as he allowed himself only the small bits left of those provided for divine service'. Occasionally 'on cold winter evenings he would beg a seat by the cheerful fire of a neighbour, and after warming his shivering limbs return, and immediately get to bed, to keep in the heat. It was one night returning thus that the old man died, comfortless, and alone; after having deprived himself of every comfort . . .' The parishioners seem to have tired of emulating so tight an example of austerity and in the year after the curate's death when the tenor bell was brought to the village from the founders at Cholsey it was turned upside down and filled with ale so that 'everyone who liked dipped a drink out of it'.

The peal at Blewbury can be heard on the west wind at the summit of Blewburton Hill, a detached, rounded hillock which overlooks the orchard country and the green vale beyond it. The earthwork capping this hill is notable for its steep artificial scarps that rise above lynchet-like terraces quite devoid of any ditch. Excavations are still in progress and will no doubt increasingly prove that this camp like most of its fifteen fellows in Berkshire can be safely attributed to the Iron Age. The finding of three skeletons in perfect condition near the surface indicates that the camp was also used as a pagan Saxon burial-ground.

On the lee or eastern side of Blewburton Hill is Aston Tirrold, a pretty hamlet set upon chalk and greensand which support an abundance of lime, elm, horse-chestnut and orchards. Most of the cottages are constructed of cob or half-timber with roofs of thatch or tiles but the gabled manor-house, a picturesque building of the time of Queen Anne, is built in a mellow red brick. The church is a little roughcast structure with some excellent fourteenth-century tracery in its windows and a few early Norman features, including a rough doorway now reset in the wall of the north aisle and blocked with a tombstone. The two splayed lancets in the chancel denote its Early English origin. Aston Tirrold has other attractions at certain seasons of the year, for here on the threshold of atomic Harwell and industrial Didcot, the annual performance of Shakespearean plays in a charming garden shines as a good deed in a naughty world.

The chalk slopes south of the orchards between Aston Tirrold and West Hagbourne rise at first gradually into a 'plain' before ascending steeply to the Ridge Way. This wide hill-side bench, although dotted with tumuli and earthworks, bears only one hamlet—the secluded Chilton. This tiny village has encountered difficulties akin to those of Letcombe Bassett and lies in a somewhat similar geographical position. Chilton, it is true, has not been threatened with destruction and the population of the parish has grown through the building of new houses for workers at Harwell but the inhabitants of the small group of half-timber and brick cottages have been hard pushed to maintain their ancient vitality. The provision of education for the infants has proved difficult and for some years recently there has not been a Sunday school nor even an electoral roll. The living of All Saints, in part a twelfth-century edifice, has been vacant since the death of the last vicar and the rectory is so dilapidated that its repair seems beyond the resources of the parish. Today the good vicar of Harwell is about to re-start the work of the church and the sympathy of all visitors will go out to the parishioners in their effort to found a new rectory and find a new rector which surely is the right of a village visited by Edward II nearly 630 years ago.

The ploughland and meadows of the lower chalk bench about Chilton are backed by the steep climb to the Ridge Way where a dry pastoral world of sheep and horses prevails. Habitations avoid the bleak summits but in the deep south-trending combes the Ilsley villages and Beedon hamlet find shelter and warmth and much-needed water.

The oldest part of Beedon—the nucleus as it were—lies isolated near the head of a deep combe but a few other houses straggle up Beedon Hill to World's End. The lonely grouping away from the busy road includes a red-brick manor of about 1700, now a farm-house or a symbol of the revival of farming on the wolds, where cows are replacing sheep. Its approaches are glorified by an almost biblical row of thatched, weather-boarded barns set neatly on brick bases, which makes one wonder if in winter ricks and stock alike have to be kept indoors against cold and tempest.

The church is a small aisleless structure consisting of nave and chancel, and dates from the thirteenth century, except, of course, the modern—but quite agreeable—porch and wooden bell-cote. In places the plaster has fallen from the outside walls revealing the original flint facing, which is much too attractive to be hid.

Inside, the deeply-splayed lancets and huge open timber roof of the nave give it a greater antiquity than the chancel but the latter is of pleasing proportions and the whole effect is harmonious. The east window consists of a beautiful triple lancet, with a richly-moulded band around its arches which spring from four pillars with foliated capitals. There were originally three more early-thirteenth-century lancets in each of the side walls but these were replaced later by Decorated windows.

Tiny Beedon is the product of a small downland parish whereas the populous Ilsley villages gather up the roads and activities of a large stretch of downland. East Ilsley, the bigger and more attractive of the two villages, stands in the flanks of a combe surrounded on all sides by broad-swelling humps of downs. The centre of wide expanses of wiry turf, it has long been the chief sheep-market of the hills and retains extensive permanent sheep-pens where in the mid-eighteenth century up to 80,000 sheep were collected in one day and 400,000 were sold in an average year. In addition to markets there were several fairs including one for wool and another for hiring. The numerous inns, of which five still survive, tell of the importance of the sheep fairs and of the local reputation for good ale, a fame no doubt much favoured by the dryness of the hills. Stephen Hemsted, who lived at the manor and tried in vain to teach the women to spin, has versified the attributes of the village:

The Thames upstream of Wallingford Bridge

The Old Mill at Abingdon, now a Restaurant

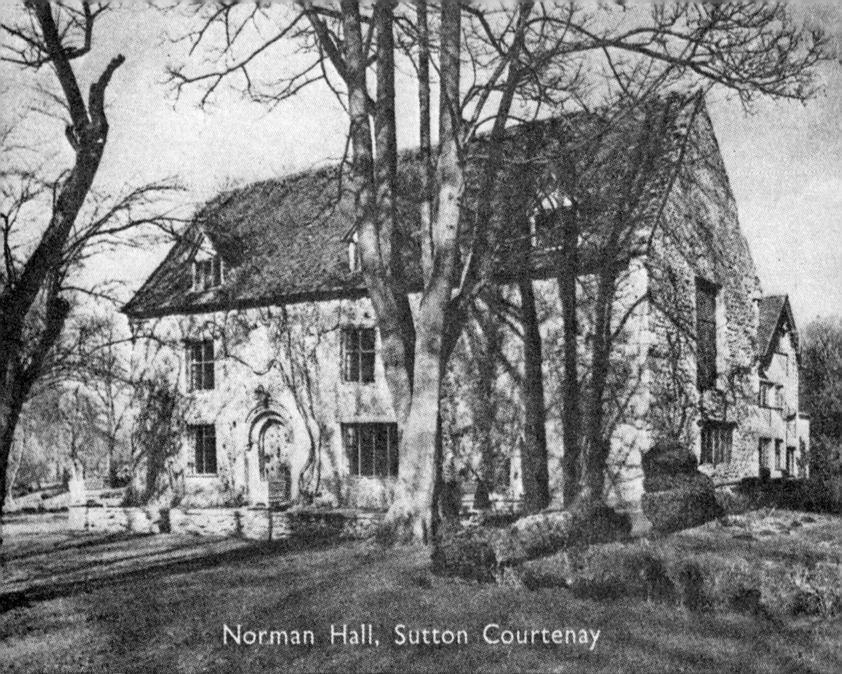

Norman Hall, Sutton Courtenay

Ruins of Reading Abbey, showing the Chapter House

Ilsley, remote amid the Berkshire Downs
Claims these distinctions o'er her sister towns;
Far famed for sheep and wool, tho' not for spinners
For sportsmen, doctors, publicans, and sinners.

East Ilsley still shows signs of its former business although race-horses tend to drive out sheep. The brick cottages are interspersed with a few handsome substantial dwellings of eighteenth-century age, which once housed the leading merchants. There is, however, nothing opulent about the church of St. Mary which stands on a slope above the village-pond and, as if mistrustful of winter gales, anchors itself by a squat tower which seems very securely rooted. The long chancel is Early English of about 1240 and shows dog-tooth moulding and some pleasant old glass, while the low square pews add further dignity to a building that is pleasant without being puzzling architecturally.

The reputation of the Ilsleys for race-horse training increased in the eighteenth century and has since spread to all the villages round. Keat's Gore, a mansion long since dismantled—at the foot of Gore Hill, was rented by the Duke of Cumberland, third son of George II, who built here elaborate racing stables and ultimately owned the largest and best racing-stud in the kingdom. He made the course and popularized the meeting at Ascot but is better known as the victor of Culloden. Many untrue stories of his supposed brutality were spread abroad with the aid of the Prince of Wales who envied the Duke's ability, but the 'Duke's Head' still swings over many an inn today as a sign of his popularity. It was at Keat's Gore that the Duke, shortly before his death, trained Eclipse, the dream horse of punters ever since.

Strings of would-be Eclipses may be seen on fine days at exercise on the downs near Gore Hill. This spot has a quite unusual charm. From the Ridge Way west of the main road the view embraces the orchard country about Harwell and the Vale of White Horse and almost all Berkshire beyond it. To the east of the road, the broad turf track swings round to survey the undulating downs near Compton and Blewbury. Here is chalk country *in excelsis*. Nothing majestic or magnificent; nothing abrupt or angular but just a rolling sea of smooth slopes above which the tiny woods rise as sharp cut as crystal and the ricks stand as clear as if made of granite. The first furrows of autumn are turned with the same precision and direction year after year as if the ploughman's marks never varied, and on every visit in each successive spring a hare doubles back on its tracks on the first bend of the hillside. Here for centuries man and nature have worked in harmony and in their long friendship is something of the joy that eternity brings.

CHAPTER VIII: The Thames near Wallingford

To his old shores the river
A new song was singing,
And young shoots were springing
On old roots forever.

LAURENCE BINYON, *Bab-lock-hythe*

THE Thames between Abingdon and Wallingford was always a nightmare for bargemen as here the river meanders wildly and has had to be straightened by cuts and dredgings. In parts the water-channel has changed its course since Anglo-Saxon times and at Culham Reach the county boundary runs south of the present stream leaving several acres of flat water-meadow and all Sutton Pool in Oxfordshire. Along this pleasant stretch of water steamers ply throughout the summer and there is no better way of reaching Sutton Courtenay than by following in the ghostly wake of a long train of abbots from the abbey at Abingdon to Culham lock.

Sutton Courtenay, lying green and cool among abundant elms and willows, was always a child of the river, remote from pack-horse, coach, railway and autobahn. Proximity to Abingdon abbey and the fertility of its own fields have been its support and the seclusion its salvation. As early as 687 the manor belonged to the abbots who later built what is now Norman Hall. The abbey subsequently gave Sutton Courtenay to the King in exchange for Andersey island and for a long time it remained in royal hands. But at different times the abbots were granted lands in the parish which formed a rectorial manor upon which was built a country retreat, today called the Abbey. Finally, Henry II gave the crown holdings in the manor to Reginald Courtenay and here in Tudor times his descendants built a third mansion called simply The Manor. Consequently the village has acquired and managed to keep no less than three manor houses, all of great interest.

Norman Hall, at other times known as the Court House and Manor Farm, has been much enlarged recently but retains the old rectangular structure with openwork-timber roof of about 1190. The hall is said to stand on the site of a royal palace of William the Conqueror and is éntered by Norman doorways one of which bears rows of dog-tooth and nail-head. The lancets are deeply splayed and the whole aspect of the building suggests a church or chapel, the fire-place being a Tudor addition.

Nearby, standing well back from the road amid elms, is The Abbey, which dates mainly from between 1350 and 1370 although an east wing was added two centuries later to form a quadrangle with the three older sides. Most of the windows have splendid masonry, especially the unaltered pointed window at the west end with its transom and flowing tracery.

The Manor is equally secluded at the end of a flower-lined avenue and two gateways, the inner of which, with two tall square pillars each crowned with a cornice and ball, is attributed to Inigo Jones. It seems that the greater part of the house was built about 1480 and the present attics added somewhat later. The front is a delightful assemblage of five pointed gables carrying barge boards carved in a vine pattern, a motif repeated in other parts of the building. The interior woodwork has an unbelievable charm, as on to the surviving pieces of original timbering has been added a wealth of 'old panelling and woodwork brought from various places' and tastefully inserted by Captain Lindsay. The banqueting hall rises airily to an open timber roof and has a minstrel's gallery with an exquisite rail of fifteenth-century workmanship. In the entrance hall, a flat half-timbered roof is supported upon oak pillars.

The delights of these domestic gems are matched by the smaller dwellings of the village which include many old-world, timber-framed cottages spaced and grouped in a half-haphazard manner along the main street and around the large village green. The gabled Jacobean house at the end farthest from the Thames, and the early eighteenth-century vicarage and the shell-shaped canopy over the doorway of the Queen Anne building near it would excite much comment elsewhere, but at Sutton Courtenay they fall so naturally into the scheme of things as to be taken for granted. And even the church with unusual skill manages to represent the whole village. There is no agreement on its architectural details as becomes its styles dating from the twelfth century onwards but its grandeur and dignity are never disputed. It is built of grey stone with a porch of brick added presumably in Henry VIII's reign. The two lowest stages of the tower belong to the twelfth century, the chancel to the thirteenth and the aisles mainly to the fourteenth but one arch in the south arcade may be the original chancel arch. Although the font has been shortened somewhat it remains a most satisfying object while the woodwork in the church, whether it be the mediaeval stalls of the chancel or old pews in the nave and aisles or the magnificent Jacobean pulpit and richly-carved chest, has an antiquity and quality typical of Sutton Courtenay. The church, it is true, needs the east window of Fairford in Gloucestershire and the village has a large fringe of new dwellings, but to preserve three manor houses and such a wealth of smaller domestic architecture and yet not to become commercialized and smug and self-conscious is a feat achieved by few villages in the drainage of the Thames.

Some three miles to the east, at the opposing bends of a great meander of the Thames, lie the Wittenhams, Little and

Long. The one street of Long Wittenham is strung out parallel with the river on a broad, flat plain of gravel and clay. A disastrous fire destroyed many of the old half-timbered houses in 1868 but a few survive, including the Plough Inn and the dovecote at the manor. At the north end of the village one larger dwelling near the church is particularly attractive with its projecting upper story while a roadside cross, now restored, adorns the southern end. The church is simple and unassuming. The early twelfth-century chancel arch retains its arabesque capitals but the chancel itself was rebuilt in the next century and almost all the windows were changed to lancets, nor has a complete rebuilding in 1850 altered their positions. Among the many details two are outstanding. In the long south transept is a thirteenth-century piscina of a most artistic design in which two winged angels, probably once with swinging censers, support a trefoil moulding so forming a canopy for the tiny sculpture of a knight lying cross-legged on the front edge of the piscina. Few if any sculptured monuments in England can be smaller than this. The other outstanding ornament is the lead font of about 1200, the lower part of which has a ring of thirty arches, each enclosing a bishop with his right hand raised in blessing. The woodwork in the church includes some stalls with fine bench ends removed from Exeter College, Oxford, and a low-pitched roof of Tudor age in the nave, which has today been ravaged by the death-watch beetle and will need extensive repairs before it is made safe.

This bend of the Thames has long been a rich source of archaeological finds, dating from the Stone Age down to Saxon times. Just south of the church in a field called Free Acre the grave of a warrior with his weapons was discovered in 1848 and excavations later revealed a large Saxon cemetery. From internal evidence it has been assumed that the inhabitants had embraced Christianity, as towards the north end of the graveyard the bodies were oriented more uniformly west to east, and in the grave of a young boy, amongst other objects was a beaker 'covered with thin bronze plates embossed with scenes from the Gospels'. Farther within the northern loop of the Thames on a wide patch of gravel the tenant of Northfield Farm during the dry summer of 1893 noticed that his crops grew stronger along certain well-defined lines and patches, and upon excavating gradually laid bare the foundations of a large Romano-British village. A great many of the objects obtained from diggings at the Wittenhams and Sutton Courtenay may be seen set out to good advantage in the museums at Reading and Oxford but the embossed beaker is in the British Museum.

Little or Abbots Wittenham is, as the name implies, a small hamlet of widely-spaced cottages, situated for the most part upon a cul-de-sac that ends in a blaze of glory near the charming gardens of a fine eighteenth-century farm-house and the church of St. Peter. Except for the fourteenth-century sandstone tower the church was entirely rebuilt in Victorian times and is interesting chiefly as the mausoleum of the Dunch family, who owned the former manor-house here for centuries. The alabaster monument to Sir William Dunch and Mary, his wife—an aunt of Oliver Cromwell—pleases the eye most, although brasses to the Kidwellys, another local family, portray civilian costume of over a century earlier.

Little Wittenham, however, is rather a means to an end, as from the churchyard, tracks lead to Day's Lock and so over the river to Dorchester, and also to Wittenham Clumps, a pair of chalk-capped hillocks rising sharply above the Thames and under various vulgar appellations forming the best-known landmark in the Oxford district. The path climbs steeply amid ploughland to the rounded beech-clad summit of Harp Hill, the higher of the two eminences, whence a short descent and a clamber over an earthwork leads to Castle Hill, the top of which has been flattened and surrounded by a deep ditch and two ramparts which, together with the entrances, remain fairly perfect. The views from the summit of either hill are beautiful and extensive. At the northern foot, just beyond the woods and the river, stretches a flat flood-plain between the Thames and the Thame and across the neck of the peninsula a strong earthwork (Dyke Hills) is clearly visible and beyond it the houses and tower of Dorchester. Of the views in other directions much has and will be written but the time of ascent is rarely mentioned. The Clumps should be climbed at the time of full moon when the woods are full-leafed, warm, scented and sighing, and in the distance bathed in cold moonlight is the 'pastoral heart of England' and the clustered lights of a score of villages and at our feet the silver curves of the Thames.

The line of the Sinodun Hills is continued in Brightwell Barrow, south of which the land drops to flatter country west of Wallingford. Here, in a district well-suited to walking, the main attraction is North Moreton, with the most perfect mediaeval church in Berkshire. Rebuilt in the late-thirteenth and early-fourteenth centuries, the little church of All Saints is in the Decorated style which is seen at its best in the Stapleton Chantry. This small gem of Decorated work was constructed about 1295 by enlarging the south chapel, and is lighted with five graceful geometrical windows, one of which rises above a lovely angle piscina. The east window here retains its mediaeval glass which still glows with a great beauty of colour and design in spite of restorations and replacements. The design consists of three panels in each of the five lights surmounted, in the upper tracery, by armorial bearings of the Stapletons. Four lights represent scenes from the life of Christ, the Virgin Mary and Saints Peter and Paul, while the fifth probably concerns St. Nicholas to whom the chapel is dedicated. St. Nicholas, wearing a mitre and green cope, lifts the murdered children from the pickle tub and above on a beam—O happy times!—hang three hams. In the upper compartment of this light the Saint in a yellow cloak gives alms through a wall to the two poor women by night. And so the scenes go on throughout the window, and once, judging from fragments of fourteenth-century glass windows elsewhere in the church, may have formed one of a series. Along the exterior of the south wall of the Stapleton Chantry, various animals and a human-headed beast are carved in the cornice.

Sir Miles Stapleton (*ob.* 1314) who built the chapel was the son of Nicholas de Stapleton of the small township of that name on the Tees. His interest in Berkshire came from lands belonging to his wife Margaret, an heiress of the Bruce family from whom Stapleton adopted the lion rampant seen in his coat-of-arms in the east window of his chantry. He served in the Scottish campaigns of Edward I and was one of the elders to whom the King entrusted the education of his son. When Edward II came to the throne Sir Miles lost his influence and many of his manorial rights to Piers Gaveston so that he became somewhat hostile to the crown and was involved in the execution of the King's favourite. Yet he obeyed the summons in 1314 to muster to the relief of Stirling and on June 24th fell with his two sons at Bannockburn, and was never buried in his chantry. His gift of twenty-five acres at North Moreton as an endowment for two priests to say mass in the chapel is still free of tithe.

For ecclesiologists North Moreton is a feast of delight but for ardent football fans it should be a place of humble pilgrimage. The church register for the merry month of May 1595 concerns the fate of two players, John and Richard Gregorie. It appears that 'Gunters sonnes and ye Gregories fell together by ye years at football. Ould Gunter drewe his dagger and broke booth their heades, and they died booth within a fortnight after.' Subsequently this tangible assistance from the sideline has declined into the modern milk-and-water yellings and had it but continued many a battle of Waterloo *would* indeed have been won on the playing fields of Eton.

There has, of course, been bloodshed on a bigger scale than Gunter's outbreak in the North Moreton country for Wallingford was for centuries a battleground and the prison of unlucky political offenders. Wallingford for a long period guarded the only easy crossing of the Thames hereabouts. At first served by a gravel-floored ford, the townsfolk built a bridge in 1141 which was replaced by a stronger structure in the reign of Henry III. It was on this bridge that special watch was kept in 1671 lest any plague-infected person from Crowmarsh or Newnham should enter. 'And throwe God's mercie our Towne of Wallingford was preserved. To God be given all glory therefoure.' In 1751 all four of the arches that were built of wood were replaced with brick and stone spans and during the next one hundred years extensive improvements were made. Today, including three small culverts on the east, the bridge consists of nineteen arches and is nearly 900 feet long. Its importance to the town may be gathered from the fact that whereas in most bridges over the Thames the political or administrative boundary runs through the middle of the crossing, at Wallingford the county boundary makes a sudden salient eastward from the Thames so as to give Berkshire control of the whole bridge and causeway.

The old town of Wallingford grew up within the protection of Saxon fortifications which comprised a raised mound and a moat on north, west and south and of the Thames itself on the east. On the north the fortifications were breached by the defences of the castle and on the other three sides by bridges. The moat was kept well filled by diverting the Moreton or Mill brook to the south and east, and by opening a sluice from the Thames into the ditches on the north and round the castle. An inquisition of 1555 tells of 'a certaine sluice or lock, built of timber, to turn the water into the castle ditches every Saturday at noon until evensong time the Sunday following'.

Whether the town came first or the earthworks is debatable, as the entrenchments may have been thrown up around the township as a protection against the Danes in Alfred's reign. Inside these defences the plan of the streets is rectangular in Roman fashion. High Street runs east to west along the line of the ancient track to the ford while the north–south road—once a wide thoroughfare—may be followed along the Market Place, St. Leonard's Square and Lower Green. Moreover, within the four smaller squares thus formed the lines of secondary rectangular street plans are still traceable.

At the time of Domesday Survey Wallingford had become a royal borough with a royal castle, which far exceeded in importance any other place in Berkshire. In 1154, Henry II held his first parliament at Wallingford and in the next year granted the town its charter, the original of which is still held by the Town Council. Within a short while the townsfolk had erected no less than fourteen churches or chapels, and as they controlled the crossing-point of the Thames of the main London to Gloucester highway they enjoyed a position and prosperity never equalled since. Yet at this time Abingdon began to arise as the great rival of Wallingford. The struggle lay between two alert communities, the one with the doubtful advantage of royal ownership and the other under the tutelage of a fast-growing monastery. Soon there was no doubt that a resident abbot was a safer asset and a better landlord than an itinerant monarch. The rivalry of the two towns had already flared up in Henry II's reign when the people of Wallingford had sallied forth and tried in vain to smash the public market at Abingdon because goods other than victuals were being sold there. So urgent was their indignation that they sent a deputation across the Channel to plead with the King, but after much legal argument the abbot of Abingdon eventually won the day. The worst blow, however, occurred in 1416 when the bridges across the Thames at Abingdon were completed and the main roads from London to Gloucester and the West now turned northward near Nuffield in Oxfordshire and continued through Dorchester to Abingdon. Wallingford dwindled under this and other misfortunes and within a few years had only a few score householders. By 1542 Leland found it in sad decay. 'The town of Walingford hath beene a very notable thing and welle waullid. The Diche of the Toun and the Crest whereon the Waulles stoode be yet manifestely perceyved, and begin from the Castelle going in Cumpace a good mile and more, and so cummith to Walingford Bridg a large thing of stone over the Thamise. . . . At this tyme there be but 3 poore Paroch churches in the Toun.'

In spite of a good malting trade, the impoverishment continued until the eighteenth century when great efforts were made to keep the corporation solvent. Towards the close of the century the bringing of two new turnpikes through the town caused a lasting revival, but today Abingdon its former rival has three times its population and half a dozen Berkshire towns exceed it in size. Yet for that very reason Wallingford has retained an attractiveness which greater growth and expansion might have ruined. And everywhere is a praiseworthy tidiness—clean streets, well-painted houses, an abundance of striking vistas of red-tiled roofs and in all a sense of civic pride which culminates in a small garden in St. Martin's Street which is an everlasting credit to its makers and a practical lesson to all town-planners.

In fact, the open spaces in the township are almost as interesting as the built-up areas. A piece of common ground in the south-west corner known as the Kine Croft—and formerly as Canecroft and Kenny Croft—was used for common grazing, but now serves for public recreation. It is enclosed by strong earthworks on two sides, the western rampart being breached by gateways said to have been cut by Prince Rupert during the Civil War. In the north-west corner is another enclosure called the Bull Croft, probably by mistaken analogy with the Kine Croft. Nearby was Portman's Moor a considerable acreage of common pasture while in the north-east near the Wharf was Hog Common.

The streets of modern Wallingford are distinguished mainly by their domestic buildings of the eighteenth century which are, most of them, either of half-timber or of brick, some being older structures refronted with a vitrified purple brick then highly fashionable. Of the eighteenth-century brick buildings, Calleva House in High Street is perhaps the most imposing but in Thames Street, Bridge House, of stone and pale brick, and Castle Priory House (now an hotel) where Justice Blackstone lived, are equally charming. Wallingford too has several pre-eighteenth-century dwellings. Overlooking the Thames is St. Lucian's a beautiful small Tudor house, with three sharp-pointed gables, of which the outer two are lighted with bay-windows with embattled parapets, while Stone Hall, facing the Kine Croft, is a three-gabled Tudor building now much restored. The Angier almshouses (founded in 1681) would be an asset to any town while the courtyards of some of the hotels, notably The George, show a respectable antiquity.

The Market Hall dates from 1670 and consists of a restored upper story of plastered half-timber supported on Doric pillars, with five windows along each of the longer sides and a central window opening on to a projecting balcony on the north. From this balcony the election results were announced, of two members up to 1832, then of one till 1885 when the borough was disfranchised. Within, reached by a magnificent oak staircase are two large rooms, adorned with several portraits and paintings and containing the municipal insignia.

Of the four churches and many chapels in Wallingford, the two most interesting are St. Leonard's and St. Peter's. The former, an eleventh-century building which was badly damaged by troops barracked in it during the Civil War, was much restored about 1700 and almost rebuilt in 1850. Yet some Norman and Transitional work survives mainly in the chancel where two fine Norman arches, and much of the walls, with some herringbone-work are almost or quite original.

St. Peter's church was entirely rebuilt in 1769 in the Renaissance style and eight years later was crowned with a most unusual needle-like spire about which some equally pointed things have been written. Even the architect considered the octagonal arcade of the tower capable of supporting only one bell, yet the building should not be despised as it covers the one and the only Blackstone, who gave to it a chalice, paten and almsdish. Sir William Blackstone (1723–80) was the author of the famous *Commentaries on the Laws of England* which went into eight editions in his own lifetime and was constantly reprinted up to 1844. The task was immense as it was the first comprehensive attempt to reduce our legal usage into a coherent statement. Coleridge wrote in the preface to his edition: 'It requires, perhaps, the study necessarily imposed upon an editor to understand fully the whole extent of praise to which the author is entitled: his materials should be seen in their crude and scattered state; the controversies examined, of which the sum only is shortly given; what he has rejected, what he has forborne to say should be known; before his learning, judgement, taste, and above all his total want of self-display can be justly appreciated.' Blackstone spent the latter part of his life here and acted as recorder but being lethargic physically he grew stout and increasingly abhorring any kind of exertion or exercise seems really to have died from the want of it. He is especially remembered in Wallingford as the man who brought the two new turnpikes through the town: one crossed the Thames at Shillingford for Oxford, and the other ran to Wantage and the Vale of White Horse.

These turnpikes partly explain the survival of many old inns at Wallingford. At the Lamb in the High Street which dates as the Bell from the sixteenth century, the landlord Sylvanus Wiggins entertained the Prince of Orange in 1688. Sylvanus's successor, a certain Thomas Clack, was possessed of three lovely daughters, one of whom married William, second Viscount Courtenay and another became the wife of Sir John Honywood, Bart. Several other inns have a sixteenth-century lineage as well as some original architecture and the names are always enthralling: The George (after St. George—with an exceptionally attractive courtyard), the Black Boy, the White Hart, the Cock, the Plume of Feathers, the Mermaid, the Green Tree and the Fat Ox. The latter, a product of the eighteenth century, seems a direct challenge to Abingdon for this town had the famous Berkshire ox which stood 6½ feet high, was nearly 14 feet long from the tip of its tail to the ring in its nose, and—whence perhaps its popularity as an inn-sign—drank 24 gallons a day.

The castle of Wallingford has suffered more than its inns and has today on its 25 acres nothing to show beyond a window and a few fragments of wall and fine earthworks all now part of a private estate. The double line of moats is still plainly traceable as well as the mound and foundations while the entrances are in their original position. The fortifications at their south-eastern corner circumscribe the ruins of the church of St. Nicholas, once an attachment to a college of that dedication. The ruins include a south wall nine feet thick, a stout tower and several windows with fifteenth-century tracery. These and several old gateways and the tall mound of the keep may be glimpsed from a narrow alley which crosses the estate from just north of its main entrance in Castle Street.

Wallingford was a royal residence in the time of Edward the Confessor, but its first great castle was built in the reign of William the Conqueror. In 1071 it began its future role as a prison for political offenders when the abbot of Abingdon was detained here on suspicion of encouraging the rising of Hereward the Wake. Its interesting connexions with royal women commenced in 1141 when the Empress Maud fled hither at dead of night from Oxford, crossing the frozen river and snow and reaching the castle at daybreak. Stephen then besieged Wallingford several times and only desisted on the signing of the Treaty of Wallingford in 1153, whereby he was acknowledged king.

King John spent much time here and carried out many repairs and improvements. Here too in 1307, Piers Gaveston, Baron of Wallingford, celebrated his betrothal to Edward II's niece by a magnificent tournament and an unpardonable display of insolence to other barons. After Gaveston's death in 1312, the King granted the castle to Queen Isabella, who made it her headquarters for a while during her rebellion with Mortimer against her husband. In 1327, after the capture of Edward, Isabella gave Wallingford castle to Mortimer and spent with him there a 'royal Christmasse'. Yet three years later when her own son overthrew her, he treated her with dignity and allowed her to pass the rest of her life very comfortably at Wallingford.

In 1361 the Black Prince married Joan, the Fair Maid of Kent, at the castle and she made it her official residence and on her husband's death held it in dower, as also later did Katherine, queen of Henry V. In 1518, Henry VIII was in residence here but his visits were rare and those of his successors rarer still. In Mary's reign the castle, which was in greater desolation and ruin than ever before, was stripped of its lead, stone and other building materials for works at Windsor Castle.

Yet the great fortress of Wallingford was to come into its own again for during the Civil War its lines of defence were restored and it regained much of its ancient strength. Even some of the arches of the bridges over the Thames were removed and replaced by drawbridges. In the spring and early summer of 1646 Colonel Blagge defended the castle for sixteen weeks at a cost of only five men slain. When he surrendered on 27 July 1646, Raglan and Pendennis were the only other strongholds holding out for the King, and they capitulated about a month later. In 1652 the Council of State ordered Wallingford Castle to be demolished and accordingly it was reduced in almost the six-hundredth year of its age. Although the castle has gone, the town's visitors can be wished no sweeter leaving than that afforded to Colonel Blagge and his men after their honourable capitulation in 1646: to march out with horses and arms, 'with flying colours, trumpets sounding, drums beating, matches lighted at both ends, bullets in their mouths and with bag and baggage'.

CHAPTER IX: Streatley and the River Pang

There is a hill beside the silver Thames,
Shady with birch and beech and odorous pine:
And brilliant underfoot with thousand gems
Steeply the thickets to his floods decline.

ROBERT BRIDGES

THE great triangle of land between the lower Kennet and the Streatley Thames belongs by right to the river Pang. It is true that the extreme southern and eastern fringes may fall to the bigger rivers but the heart of the district drains solely to the diminutive stream which in wet years sweetens the vast hollows near Ilsley and in dry summers may be almost waterless as far as Bucklebury. To approach the lower Pang from Compton and northward is to step from the baldness of chalk to a land of hedgerows and woods upon deposits of gravelly clay, and the spaciousness of the one detracts from the homeliness of the other. In fact, the drainage basin of the Pang is essentially not downland but Chiltern country and to appreciate its unity it should be approached from the Chiltern side. Its sameness then becomes striking: the profuse stretches of wood, coppice and park; the small hamlets of mellow brick; the palatial, widely spaced farms, and the wide green valley-floor which for such long distances may be disappointingly empty of the sparkling, willow-lined watercourse which its size deserves.

Streatley forms both a foil and an introduction to the Pang, as it shows the beauty of river reflexions and the sylvan nature of the continuation of the Berkshire hills on the other side of the Thames. Here, in a gorge-like gap cut right through the upland, Berkshire and Oxfordshire hold hands at a bridge beloved of artists. Around are the richly-timbered meadows and nearby, the woods of Cleeve lock and the small reed-braided islets where the water tumbles over the weirs.

Streatley has laid at an obvious crossing of the Thames since time immemorial as here the routes of the Berkshire downs converge on their way to the Chilterns. Two Roman milestones are said to have stood between Streatley and Aldworth and the Romans used the rectangular camp on the summit of Lowbury Hill where they left so many oyster shells that the eminence is known locally as Oyster Hill. The river was then forded, probably with the help of a raised causeway but subsequently it was crossed by a ferry, which at one time was owned by the prioress of Goring. In 1674 about fifty persons returning from Goring feast to Streatley were drowned in the river yet no bridge was built until 1838.

Near this bridge stands an old water-mill with steep gables and high set dormers and alongside huddle the sheds of boat-builders, an occupation which retains its vitality in all the larger Thameside places of Berkshire. Admirers of Kenneth Grahame will remember how Rat and Mole on leaving the main stream, 'passed into what seemed at first sight like a little land-locked lake. Green turf sloped down to either edge, brown snaky tree-roots gleamed below the surface of the quiet water, while ahead of them the silvery shoulder and foamy tumble of a weir, arm-in-arm with a restless dripping mill-wheel, that held up in its turn a grey-gabled mill house, filled the air with a soothing murmur of sound, dull and smothery, yet with little clear voices speaking up cheerfully out of it at intervals.'

Those parts of Streatley away from the Thames attract more for their setting than for their own virtues. The church with its late Perpendicular tower is prettily situated near the river while the village itself spreads out along the highway and up the steep slopes re-echoing its noises. The whole appears to perfection from Streatley Hill which is best reached by a clamber up a wide footpath leading from off the main road. The scenic virtues of the middle Thames are summarized in the view: the willows and poplars along the reflective river; the dead flat stretches of riverine meadow; the abrupt valley-slopes, whitish with chalk, patched haphazardly with dark clear-cut woods and indented at intervals with entrancing combes, some high up the slope like small shaven niches and others tremendous coves rising sheer from the valley-floor to the narrow ridges between them. The whole landscape resembles a sea-strait where the waves have carved cliffed bays in the chalk and, on the retreat of the ocean, the former coastline has been smoothed by rain-wash and tamed by the growth of vegetation.

This gap through the hills is one of the busiest gateways in England and through it a constant succession of traffic hurries to and from London and the upper Thames and the West. Its easy gradients induced the main railway to follow it on the way to Bristol although the rival route up the Kennet valley is much less circuitous. It had much to do with the creation of Didcot and Swindon and, of course, with the building of those Tudor-style houses at Steventon which were used for meetings of G.W.R. directors. Yet the outward expansion of the residents of Reading and London seems to weaken at the gap which forms as it were a safeguard to the Thames valley upstream of it. However, many are the people who at dawn dash feverishly to their metropolis and return each evening to sleep on these valley-sides, so willingly giving the lie to the bantering poet:

> The air is clear, the day is fine
> The prospect is I know divine
> But most distinctly I decline
> To climb the hill at Streatley.

Lower Basildon shares this lovely Berkshire bank with Streatley although here, a mile or two downstream, the

Thames winds across the valley-floor to hug the steeply-hanging woods of Combe End in Oxfordshire. Basildon church stands near the river and the ancient ferry while Basildon House overlooks it from the higher wooded slopes. The baroque lodges on the main road were built in 1832 when the mansion itself—then about seventy years old—underwent a thorough restoration, including additions to its fine plasterwork ceilings. In recent years the house seems to have gone to decay, but will, let us hope, yet be restored to all its old splendour.

One of the registers at Basildon records the death of Jethro Tull in the year 1741 and adds 'This Jethro Tull Esq., was the author of a valuable book on agriculture entitled *Horse Husbandry*'. Tull was, indeed, outstanding among a long line of Berkshire agriculturalists which continues to this day. His life may be briefly told. Born and buried at Basildon he was educated at St. John's, Oxford, and Gray's Inn but he never practised at the Bar, probably because his father's death in 1699 necessitated his return to look after the family property in the Thames valley. An accomplished musician, he took to agriculture, as he himself says, 'not by choice, but by a sort of necessity'. By 1701 he had already invented and perfected the seed-drill for which he is famous. Eight years later ill-health caused him to move to Prosperous Farm, near Hungerford, where the knowledge gained from methods of cultivation in France allowed him to perfect his system of intensive pulverization and preparation of the soil, whereby he grew wheat successfully for thirteen consecutive years on the same piece of land without manuring.

In 1731, he published his experiences in a book called *Horse-Hoing Husbandry* which unfortunately attracted a great deal of adverse criticism to which he was morbidly sensitive. He died in 1741 and was taken to Basildon for burial, although here, as at Prosperous Farm, the workers strongly disliked his methods. As late as 1822 William Cobbett thought sufficiently highly of *Horse-Hoing Husbandry* to edit it and it is pleasant to record that shortly after Tull's death his book was translated into French and his system followed by Voltaire at Ferney.

The richest agricultural land in the Basildon sector or Berkshire is that reached by a steep, picturesque road which runs up through the beech woods and skirts the perimeter of a deep cuspate combe from Streatley to Aldworth. Long before Aldworth is reached the tree-growth thins out and the country expands into chalk-land although the flints in the buildings still suggest the proximity of surface deposits.

Aldworth may be a mere village but it does what it does in a very big way. Its canopied well, 372 feet deep, is one of the deepest in England. Its churchyard yew, a gigantic whitened stump 27 feet in girth, is probably the oldest living tree in the country and although it has quite lost its bark still sends forth green shoots. The church contains a collection of the largest and most mutilated monuments to one family in any church in Britain. Admittedly there is much else in the well-kept building, including four fine carved pew-ends and an artistic stone-carving in the vestry, but the extraordinary effigies are the main attraction. Three knights lie under crocketed canopies with ogee curves and flowerets on the north wall of the nave and two others and a lady under similar canopies in the aisle opposite. In addition, two large table tombs, one with two figures, occupy the arcade of the nave. The popular rhyme for them ran:—John Long, John Strong, John Everafraid, John Neverafraid, though it is doubtful to which the names applied. Their identity remained uncertain until a fourteenth-century seal bearing the name of Isabella de la Beche and three small shields was ploughed up near the site of the ancient manor. Subsequently it was learned that Queen Elizabeth rode here pillion behind the Earl of Leicester to see the monuments, as the diary of Captain Symonds records. 'May 2. 1644, Aldworth vulgo

Alder, In ye E ende of ye S yle did hang a table fairly written in parchments of all ye names of ye Family of de la Beche, but ye Earle of Leicester coming with ye Queen Elizabeth in progresse took it downe to show it her, and it was never broughte againe. Ye common People call ẏe statue under ye outside of ye churche John Everafraid, and say further that he gave his soule to ye Divil if ever he was buried either in Church or churchyarde, so he was buried under the Church Wall under an Arche.'

This outer arch is blocked today and the effigy gone whereas the nine interior monuments survive although sadly mutilated and damaged in Puritan times, one of them being now a mere torso, and others without an arm or a leg or two. The possible identification of each effigy is minutely discussed in a typescript volume kept in the church but the extraordinary size of some of the recumbent knights seems quite inexplicable. The earliest monument, that near the north door, probably represents Sir Robert de la Beche who was knighted by Edward I about 1278. The last is to Sir Nicholas, a constable of the Tower who died in 1346. In all probability most of the effigies were carved at much the same time and presented by a de la Beche in the middle of the fourteenth century, the most likely donor being Edmund, Archdeacon of Berkshire, who held the manor from 1346 to 1365. Yet differences in the quality of the stone are noticeable and some of the monuments were obviously not intended for their present positions. It would be pleasant to know the thoughts of the villagers as these 'giants' turned up in batches, and gradually threatened to outnumber the normal congregation.

From Aldworth a by-road leads southward to Beche Farm, a cluster of red-tiled buildings standing on the site of the castellated manor and on the line of an ancient earthwork. Thence the Pang is reached near Hampstead Norris which has much the same history as Yattendon its neighbour, both coming early under the Norreys family. Hampstead, however, grew partly as a route centre and has been since 1882 on a main railway whereas Yattendon remained in strict seclusion and flourished as the seat of manorial lords.

Yattendon breathes an air of well-being and has managed to keep some charming half-timber, and mellow brick houses, such as the haunted Rectory and the Grange, and the much older stone-built malt house. The concentration of dwellings about the village square heightens and facilitates the tidiness while the recent munificence of the lords of the manor is seen at every angle.

The parish has always been in good hands. The de la Beche family held it until 1365 and the Norreys from 1441 to the late-eighteenth century. The first John Norreys of Yattendon, who rebuilt the church and the manor house, had a list of offices in the royal household that sounds more like an incantation. Another Sir John enlarged the park and entertained Henry VIII here in 1520 but was later beheaded for alleged intimacy with Anne Boleyn. His sons were well treated by Queen Elizabeth, one being made Baron Norreys of Rycote and another—also Sir John—excelled himself in Flanders, France and Ireland and went with Drake to Spain. The story of this warrior, including a mention of 'his father's suffering' for the sake of Elizabeth's mother, may be read on his marble monument in the church, above which hangs his helmet and below it his rapier.

In 1784 the manor was sold to Giovanni Andrea Gallini, a native of Florence who became a famous dancer at the Haymarket Theatre and who styled himself 'Sir John' after being made a Knight of the Golden Spurs by the pope. Gallini rebuilt the manor house on its original site practically as it is today, a square dignified structure of red brick.

Eventually in 1876 the manor was bought by Alfred Waterhouse, the eminent architect whose works especially adorn Manchester, Liverpool, London and Cambridge. He built the mansion in Whiteknights Park, Reading and in

1877 erected Yattendon Court on a hill-top site just west of the village, which during the diggings for the foundations revealed a Bronze Age hoard and two large balks of oak which had once supported a beacon post. The Court was replaced in 1925 by a Tudor-style half-timbered building on the same pleasant site.

In the meanwhile the Manor House had had notable occupants. In 1881, Robert Seymour Bridges, a London physician, had so bad an attack of pneumonia that he resigned his medical posts and shortly afterwards came here to the Manor, a 'pleasant old red-brick house' with 'just the combination of beauty, simplicity, and remoteness suitable to a poet of the Miltonic order'. Here he married a daughter of Alfred Waterhouse and spent the first twenty years of his married life. At Yattendon, Bridges wrote many of his best poems and the Manor became the mecca of aspiring poets. In 1904 Bridges left the village. Yet his heart was always here and when he died in his eighty-sixth year he was buried under the churchyard cross which he had had erected over the grave of his mother. A tablet in the church, over the seat he used for so long, records that he was Poet Laureate of this Kingdom and for eighteen years precentor in this church.

The significance of the last sentence—written by Bridges himself—can only be understood by the older inhabitants of the parish. Here Bridges and Professor H. Ellis Wooldridge edited the *Yattendon Hymnal* in an attempt to restore to use old melodies neglected or long forgotten. What these authors wrote of a nation—that its excellence 'in music can have no other basis than the education and practice of the people . . .' —they applied to this particular parish and Yattendon choristers became a wonder of the shire.

Robert Bridges was, however, but part of the spiritual revival of the neighbourhood. The Waterhouse family made the village 'a visible testimony' to their 'sense of the obligations of a landlord'. The church of SS. Peter and Paul, erected in the Perpendicular style by John Norreys in 1450 and restored four centuries later, was carefully tended, the tower being rebuilt, a few small additions made and the interior fittings, already tasteful and elaborate, were repaired and increased. The rector, Henry Charles Beeching, later Dean of Norwich, was also a poet and is best remembered for his 'Going Down the hill on a Bicycle' and 'Prayers', which begins

> God who created me
> Nimble and light of limb,
> In three elements free
> To run, to ride, to swim;
> Not when the sense is dim,
> But now from the heart of joy,
> I would remember Him:
> Take the thanks of a boy.

Under such a stimulus the whole village was re-vitalized. The village well glowed under a graceful canopy, the annual revel or feast grew into a refined fête and even into an historical pageant; handicrafts were revived and Yattendon copperwork adorned local churches and found its way to Cala, South Africa, where a large copper lectern-cum-pulpit beautifies the church of the Ascension. More recently with great assistance from Lord Iliffe a new village hall has arisen to centralize the activities of Yattendon and Frilsham.

At Frilsham the Pang flows past an almost circular churchyard and drives its first mill, at least in wet seasons although many a recent year has resembled that of two centuries earlier when a duck made her nest under the mill-wheel and hatched a brood before a drop of water had passed. Downstream the Pang may be followed to Marlston, where a Roman villa has been found, and so on round a great curve to the east of Bucklebury. Here all the higher areas are plastered with sandy, gravelly deposits which support extensive woods mainly deciduous with a most varied flora, including the spurge-laurel and the pendulous, shade-loving Solomon's Seal.

Much of the charm of Bucklebury depends on its woods or common which clothes the sands on the high ridge to the south. The Common is five miles long and is traversed lengthwise by a route which begins at Wood Gate in the east in a mile-long avenue of splendid oaks, and which enters the common proper at the Blade Bone Inn. Crosswise tracks abound and most of the 268 footpaths said to exist in the parish are here. Chapel Row used to be noted for sports and horse-shows while the Common was until recently the home of wood-turning. These now seem to have died and worse still the woodland has been unfrocked and disgraced. Bracken, heather and gorse abound but most of the lightsome scattering of birch and the denser patchwork of thickets have been cleared, as a site which the Parliamentarians found so convenient for assembly during the Battle of Newbury in October 1644 proved equally attractive to their more destructive successors three centuries later. Today also the early squatter settlements of the 'broom squires' have thickened into a fair sprinkling of dwellings around the perimeter of the Common. The traditions of horse-play and murder of the turbulent nomads have long since faded into gentility, but one delightful tale of the hunt keeps green. Merry Tidbury, an old hoop-maker, when busily working in Carbin's Wood, was asked by a fox if any hounds were drawing the Wood. Tauntingly Merry replied 'Craven!' 'Well,' said the fox, 'I must be off; if it had been the South Berks I'd have stopped and 'elped 'ee make a few withies.'

The dispersed houses about the Common have kept well clear of the church and the few picturesque cottages in the valley below, partly because this early nucleus stood on a site that was always liable to be flooded. Here near the Pang are a foundry that was working before 1717 and a Georgian vicarage which in that capacity succeeded the old Glebe Cottage.

The church of St. Mary the Virgin stands in a tidy churchyard with an abundance of wooden cross-beam tombs so typical of the Pang valley. An elaborate south doorway of 1170, rich with carvings of faces interspersed with leaves, leads into a cheerful interior partly Transitional and mainly late Perpendicular in style. The chancel was much altered later for an inscription on a tie beam reads '1591 Francis Winchecom Esquier build this'. But it is the incidentals which are so intriguing. The chancel has a small annexe, added in 1705, to accommodate the pews of the lord of the manor, with a squint into the nave which is now closed presumably to stop his thoughts from wandering like those of other mortals. The window of this recess contains a glass-panel of 1649 showing a sundial and a very realistic fly. On the walls of the chancel near mural monuments to the Winchcombe family are pieces of armour, the finest being a helm with the Winchcombe crest of a roebuck's head with a spray of leaves in its mouth. The pews in the aisle are still delightful and the great chest, perhaps from Reading Abbey, is a gem of chamfered security. Outside, high up on the tower corner, are small carvings of a crucifixion, a Maltese cross and a figure combing a wheel—a rebus of the Winchcombes. Yet to many the most intriguing memorial in the church is a flat slab in the chancel floor bearing the words:

> Here lyeth the Body of Frances Lady Viscountess
> Bolingbroke, Daughter of Sir Henry Winchcombe Bart.,
> who departed this life the 24 day of October A.D. 1718.
> *Aet.* 39

The Winchcombes came into the manor about 1540 when John Winchcombe, son of Jack of Newbury, built a new manor house on the site of the retreat of the abbot of Reading Abbey and adorned to this day with the fishponds dug by the monks. The manor acquired national fame when Frances, daughter and heir of Sir Henry, married in 1701 Henry St. John, an eloquent Tory M.P. who came to live here. The beautiful lady had joined herself to a husband whose earlier life had been particularly blameful and who regarded all women as his natural prey. St. John had an overpowering grace and urbanity which made him a perfect 'woman's man' yet the good Frances and Bucklebury seem to have chastened him for a while and here, during intermittent visits from 1701 to 1714, he adopted a pose of a country squire. As he himself wrote 'in the midst of business, Bucklebury runs in my head'; 'I am ready to go there at an hour's warning.' On his wife's large fortune, he kept a fine establishment in London and Bucklebury and constantly travelled between them. Many eminent politicians and writers came to the Manor, including Harley, Pope, Prior, Arbuthnot and Swift. St. John had already been made Secretary of State with a salary of £5,000 a year when Jonathan Swift came here early in August 1711, and found 'Mr. Secretary was a perfect country gentleman at Bucklebury: he smoked tobacco with one or two neighbours; he inquired after the wheat in such a field; he went to visit his hounds, and knew all their names; he and his lady saw me to my chamber just in the country fashion. His house is in the midst of near three thousand pounds a year he had by his lady. . . . She is a great favourite of mine.'

In 1712 St. John was made Viscount Bolingbroke and thereafter his visits to Bucklebury grew fewer and fewer. He had never broken loose from his past and even in 1705 he could write to Thomas Coke, M.P. for Derbyshire, 'Really Tom you are missed: whoring flags without you.' In 1714 he was dismissed from office and retired to Bucklebury but soon afterwards fled to France where he found a wealthy middle-aged widow to his liking. Only then did Frances despair and she died of a broken heart in the prime of her life and left an estate heavily saddled with debts, to her godson. Descendants of the Winchcombes still own the manor but the old house was destroyed after a fire about 1830 except the great kitchens, brew-house and stables, the last-named bearing the date 1626 and the H. W. for Sir Henry Winchcombe. The magnificent oak avenue near the Blade Bone Inn must also be associated with the manor as it was probably planted by Bolingbroke to commemorate Marlborough's victories.

The nearest neighbour to Bucklebury is Stanford Dingley which lies athwart the Pang two miles downstream. Here fine Spanish chestnuts shade the little church of St. Denis, which retains a good deal of Transitional work, including some large piers. Worth noticing also are the deeply-splayed quatrefoil in a circular window, the ironwork of the south door and the wall-paintings some of which in plan at least are original thirteenth-century work.

The road north of the church follows the Pang valley and in a mile or so gives a fine view of Bradfield College sitting sedately amid a well-wooded park on the opposite hill-side. Bradfield had had notable residents long before the Rev. Thomas Stevens in 1850 turned the unoffending manor house into a college. John Pordage, a rector here two centuries earlier made unusual progress in mysticism and on one occasion when preaching fell into a trance and rushed home where he found his wife 'cloathed all in white lawn with a white rod in her hand. Ten other women came in and all fell to dancing the Mays about the flower pots.' Pordage was vicar at Bradfield when Elias Ashmole married Lady Mainwaring and as lord of the manor 'enjoyed his wife's estate though not her company for altogether'. Ashmole, however, had no time for heresy hunting as he spent most of his time in studying and in quarrelling violently with his in-laws. His pursuit of botany led to a friendship with John Tradescant of the Botanic Gardens at Chelsea, who bequeathed a museum to him, the same that formed much of Ashmole's bequest—now grown into the Ashmolean—to the University of Oxford. His diary for February 17th 1683, when he was living at Englefield, runs: 'The last load of my rarities was sent to the barge and this afternoon I relapsed into the gout.'

The troubles of the Rev. Thomas Stevens, founder of Bradfield College, were mainly financial and at one time when the staff equalled or exceeded the pupils, he is said on being asked by a master for salary to have advised the poor man to say the Nicene creed. Things had not improved much when H. B. Gray became headmaster in 1880 yet within thirty years he had set the school well on the way to its present prosperity. In 1890 Gray supervised the construction in a nearby chalk pit, of a Greek theatre modelled on that of Epidaurus in the Morea. The first performance was held that year with Gray in the leading part and others have followed triennially in a setting greener than any Greece can show.

From Bradfield the same straight road north of the river proceeds through lonely woods and skirting the grounds of Bere Court and of the Nautical College descends with a flourish to the church at Pangbourne. The original village sprang up on the flat deltaic land at the junction of Pang and Thames but today the delights of the valley have attracted numerous houses in a variety of styles, ultra-modern, Edwardian and Victorian, including the dwellings directly facing the main reach of river, known to architects as 'The Seven Deadly Sins' and to mere mortals as 'The Seven Havens of Comfort'.

Below the wooded gardens of hill-side Pangbourne lie two deeply-contrasting worlds: the world of the highway and the world of the river, and both have been described exquisitely by Kenneth Grahame who lived near the church and the old timbered forge in Church Cottage where stands the old village lock-up which he used as a toolshed. Descended from Robert the Bruce, Kenneth Grahame was born in Edinburgh in 1859. At the age of twenty he became a clerk in the Bank of England and proved so successful that in 1898 he was made Secretary of the Bank. Alongside this business success he won a name for himself as a writer of rare insight into child mentality expressed in 'subtle and evocative prose'. *The Golden Age* was published in 1895; *Dream Days* followed in 1898 and *The Wind in the Willows*, which was gathered together in book form at Cookham Dean, in 1908. Much of this last work was originally written in letter form to his only son Alastair who later in life was killed by a train while an undergraduate at Oxford. Kenneth Grahame died in 1932 and lies with his son in one grave at Oxford. His epitaph, although he of all people needed none, includes the words 'leaving childhood and literature the more blessed because of him'.

At Pangbourne, countless readers will recall how Water Rat, Mole and Toad were strolling along the main road easily when 'The "Poop-poop" rang with a brazen shout in their ears, they had a moment's glimpse of an interior of glittering plate-glass and rich morocco, and the magnificent motor-car, immense, breath-snatching, passionate, with its pilot tense and hugging his wheel, possessed all earth and air for the fraction of a second, flung on enveloping cloud of dust that blinded and enwrapped them utterly, and then dwindled to a speck in the far distance, changed back into a droning bee once more.' And how the admiring Toad sitting in the middle of the road exclaimed 'Glorious, stirring sight! The poetry of motion! The *real* way to travel! The *only* way to travel! Here to-day—in next week to-morrow! Villages skipped, towns and cities jumped—always somebody else's horizon! O bliss! O poop-poop! O my! O my!'

But the real world at Pangbourne is the river with its smooth cliff-hung reach and the lock and lasher and the bridge to Whitchurch with everyone messing about in boats —'By it and with it and on it and in it.' Who could ever

The Thames Valley between Pangbourne and Streatley

Bisham Abbey, near Marlow

Heralding the Hocktide Festivities at Hungerford

Smyth's Almshouses, Maidenhead, built 1659

afterwards forget how 'On either side of them, as they glided onwards, the rich meadow-grass seemed that morning of a freshness and a greenness unsurpassable. Never had they noticed the roses so vivid, the willow-herb so riotous, the meadow-sweet so odorous and pervading. Then the murmur of the approaching weir began to hold the air, and they felt a consciousness that they were nearing the end, whatever it might be, that surely awaited their expedition.

A wide half-circle of foam and glinting lights and shining shoulders of green water, the great weir closed the backwater from bank to bank, troubled all the quiet surface with twirling eddies and floating foam-streaks, and deadened all other sounds with its solemn and soothing rumble. In midmost of the stream, embraced in the weir's shimmering armspread, a small island lay anchored, fringed close with willow and silver birch and alder. Reserved, shy, but full of significance, it hid whatever it might hold behind a veil, keeping it till the hour should come, and, with the hour those who were called and chosen.'

Surely Berkshire offers no sweeter thing than to float on the Thames at Pangbourne and as the shadows lengthen over the water to sip hot coffee and read again *The Wind in the Willows*. 'O Mole! the beauty of it! The merry bubble and joy, the thin, clear happy call of the distant piping! Such music I never dreamed of, and the call in it is stronger even than the music is sweet! Row on, Mole, row! For the music and the call must be for us.

'The Mole, greatly wondering, obeyed. "I hear nothing myself," he said, "but the wind playing in the reeds and rushes and osiers."'

CHAPTER X: Hungerford and the Middle Kennet

Come live with me, and be my love
And we will some new pleasures prove
Of golden sands, and crystal brooks,
With silken lines and silver hooks.

Let coarse bold hands from slimy nest
The bedded fish in banks out-wrest;
Or curious traitors, sleeve-silk flies,
Bewitch poor fishes' wandering eyes.

J. DONNE, *The Bait*

OF all the tributaries that feed the Thames the Kennet is the most copious and beautiful. Entering Berkshire near Hungerford from the chalk downs about Avebury, its waters run crystal-clear and plainly show the famous trout lying in 'a cool curving world' rippling 'with dark ecstasies'. Poplars, hazels and willows shade its banks and beyond the marshy, floodable meadows, the valley-sides sweep upward to corn-land and to wide commons interspersed with parks while on the far southern horizon the downs of Inkpen form a sombre background to a smiling valley. In the chalk country of Wiltshire the roads keep close to the river but from Hungerford downstream, where the strip of damp alluvium widens, they avoid it with unnatural cunning and river-crossings become increasingly difficult. Hungerford and Newbury control the passage of the full-grown Kennet and between them collect up all the thoroughfares hereabout. Yet whereas Newbury is of and on the Kennet, Hungerford has carefully expanded away from it, just as if its early citizens could not forget the (false) tradition that Hyngwar the noted Saxon was drowned in a ford here in 870.

In fact Hungerford lies mainly on the river Dun just before its junction with the Kennet and on what was once the edge of Savernake Forest and up to 1895 the administrative territory of Wiltshire. It is—saving its grace—a relative newcomer which has grown up mainly on the southern slopes of the valley and has incorporated the ancient Charnham Street (or Celdrington) which stands between the Dun and Kennet, and the equally old Eddington which guards the Kennet bridge. As for so long in history, many roads still converge on Eddington bridge but much credit must also be given to the little river Dun for at Hungerford the valley of this small stream attracted both canal and railway and led them safely to the Kennet. These modern lines of communication never attempted to follow the youthful Kennet through the great chalk downs near Marlborough but slunk around their edge on the way to the west. After the opening of the canal late in 1810, Hungerford benefited from being on the quickest line of water-traffic between London and Bristol and henceforth it became the western entrance or exit of the main Kennet valley. The railway duly followed the canal and, spanning the main street with an iron bridge, changes direction and enters or leaves, as the case may be, the flat floor of the vale of Kennet.

The amazing thing about Hungerford, however, is not its nineteenth-century revival but its organization as a real community ever since it enters into recorded history. Hungerford itself was not mentioned in *Domesday Survey* yet less than a century later it had a 'community of burgesses' with a common seal and enjoying certain 'ancient usages'. In the thirteenth century the manor belonged to Simon de Montfort and from him the Hungerford people declare that they received a charter of herbage for sheep and pannage for swine. Tradition also has it that Edward III granted to the burgesses their first royal charter and that John of Gaunt gave them fishing rights extending from 'Elder Stub to

Irish Stile', which with few exceptions included all the middle Kennet. To confirm this gift he gave a horn which along with the fisheries the townspeople still hold and as if to keep his memory evergreen they sport his arms, the Crescent and Star, and name their fire-engine after him.

To this day, the affairs of Hungerford are in the hands of a Hocktide jury of twenty or twenty-four, chosen on each Easter Tuesday by the commoners who form the Hocktide Court. The ancient ceremonies of government are then performed with much of their former glory, beginning on Friday in Easter week with a 'Macaroni supper' held at the John of Gaunt inn which belongs to the town. Before the supper the Constable receives all the rents of the communal properties and the accounts being audited the company regale themselves with macaroni cheese, watercress and punch. On the following Tuesday the Hocktide jury assembles at nine o'clock in the town hall, while for an hour previously the horn has been blown as continuously as possible from the window, and the bellman or assistant bailiff, dressed in uniform of a grey coat with scarlet facings and brass buttons, and a tall hat with a gold band, has perambulated the town crying 'Oyez! Oyez! Oyez! All ye commoners of the borough of Hungerford are requested to attend at your court house at nine o'clock this morning on pain of being fined. God save the King!' At the same time those commoners who do not wish to attend the court pay the bellman one penny, a relict no doubt of the shilling fine once exacted for non-attendance.

At nine o'clock the court assembles and the Constable takes his seat in an ebony chair, elaborately and skilfully carved. The jurymen are summoned, a foreman selected and the jury sworn and empanelled. The Town Clerk (formerly called Seneschal) reads out the 'Ancient Customs' and recites the provisions of John of Gaunt's grant whereupon the assistant bailiff rings his bell and cries out, 'All ye commoners of the borough of Hungerford draw forward and answer to your names or you will be fined.' The list of commoners is then read out and fines are received on behalf of absentees, almost any burgess being willing to produce the necessary penny to ensure that a forgetful neighbour shall not lose his right of pasture, usually for two cows and one horse, for the ensuing year. The Constable proceeds to submit the accounts, which include the various rents and even a five-shilling charge on anyone setting up in business during the last twelve months, and the court prepares to elect the officers for the ensuing year. These consist of, first a Constable, next a portreeve who collects the quit rents, a bailiff who with the aid of a black silver-mounted staff of 1688 collects the market dues, an assistant bailiff, three water bailiffs, three overseers of the common lands, one hayward, three keepers of the common coffer, two tithing men (out of four in office) and two ale tasters. Today the two searchers and sealers of leather and two tasters of fish and flesh are no longer deemed necessary. After the elections the commoners may propose new by-laws or make complaints, and during this part of the ceremony two tithing men call at the Constable's house for the tutti poles, which still show signs of faded colour and gilding and which are decorated for the day with gorgeous blooms and long streamers of ribbon. Armed with these and accompanied by a man carrying a basket of oranges, they visit the schools where they distribute the fruit and beg a half-holiday for the children before going on to the workhouse to dole out more oranges. They expect a coin from every house to pay for the oranges and have the right to kiss every lady in the house, at which honour she is presented with an orange stuck on the spiked end of the tutti pole. At lunch, which takes place at the Three Swans on the site of the old manor house, the Constable again presides, and oranges and hot pennies are thrown out to the children in the streets. Every commoner drinks of 'ye ancient Plantaganet punch' and newcomers or 'colts' are shod by having a nail driven into their sole for which they contribute to the cost of the punch.

On the following Friday the proceedings close with a Court Leet for the manor of Sandon Fee. Another Court Baron is held in the Town Hall and an evening banquet follows at which the Constable again sits gracefully enthroned with the horn suspended between the two tutti poles. At the stroke of midnight he proposes 'The immortal memory of John of Gaunt', which is drunk in silence, after which 'Auld Lang Syne' and 'God Save the King' are sung. To a blast on the horn, the Constable leaves the building and seated in the chair with an escort of officials he is borne home, where his wife is supposed to provide a coffee breakfast for the party. So the ceremony ends. The horn used in them today is somewhat battered and is inscribed 'Jehosphat Lucus was Cunstabl 1634'; 'John a Gaun did give and grant the Riall Fishing to Hungerford towne from Eldren Stub to Irish Stil excepting som several Mil Pound [es]'. The borough also possesses a much older horn said to have been given by John of Gaunt and bearing the mutilated inscription 'Hungurford' and 'Actel' or 'astel'.

The present rights and liberties of the borough of Hungerford were not acquired without a struggle. The documents of 1433 and 1466—still in the Town chest—affirmed certain customs and franchises and were kept with the charters of John of Gaunt and Simon de Montfort and various minor parchments inside a little chest within a larger coffer. In 1572 a certain John Lovelake, hitherto so zealous a burgess that when Constable 'he went down to the Dun with bow and arrows to vindicate the right of fishing there' against an intruder, appears to have gained possession of the small chest by dishonest means, and the precious charters of John of Gaunt and Simon de Montfort have been missing ever since.

A commission of investigation—rather surprisingly—ruled against the borough and although Elizabeth graciously made an order in the year following that the townsfolk should continue to enjoy their ancient privileges she carefully avoided defining them. As endless litigation on dues and tolls and tithes followed, in 1612 the people of Hungerford decided to purchase the rights in question. This they did by means of trustees to whom in 1617 was finally conveyed the manor, with all rents, pleas, fishing and fishery, and perquisites of the borough court. Today the trust property includes the Corn Exchange, the Town Hall, the markets and fairs, the fishing, the John of Gaunt inn, the rents of assize, the common rights of Port Down, Freeman's Marsh, a few sand-pits and withy beds and Church croft, the last-named being the gift of John Undewes at a nominal rent of one rose as 'a place to sport therein'.

Today the town no longer keeps its own stocks of bees and stud bulls but it retains its traditional civic spirit and offers amenities far greater than those of most other rural towns of its size in Britain. The fisheries remain a unique and splendid municipal possession. In Elizabethan times the Kennet yielded a great store of fish 'especiallie trowtes and crevices', the former being 'accompted the beste troute within this land'. In 1910 the river was re-stocked with 80,000 trout of varied grades up to 8 inches long and in some recent years the town has made over £100 profit on the fisheries. Brown trout spawn and abound in the Kennet as in no other part of the Thames drainage, but the eels and roach and dace are also superior in flavour and often in size while the grayling need competent cooks more than eulogies.

Modern Hungerford has few old buildings partly because of several great fires in the reign of Charles II. It was, as became its position by the Bath Road, always well blessed with inns and hostelries. The Bell Inn first appears in the records in 1494 and the White Hart in 1686, while actually on the Bath Road and formerly near a ford and footbridge over the Kennet is the Bear Inn which was granted with the manor of Chilton Foliat, to Anne of Cleves in 1540 and to Katherine Howard in the following year. The Bear was the meeting place in December 1688 of William of Orange with the commissioners of James II and about 1750 became a well-known posting station. Just before the coming of the railway in 1847 nearly fifty coaches used to pass through Charnham Street daily. Today the visitor will find a few attractive Georgian houses amid many post-Georgian as Hungerford underwent a distinct revival in Victorian times when the Town Hall was rebuilt. The old church of St. Lawrence after generations of neglect finally collapsed during a great fall of snow in 1814, and was replaced two years later by a Georgian Gothic structure, which has evoked warm praise from modern architects. It is indeed a likeable building as are most structures artistically designed in Cotswold stone and has a most happy position on the banks of the Kennet and Avon Canal not far from the river Dun. Yet many will deplore the passing of the old church which is shown in prints as an intriguing medley of styles and which would have given to Hungerford a touch of the architectural antiquity that its civic awareness deserves.

Such a treasure exists at Avington just off the Bath Road three miles east of Hungerford, where in quiet seclusion on the meadows beside an arm of the Kennet is the finest Norman church in Berkshire. The little aisleless, towerless building is all twelfth century except the Tudor porch and the vestry which is modern, and a few Early English insertions. The plan is plain rectangular, measuring about 75 feet by 15 feet, so that the whole consists of five bays (two in the chancel and three in the nave) each nearly 15 feet square, which was once presumably the height to the crown of the chancel arch. The actual sanctuary is pure Norman with three rounded windows on the east and one in each flanking wall but the arch once separating it from the adjoining bay has gone. The chancel was once actually or intended to be vaulted as the springing of the ribs remains at the angles as well as two corbels carved as an ox and lion perhaps after the evangelists SS. Luke and Mark. The remaining chancel arch, although broken, is a delight of beak-heads and cats' heads, and the capitals supporting it are incised with human faces with large oval eyes. The south doorway is still richer and in spite of the mutilation of its outer hood is wonderfully pleasing, nor does the sixteenth-century door disgrace it. The cylindrical stone font refuses to be outdone in ornamentation and is elaborately but rudely carved with arcades with grotesque figures many of which have very short legs and appear to be wearing loose-fitting ankle-length trousers. The little church has other items of interest, but it is the completeness of the survival which pleases, not least in a part of the county that has lost so many of its original religious buildings.

The country south of the Kennet has no parish church as fine as Avington but its less-frequented ways are peaceful after the roar of the Bath Road and the last chalk bastions in south Berkshire, once visited, have an irresistible charm. Inkpen, the gateway to the Beacon, spreadeagles unassumingly about its church and rectory, the former richly and tastefully restored with a wealth of handsome woodwork, and the latter a stately Queen Anne mansion of brick in grounds adorned with avenues of yew and beech converging upon a viewpoint to the southern hills. Inevitably all eyes at Inkpen turn to the south where the chalk escarpment rises sharply to over 900 feet and gives with the ascent a spacious horizon filled with chalk landforms and refreshed in summer with a fitful breeze.

The summit of the chalk just exceeds 950 feet at Inkpen Beacon and eastward after dropping a little at Walbury Hill rises at Walbury Camp to 975 feet, the highest point of the chalk in Britain and eleven feet higher than its greatest rival Milk Hill on the Marlborough Downs. The Camp is surrounded by a strong earthwork showing clearly its main gateways and has yielded various borers, axes and scrapers of flint to augment the collections at Newbury and Reading. The adjacent Walbury Hill is capped with a fine long barrow on which stands the Combe gallows, an eerie landmark—surely once a beacon post?—which is kept in good repair, under the obligations of the lease, by the tenant of Eastwich Farm.

The views are superb: to the north the Kennet valley growing more wooded downstream; to the south, in a vast amphitheatre of shaven slopes lies Combe, a Berkshire hamlet since 1895 with its spiritual affairs still under Winchester, and beyond it the bare rolling downs of Hampshire. But here we are trespassing on the province of A. G. Street who describes how 'south of that gibbet post lies a country of poverty and desolation, a country of juniper bushes and rabbits, a land of steep, barren slopes on which the chalk shows through the thin turf continuously, a country in which very few acres are worthy of man's effort. But looking northward the contrast was very sharp. Below me, miles below me, lay the Kennet Vale, by comparison a land flowing with milk and honey, a land of rich farms, prosperous villages, snug churches and kindly meadows. . . . From this high shelf of down everything in the lovely countryside far below appeared as in miniature. . . .'

The largest settlement immediately below the northern flank of Inkpen Beacon is Kintbury which stands on the chalk overlooking the valley-floor just before the Kennet traverses a belt of coarse grass and marshy tree-growth known as the Wilderness. This site has been occupied since early Saxon times as coins of Eadred have been found with skeletons in the churchyard, and many other burials have recently been discovered. A charter, also of the tenth century, tells how

Wulfgar left his lands at Inkpen to his wife Aeffe that she might enjoy the produce of three parts of it, and give the fourth part to the 'servants of God' of the 'holy place' at Kintbury for the good of the souls of himself, his father and grandfather. On Aeffe's death her share also was to go to the 'Holy place' to aid the salvation of the same males, for Wulfgar's womenfolk apparently had no need of intercession or were quite beyond praying for.

Kintbury today has a happy balance of both sexes and although still a village has acquired the air of a town and spreads townlike along several roads south of the church and canal. The little cruciform church of St. Mary the Virgin is mainly a much-restored twelfth-century structure of which the south doorway seems as good as original. The large parish it serves stretches on both banks of the Kennet, forming as it were two agricultural flanks to a semi-industrial vale where the river has always been a source of power. Two grist mills were working in Norman times and in succeeding ages tucking and tanning and wool-dyeing arose, and in the eighteenth century a silk factory was founded. Today the most noteworthy manufacture is of whiting for shoes from the chalk. The strong agricultural interests are reflected in the mellow old farms scattered over the parish and in the mansions, which with their parks and cottages, form outlying hamlets. Wallingtons, a palatial brick building partly of the seventeenth century, is to the south what Elcot House is to the north and between them at Wawcott are the kennels of the Craven Hunt.

East of Kintbury the chalk disappears beneath a mantle of clays and sands and gravels on which tree-growth abounds. Here we again cross the threshold from the downs, with their rarities, such as the musk-orchid, spring crocus and spiked Star of Bethlehem—to the ranker, more varied flora of heath and woodland. These wooded tracts were never natural routeways and today are criss-crossed by tall-hedged or sunken roads well-suited only to leisurely travel and to the discriminate traveller.

A typical winding route leads from Kintbury to Hamstead Marshal a tiny rural village that was for long associated with the Marshals of England. Later, in Tudor times, Catherine of Aragon, Cardinal Wolsey, Jane Seymour and Catherine Parr all held lands here for a while but it was left to Lord William Craven—the man who loved fighting fires—to erect in the seventeenth century a truly magnificent house. The first architect of the mansion, Sir Balthaser Gerbier, died soon after it was started and it was probably completed under the guidance of Captain Wynne. It was created as a miniature castle of Heidelberg in memory of Elizabeth of Bohemia whom Earl Craven adored, but, sad to say, even the Earl could not prevent it from being utterly ruined by fire in 1718 and today only a great garden wall and nine pairs of entrance piers remain. One pair has been removed to Benham Place across the Kennet, three pairs stand in grand isolation in the park, and five others are in the garden wall. Some of the gate piers of brick are adorned with scalloped niches and fine urns while those of stone (in the garden surround) have equally fine urns and fine cones and beautifully carved panels of fruit and flowers, some of which hang almost free from the pillar.

Hamstead Park was mentioned in *Domesday Survey* and more frequently about 1230 when Henry III stayed here with his brother-in-law William the Marshal, Earl of Pembroke. The present park is said to contain patches of ancient forest but its greater acreage is fine English parkland moulded by the valley of a small stream. At its north-western corner, near the site of the old manor house, is the parish church, which could hardly be better cared for and has a wealth of warm woodwork. From near it a long avenue rolls majestically eastward through pasture and bracken to Hamstead Lodge and so over more parkland to the village of Enborne.

Although for centuries in Kintbury Hundred, Enborne has profited more from nearness to Newbury. Most of its old brick cottages are scattered at wide intervals about what was once an important sheep-drove from the Hampshire Downs by way of Newbury bridge to East Ilsley. During the first battle of Newbury, Enborne was near the thick of the fighting as the Earl of Essex, marching south of the Kennet from Hungerford, took up his quarters for the night and opened his attack next morning from high ground just south of the village. Strangely enough, the church of St. Michael at Enborne was unmolested and with its Norman nave and traces of old frescoes remains a tidy, attractive building. But Enborne has had fame thrust upon it for other than historical or architectural reasons. To the south, between the ridge on which the battle was fought and the Hampshire Downs, lies the wide deep valley of the Enborne river, a headstream of which rises near Inkpen Beacon and forms for many miles the county boundary. Recently plans which failed to materialize in 1910 have again been brought forward to dam the valley and to convert the lower parts of its middle course into a reservoir for the water-supply of London. The sites of numerous farms and cottages, and vast stretches of good cropland will disappear beneath the lake, although in summer when the water-level falls, former residents will have the doubtful pleasure of seeing their ancestral acres coated with Enborne mud. This lake will then creep again like an autumnal tide up all the embayments of the foothills, and no boat or float will stir it as the strictest privacy will be necessary to prevent pollution. So over 5,000 acres of productive farmland will be utterly lost, while on Welsh hills floods scour the sterile landscape and the waters of a hundred Enbornes run to waste. Although late in 1949 it appeared that the plan was being abandoned, the fears of the people of Enborne should not be lulled by a temporary victory, for the threat will be on again before the turn of the century. Then, as now, there is salvation in the voice of the poet:

> And I saw in a vision the worm in the wheat
> And in the shops nothing for people to eat
> Nothing for sale in Stupidity Street.

CHAPTER XI: *Newbury and the Lower Kennet*

The Chesshyre Laddes were bryske and brave
And the Kendall Laddes as free
But none surpass'd, or I'm a knave,
The Laddes of Newberrie.

'Ballad of Flodden Field'

THE roads of all central Berkshire focus on the narrow bridge at Newbury over which an incessant stream of traffic moves south to Basingstoke, Winchester and Salisbury and north to Oxford, Wantage and Swindon. In the town these longitudinal lifelines are crossed rectangularly by the main Bath Road, while from all the neighbouring hills and vales, folk flock in to see the shops and to enjoy a brief hour of urban excitement. The animation heightens on market days and culminates on race days in a vast concourse which collects and disperses with an intentness borne only of great hopes or deep despair.

The Romans seem to have begun it all, for they built a road from Gloucester and Cirencester along the Lambourn-Kennet watershed to Speen and so on to Silchester. No doubt older tracks, including that from Streatley Hill, also came here but the Roman road was the first of national importance and beside it Speen or *Spinae* grew up as a posting station. Before the end of the Roman occupation people were probably living on both banks of the Kennet as the presence of pile dwellings shows they had done many centuries earlier; and in 1856 nearly one hundred skeletons and various quantities of pottery of Roman age were excavated at the goods yard of the railway station.

In Saxon and Norman times Newbury expanded mainly

southward where the valley-floor was higher and less liable to flood, in all of which it closely resembles Hungerford as both early incorporated an old nucleus between two rivers and proceeded to expand up the bank facing away from the sun. During these periods the Kennet increased in value, giving the people lush water-meadows and plenty of power for milling. Yet Newbury grew rich on cloth and not on corn.

At the very beginning of the thirteenth century a fulling mill was active here and long before its close St. Bartholomew's Fair had begun. Some of this progress was due to foreign influence as the town early seems to have sheltered an alien colony within its boundaries. The learned Dr. Twisse, rector in 1620 and a native of Speenhamland, was the grandson of a German and son of a clothier. By the fifteenth century, the cloth trade supported eminent clothiers and an abundance of humbler fullers and kersey-weavers. The manufacture reached the height of its fame in the time of Jack of Newbury and of Thomas Dolman, the son of a foreman of Jack's, and builder of Shaw House.

Jack of Newbury acquired a picturesque fame and a popularity similar to but much earlier than that of Dick Whittington. The stories told of him bring to mind Dekker's shoemaker and although most of them are legendary they make happy reading. He was in fact an apprentice who had changed his name from John Smalewoode to John Wynchcombe and who had progressed rapidly after marrying a master-clothier's widow. His business grew to an extraordinary size and 'Winchcombe's kerseys' were the finest of the day. He is said to have fitted out one hundred of his journeymen to fight at Flodden where the 'laddes of Newberrie' did well, yet rumour has it that his modesty would not allow him to accept a knighthood. Of the early books written on him the chief was Thomas Deloney's *Pleasant History of John Winchcomb, in his younger yeeres called Jacke*

A corn[illegible] Newbury from the Churchyard

St. Lawrence's, Reading, from the Market Place

of Newberie, the famous and worthy clothier of England (1597), which had already run into fifteen editions by 1700.

As Deloney was a silk weaver of Norwich his description of textile processes is more accurate than his story, in which he describes the visit of Henry VIII, Queen Catherine, Cardinal Wolsey and other members of the court to Jack of Newbury's workshops. The King and Queen dined with the clothier, all the floor being covered with broadcloths of azure colour instead of green rushes and the banquet served in glass dishes. Afterwards the weavers sang for the King, who gave them 'an hundred angells to make cheere withal' and leave to fetch four bucks out of Donnington Park every year.

After inspecting some of the workshops their majesties were met by a large group of children, who earned their living by picking wool. Each gave to the King a gillyflower, and all so impressed the Queen that she exclaimed 'Certainly I perceive God gives as fair children to the poor as to the rich, and fairer many times,' and decided to take two of them to wait upon her. 'Fair Katherine,' said the King, 'thou and I have jumped in one opinion,' whereupon he took four more, sent twice that number to universities, and other nobles following his example, not one child was left to pick wool. The rhyming description of the workshops—taken by Deloney from some popular ballad—is far less fanciful although grossly exaggerated.

'Within one room being large and long
There stood two hundred loomes full strong:
Two hundred men, the truth is so,
Wrought in these loomes all in a row.
By every one a prettie boy
Sate making quils with mickle joy.
And in another place hard by,
An hundred women merrily

Were carding hard with joyful cheere
Who singing sate with voices cleare.
And in a chamber close beside,
Two hundred maidens did abide,
In petticoats of stammel red,
And milk-white kerchers on their head:'

. . . . .

After these spinners, who sang like nightingales, came the children who picked wool, the rowers who raised the nap of the cloth, and the shearmen who cropped it. But in addition

'A dye-house likewise had he then,
Wherein he kept full fortie men:
And likewise in his fulling mill,
Full twenty persons kept he still.'

These fancies are hard to replace with facts, yet we know that the younger John Winchcombe, who succeeded his father, was given in 1539 a single order for 1,000 pieces of cloth by Thomas Cromwell. Fortunately, the greater clothiers have left visible signs of their wealth. Jack of Newbury's house stands in the present Northbrook Street next door to the Jack Hotel and retains, in the side court, an old gabled face with two overhanging stories of half-timber and herringbone-brick, the lower being enriched with curved brackets and a wooden-framed oriel window.

The church of St. Nicholas was completely rebuilt in stone by Jack of Newbury and John his son between 1509 and 1533, and, apart from a modern vestry and slight internal restorations, remains a handsome, unified Tudor structure. The brasses under the tower include one to Jack of Newbury, which bears figures of himself and his wife, with the inscription 'Off yo charite pray for the soule of John Smalwode als Wynchcom and Alys hys wyfe which John dyed the XV day of february a d m MCCCCCXIX'. John is shown dressed in a fur-trimmed coat, belt and pouch, and his hands in prayer. Below the inscription are the figures of a daughter and two sons, one of whom is the John who followed his father in the business and became the owner of Bucklebury manor, where a fine portrait of him is still kept by his descendants, and was thought by Swift to be of the great Jack himself.

Another building in Newbury connected with its greatest clothier is the Litten chapel of the old Hospital or Priory of St. Bartholomew which stands in the street of that name. Today the chapel consists of a plain rectangular room with old yet much restored windows, and its main interest lies in its elaborate Tudor timbering supporting its gabled roof, and especially in two richly-carved queen-post trusses. Here Jack of Newbury was married but in later years the chapel became part of the grammar school and has continued in secular use.

Whereas both of the Winchcombes dwelt in popular fashion near their workers, their great rivals the Dolmans seemed urged by a different ambition and having made a fortune soon moved out to more palatial quarters in the suburbs. Thomas Dolman built Shaw House, a charming gabled mansion of red-brick faced with well-cut limestone and designed on a clever H-plan. The stone-mullioned windows, including two grand bays on the east, combine with a colonnade on the north and stately porch on the south to make the finest Elizabethan dwelling in Berkshire. Upon it Dolman spent £10,000 and the cloth-workers, seeing the expenditure of capital which might have purchased wool, invented the rhyme,

> 'Lord have mercy upon us, miserable sinners,
> Thomas Dolman has built a new house,
> And turned away all his spinners.'

The clothier 'fearful of the lashes he expected to receive from the envy of his neighbours,—inscribed more than one apposite sentence . . . above his superb stone porch, as spells against those ill-wishers whose peculiar malice he dreaded'. They remain there to this day, the one in Greek over the main door meaning 'Let no envious man enter here', and that in Latin on the portico signifying 'The toothless man envies the teeth of those who eat, and the mole despises the eye of the roe.'

The death or retirement of the Winchcombes and Dolmans did not entirely upset the local cloth trade which struggled on for another two hundred and fifty years, but it never again reached any importance. In 1601, the Guild or Fraternity of Weavers, which had existed for many generations, was granted a royal charter as 'The Fellowship of the Weavers at Newbury', and, in a stilted way, did its best to bolster up the declining cloth trade and to cheer its members with good food on its feast days. Its insignia or regalia hangs with the original charter and many other documents in a glass case in the former Cloth Hall. The Cloth Hall itself, apart from restorations, dates from the early seventeenth century. It is a long, narrow rectangular building with an overhanging first floor supported by decorated brackets and carved wooden pilasters. These pilasters divide the longer walls into six bays while similar pilasters adorn the modern porch. The building rises to an attic with a tiled roof and is kept weather-wise by a wrought-iron dragon which swings menacingly from the western gable. Today the Cloth Hall is a pleasant museum where the treasures of the locality from the Stone Age onwards are most carefully exhibited.

The museum holds a great many relics of the two battles fought at Newbury during the Civil War. The battlefields themselves make pleasant walks in all the warmer months of the year. The first battle was fought on the 20 September

1643 on the plateau between Crookham Heath and Greenham Common south-west of the Kennet bridge. Here Charles intercepted the London trained bands under Essex retreating homeward after the siege of Gloucester. The Parliamentarians attacked from the neighbourhood of Enborne in the usual triple thrust. On their right they were driven back by Rupert's cavalry; in the centre they crept slowly forward on to the common; on their left, near the Kintbury road, they gained high ground overlooking the Royalists, and here it was that Lord Falkland and the Earls of Carnarvon and Sunderland were killed. At dusk the battle was still undecided but Charles withdrew during darkness leaving the London road open.

At a crossroads on the top of Wash Hill on the Salisbury road one mile out of Newbury stands a monument to Lord Falkland and other illustrious royalists. Only Falkland is mentioned by name but the symbol *x* and crown refers to the Earl of Carnarvon and the S and crown to the Earl of Sunderland. Falkland has caught the public imagination in much the same way as Sir Philip Sidney did. He had an intellectual mind which could see too clearly both sides of a problem, and was blessed with a gentleness and tolerance that made him a student more than a soldier. By 1643 he was heartily sick of war and at the siege of Gloucester among friends he would relapse into silence and with frequent sighs 'would with shrill and sad accent ingeminate the word Peace! Peace! . . .' At Newbury he rode fearlessly at a gap in a hedge raked by the enemy's fire and fell in 'a death scarcely distinguishable from suicide', so closing 'his eyes to the horrors his mind could not tolerate'. He was buried under a graceful marble monument in a chapel of the lovely church beside the Windrush at Burford in Oxfordshire.

From a minor road west of the Falkland monument at Newbury a footpath leads between the houses to the heart of the battlefield and reveals the town in all its glory with the converging valleys and the high wooded hills beyond. Such a view, with the evening sun lighting the route eastward to London and home, met the eyes of the Parliamentarians as they breasted the lip of the hill. There too in the distance at the foot of the northern valley slope is the site of the second Battle of Newbury.

On this occasion a large Parliamentarian force under Essex and Manchester with Waller and Cromwell as captains marched west to prevent the relief of Sir Charles Boys who was besieged in Donnington castle. By the time the Roundheads reached the Newbury end of Bucklebury Common, Charles had already relieved the garrison at Donnington and had taken up a position between the Lambourn and Kennet with Shaw House and the castle as part of his defences. The battle on the 27 October 1644 was, as so often happened, won by both sides and Charles stored his guns and ammunition in Donnington castle until he saw an opportunity of removing them to Oxford.

Shaw House, at this time owned by Humphrey Dolman, bore the brunt of Manchester's attack but although fierce fighting went on in the garden, its defences held out till night stopped the struggle. The building is now a school and inside the window at its south-east corner is a bullet hole with an inscription in Latin saying that the bullet itself on the morning of the battle narrowly missed the King. In the garden the defensive ramparts still exist as yew-shaded walks and continue round the house except on the north side. In addition, a set of four old cannon captured during the battle are mounted in an opening of the surrounding wall. After the fight the Dolmans collected another rhyme:

> 'King and Law
> Shouts Dolman of Shaw,'

and at the Restoration Dolman junior was given a knighthood.

Donnington castle which played so large a part in the second battle of Newbury was built about 1386 by Sir Richard Adderbury on a site guarding the northern flanks of the Kennet valley. Thomas Cromwell stayed here, as also did Edward VI; Henry VIII visited it and Queen Elizabeth took steps to prevent poaching in its extensive deer park. During the later years of the Civil War, Sir Charles Boys held it for the King until, after a siege of eighteen months, he was given an honourable surrender in April 1646. The castle was already badly damaged and within a year or so was in ruins. Today only the massive embattled gatehouse remains above ground. This consists of an entrance gateway flanked by two stout circular towers with stages divided by string courses some of which bear huge grotesque heads. Behind the ruin stretches a dwelling, dating in part from the time when the castle was demolished.

After the Civil War the citizens of Newbury led a quieter life and although the cloth manufacture was failing, seem to have flourished on agriculture and other trades. The visible signs of late-seventeenth-century expansion range in nature from cottages to chapels and almshouses. Some of the courts off Bartholomew Street have old half-timbering while on the banks of the river at West Mills is a row of cottages rising at one end to a gabled tile-hung face with an overhanging bay-window. Far grander is a dignified house (dated 1669) in Northbrook Street which, above a modern shop-front, is divided into symmetrical bays by pilasters and is surmounted by gables with their original barge-boards. In, or just off, Bartholomew Street are the oldest of the many surviving almshouses in Newbury. Adjoining the former Litten chapel stands St. Bartholomew's Hospital, an almshouse consisting of a long range of brick buildings designed on an E-plan with projecting wings and gabled roofs and a main entrance porch adorned with royal arms. The cost of its erection in 1698 came out of the revenues of the old hospital and its plan seems to have been copied from the almshouses which had been built on the opposite side of the road over twenty years earlier by Alderman Jemmett of the Brewers' Company of London.

The latter, which occupies the site of property belonging in 1550 to John Winchcombe, forms quite the prettiest building in Newbury. Together with the nearby Bartholomew Manor and various intervening dwellings, it has recently been acquired for the Middlesex hospital and has been converted into delightful homes for retired nurses. This succession of picturesque fronts facing across the narrow street to the façades and sides of various almshouses, new and old, makes Argyle Road the envy of all Berkshire towns.

A more unusual building of this century is the Corn Stores which recalls the gallery of the checker of Abingdon Abbey. Long, low, tiled and of brick, it is distinguished by a covered wooden gallery on its first floor which is reached from the ground by lateral staircases and gives access to the upper rooms. Other examples of contemporary architecture are mainly concerned with Nonconformity.

These include a Congregational chapel founded in 1662 and remodelled a century later, and Waterside Chapel, once Presbyterian and then Unitarian, which retains its picturesque gabled exterior almost as it was in 1697, although its old fittings—even the box pews with raised corner seats for children—have just been sold.

In the eighteenth century Newbury was for the most part prosperous. It did a good trade in shalloons 'for the lineing and insides of men's cloathes' and as Defoe also said, retained 'A manufacturing genius'. The Kennet after its improvement in about 1720 soon carried much traffic, especially of malt and corn downstream, while the London coach now sped to London in little over twelve hours. Yet the prosperity did not always lead to the beautification of the old town as many of the picturesque tile-hung cottages on the main street were re-faced in brick. A large house in Northbrook Street and another close to the bridge have a pleasant brick dignity, but the most striking structure of this age—apart from the entrance gates to the churchyard—is the former Kimber's Almshouses in Cheap Street. These were built in 1795 in a pattern of blue and red brick with recessed arches by the John Kimber who left charities for ten apprentices. The almshouses near Bartholomew's Hospital, known as Raymond's Buildings, were founded in 1796, but suffered damage during the last World War.

If, however, central Newbury has relatively few outstanding dwellings of Georgian times, the suburbs make full amends. Along the Bath Road comfortable houses arose. The Dower House itself is stately Queen Anne but beside it is an 'early Gothic revival'. The latter is a smaller copy of Donnington Grove, which was completely Gothicized inside and out about 1783 by William Brummel, father of the famous Beau. The former theatre, now a storehouse near the Bacon Arms, was a worthy addition to the life of the town and has notable connexions. John Wesley, after preaching from the pulpit of the parish church on his first visit, attempted to use 'the playhouse' on a second visit in 1770 but was refused as 'the good mayor would not suffer it to be so profaned'! A decorated ceiling from the theatre survives at Sandleford Priory, which is by far the most magnificent 'Gothic revival' style mansion hereabouts. It was built in 1781 for the wealthy Elizabeth Montagu who had long been famous as the most brilliant and witty hostess of her day and as the leader of 'blue-stocking' assemblies in London at which talk on literature and art replaced cards and gossip. The mansion was designed by James Wyatt and incorporated parts of a mediaeval priory. The old chapel became an 'eating room' and was joined to the main new building by a 'fine oval room of the Adam type', where Miss Montagu, although over seventy, still delighted to talk *belles lettres* up to the time of her death in 1800. She did much to raise the standard of 'polite' conversation in her day—a remarkable achievement in such an age—but her taste in architecture was less single-minded as externally Sandleford Priory is a collision between Classic and Gothic, from whose tortuous, cemented surfaces lovers of stone will fly to Wren and Inigo Jones.

It would need the wit of twenty blue-stockings to glamorize the growth of modern Newbury. The completion of the Kennet and Avon canal in 1810 was a profitable Christmas present to the town; barges were built here and, coal now being cheap, much agricultural machinery was made. Silk and paper replaced cloth as a manufacture although as late as 1811 John Coxeter, manufacturer of Greenham Mills, Newbury, made the famous Throckmorton coat and so won a wager of one thousand guineas for his patron. The race-meeting was founded about 1815 and at first seems to have been largely local. Simultaneously almshouses sprang up right and left to testify more to the wealth of the donors than to the poverty of the people. With the coming of the railway in 1847, Newbury's population soared and numbers of worthy citizens soon began bobbing backwards and forwards to London. Yet the tempo increased unbelievably in the twentieth century; tentacles of houses stretched out round the commons and fir-decked sands to the south; and the great God Equus grew in stature after 1905 when the race-course was modernized. The motor traffic has become enormous and converges still on that narrow bridge over the Kennet as surely as if it were a defile through a mountain range; and the terra-cotta statue of Queen Victoria, given to the town by Lord George Sanger, has been carried from Cheap Street to Greenham Park, so now there is no one left to exclaim 'We are not amused!'.

* * * * *

THE LOWER KENNET

The unfettered traveller leaving Newbury for the north instinctively makes for the Lambourn valley or for the delights of Snelsmore, an attractive birch-scattered common of bracken and heather which has escaped serious mutilation and far exceeds Bucklebury in naturalness. Yet no choice is open to the visitor moving eastward down the Kennet Valley as the Bath Road has for centuries brooked no rivals, and runs with devastating efficiency straight to Reading. Along it, the ribbon-development outside Thatcham demonstrates the vitality of local industries but hardly prepares one for the older or Georgian part of the village, which centres upon a large market-place and continues eastward past a few half-timbered cottages and an ancient little chapel. The newer houses and the market square actually lie athwart the line of the Roman road from Silchester to Speen and here excavations in the gravel have revealed a Roman village that appears to have come to a very sudden end. On the site of one house much broken crockery was unearthed, some pieces burnt black, others with their original red colouring just as if it had crashed during the burning; in a house opposite, a flint-walled well of Roman age contained the remains of a padlocked coffer and various plates and a flagon and bowl mainly of pewter, which seemed to have been hurriedly thrown into the well just before an enemy raid.

By Saxon and Norman times Thatcham had outgrown Newbury and during the reign of Henry I it was holding a market which was confirmed by a charter of Henry II and protected from the jealous interference of its neighbours. Yet Newbury expanded greatly with the kersey trade and Thatcham slumbered throughout the reigns of the Tudors and Stuarts. Today it has only two pre-Tudor buildings. The church of St. Mary the Virgin, which overlooks the

Kennet meadows, existed in Saxon times, but has no stonework earlier than a fine Norman south doorway and those parts of the chancel retaining the Early English additions made by Simon, Abbot of Reading. The eastern extremity of Thatcham is graced by a little chapel of ease founded about 1304 and endowed four centuries later as a blue-coat school by Frances, Lady Bolingbroke. The charming structure has richly-moulded niches and windows and a timber roof of the fifteenth century.

Thatcham must not be left without paying homage to Francis Baily, her most brilliant son. In 1796 Baily went as an explorer in the unsettled parts of North America and his journals were subsequently published. During the next thirty years he worked on the London Stock Exchange, making a large fortune and writing three detailed books on leases, assurance and life annuities. At the age of fifty-one, with two minor reputations made, he retired to study astronomy, having already founded the Royal Astronomical Society and been its president for four years. He then proceeded to win a reputation most men would envy. He remodelled the *Nautical Almanack*, determined the length of the second's pendulum, and fixed the standard of length, this last just six weeks before the existing standard yards were destroyed by fire. Baily became known as 'the man who weighed the earth' or calculated its density, but he also revised the catalogues of the stars, formed a new standard catalogue of 8,000 stars and observed the phenomenon during an eclipse today called Baily's Beads. On his death in 1844, his relatives preferred him to lie in Thatcham church rather than Westminster Abbey, as may be inferred from the tablet beneath the tower.

East of Thatcham the Bath Road keeps well above the valley-floor which for miles consists of coarse ill-drained pasture and marsh, broken only by a few vast factories, by gravel workings, and the civilizing influence of an occasional mill. At Woolhampton, the village has been savaged by the highway and the attention turns to Douai School and the incomplete abbey church being erected so skilfully by the Benedictines.

Yet Aldermaston, on the opposite side of the Kennet valley, has not been blasted by road-widening and remains quite the most unspoilt village in this part of Berkshire. It is a medley of brick and tiles alining a single street which slopes from the seventeenth-century Hinds Head up the hill to the entrance lodges of Aldermaston Court. A fire in 1843 destroyed the old Jacobean house, but a fine carved oak staircase, some ancient glass and several chimney stacks were incorporated in the present building while the original stables also survive. The park itself is well wooded and shows traces of Grim's Bank as well as more perfect mediaeval fishponds.

The village church adjoins the mellowed brick wall of the park which almost reflects its weather-beaten exterior so much encouraged by patching and mendings. The architectural features include a fine late Norman doorway with much cable-moulding and bird-adorned capitals, and triple Early English lancet which contains two circular panels of thirteenth-century stained glass; the first depicting the Annunciation with figures in white on a blue ground; and the second the Coronation with the ground again blue and the flesh of the figures tinted. The walls are decorated with paintings, some of which are old, notably the large fresco on the south wall of St. Christopher with the Infant Christ in his hand and a mermaid and fish below his feet. The church shelters many memorials to the Forsters, who owned the manor for three centuries, and here several times entertained Queen Elizabeth. Of them all, the finest is the alabaster tomb to Sir George Forster and Elizabeth his wife 'wiche Elizabeth dyed the VII day of december in the yere of our lord god MCCCCCXXVI . . . '.

Sir George's feet rest on a hind and his head on a helm while his lady has the comfort of a pillow supported by angels and the solace of a pet dog tugging at her cloak. The sides of the tomb are elaborately carved into niches holding their twelve sons and seven daughters.

Aldermaston has further attractions. The gardens seem to reflect the skill of John Stair who here in 1770 first propagated the William pear; the old mill to the north stands on a lovely site where the braided Kennet is joined by the Enborne; and Aldermaston wharf also offers endless hope of waterside activities. Yet most of the land and dwellings near the wharf are in Padworth parish and communes parochially with a church and manor perched high up the hill-slope a mile to the south. Padworth House is Georgian Gothic, with elegant interiors, while the little church is unaltered Norman except the modern porch and vestry and several windows which were inserted about the time when light was first needed for reading printed books. It stands defiantly on the lip of the hill like a Swiss church on an alpine terrace but sad to say is often kept locked. It has two fine moulded Norman doorways which agree favourably with the large chancel arch. The dignified plainness of the interior walls is quite unaffected by a few mural monuments and the traces of old paintings. The glass is modern but relegated to the porch is a delightful grisaille panel probably of fifteenth-century Flemish workmanship. To those who like little things, St. John the Baptist's at Padworth, in spite of modern fittings and external distempering, will become a firm friend.

Ufton Court which lies in the forested park barely a mile eastward would be befriended by all were it open to the public. A mansion with nineteen gables, the most picturesque of Elizabethan times in Berkshire, it was built about 1570 around parts of an older house. Its traceried windows and overhanging upper story and the succession of pointed gable and massive chimney have a beguiling air of irregularity which breathes charm and picturesqueness. The interior is equally rich having no less than three priests' hiding-holes, and, on the human side, boasting of literary connexions with Bolingbroke, Steel, Pope and others. The northern part of the mansion was enlarged in 1715 for a belle of London society, Arabella Fermor, who had just married Francis Perkins, whose ancestors had held the manor for over three hundred years. Arabella was the Belinda of Pope's *Rape of the Lock*. The poem arose from the action of young Lord Petre in cutting off and stealing, unbeknown to the lady, a lock of her hair. A quarrel followed and a friend suggested to Pope that it might be healed by a poem. In fact, Arabella was enraged against Pope, a mere stranger, for presuming to interfere as well as for the wording of certain phrases. Yet when in 1714, he altered and enlarged the poem and added a dedication to the lady herself she quite forgave him. *The Rape of the Lock* was at once hailed as a masterpiece. Three thousand copies were sold in four days and Pope became the richer by £15.

East of Ufton the valley of the lower Kennet is passing into nonentity—a broad flat pastoral vale which underwent a great revival in Victorian times. The smoke of Reading is already on the horizon before one is half aware of it but there is still a rural escape north to the Thames up an ancient valley past Englefield. It is always a pleasure to re-visit the manorial tidiness of Englefield if only to see the approach to the church and those exquisite monuments, for who could not admire the Jacobean composition to 'John Engefilde Esquire' or the Georgian sculpture showing Mrs. Mary Benyon stricken down suddenly by death? Thence, through shady avenues, the road leads down to Pangbourne and to the—but 'I *don't* talk about my river! You *know* I don't! But I think about it. I think about it—all the time!'

CHAPTER XII. Reading: The County Capital

Summer is a-coming in!
Loud sing cuckoo:
Groweth seed and bloweth mead,
And springeth the wood now.
Sing cuckoo, cuckoo.

Ewe bleateth after lamb,
Loweth after calf the cow;
Bullock starteth, buck verteth;
Merry sing, cuckoo,
Cuckoo, cuckoo.

MONASTIC READING

'EQUAL, if not superior to any spot in the county of Berks, for richness of soil, and pleasantness', so, says John Man, was the site of Reading Abbey. 'Placed on the ridge of a hill, running east and west, it commands a beautiful view of the adjoining country. On the north, the hill descends by a gentle declivity, to a range of meadows, covered with the choicest herbage, and watered by the majestic river Thames, beyond whose boundary the Oxfordshire hills, fringed with trees, and variegated with all the luxuriance of cultivated nature, formed a background to the prospect.' East and west the view is more extensive, comprehending the beautiful vale of Thames; on the south it is more restricted 'but more picturesque, the river Kennet gently gliding along its banks. On the opposite side of the river was park, and beyond this the ground rises gradually affording a delightful view of a finely wooded country bounded by the distant hills of Hampshire. Such was the spot which Henry chose for the erection of this once celebrated abbey. . . .'

Yet historically Henry I must be denied the wisdom of the selection for the value of the site had been noted four centuries earlier. Here a large gravel terrace stretches along the west bank of the Thames and stands conveniently about thirty feet above flood-level. This terrace is crossed by the Kennet which cuts it into two unequal parts—a long narrow strip to the north and a wide plateau to the south. The northern strip formed a palpable hillock fended on three sides by waterways which acted according to circumstances as defences or highways. So favourable a site was early occupied in Saxon times but then lay wide open to upstream attacks by Danish pirates who captured and fortified the place in 871 and on a later visit in 1006 probably destroyed a convent here.

When Domesday Survey was made, Reading had six mills yet was far below Wallingford in importance. Nor was it until 1121 that the town had greatness thrust upon it; for in that year Henry I founded the abbey, and gave it by charter soon afterwards 'woods, arable lands, pastures, meadows, waters, mills, fisheries, churches, chapels, churchyards, oblations, tithes and a mint'. The abbot was granted a fair on the feast of St. Lawrence and, at the special request of the Empress Maud, the hand of St. James, a relic which attracted hosts of pilgrims. The great buildings on the peninsular site gradually took shape but before their completion the royal founder had died and had, at his own request, been buried before the high altar.

Henry II also took much interest in the abbey and in 1163 assisted at the consecration of its church by Thomas à Beckett. He granted the abbot a fair on St. James's day and royal protection to all attending it. The large Benedictine abbey henceforth played a regular part in national affairs as became its proximity to Westminster. King John came here several times as did most of his kingly successors for the next four hundred years. Here in 1359 John of Gaunt married Blanche, heiress of Lancaster, an event celebrated in Chaucer's *Dream*. In its peaceful and healthy buildings parliament sat in 1440, 1452 and 1461–2, and the worthy abbot had only to cross the cloisters to take his rightful seat in the council. And so the story goes on until at the dissolution the abbey had outgrown and outlived almost all its English contemporaries, and had revenues amounting to £2,000 a year. Yet the end of the monastic life when it came was dramatically brutal. Hugh of Faringdon, the thirty-first abbot, fell foul of the commissioners and was flung into the Tower on a charge of high treason. In the November of 1539, after the semblance of a trial, he and two other Reading priests were hanged, drawn and quartered before their own gateway. Pensions were given to a few of the older monks but most of them were ruthlessly turned out to fend for themselves and to leave the place unencumbered for the use of Henry VIII, the new owner.

The former abbey now became the occasional residence of succeeding monarchs until the troubles of the Civil War rendered it uninhabitable by royalty. By order of parliament, in 1650 a survey was made of the premises, which included, among numerous large gardens, orchards and closes, an 'abbey-house with the appurtenances, called Reading abbey, consisting of two sellars, two butteries, a hall, a parlour, a dining-room, ten chambers, a garret with a large gallery, and other small rooms, with two court yards, and a large gatehouse, with several rooms adjoining, and a small gardine with an old small house, . . . and a stable with sellars . . ., and a small tenement, and a dove-house . . . which said abbey in all by measurement two acres, value per annum fifteen pounds.

'There is on the east side of the said mansion house a great old hall, with a very large sellar under the said hall, arched, with some other decayed rooms, . . . with the ruins of an old large chapel, a kitchen, and several other rooms, fit to be demolished, the materials valued at two hundred pounds. The ground on which the ruin stands is by estimation eight acres and a half, valued at eight pounds two shillings'.

The survey proceeds with several small tenements, a malt-house, 'a large barn, formerly a stable, in length 137 feet, in breadth 30 feet, bounded by the Hollow-brook south, . . . a granary standing over the said Hollow-brook, and a porter's lodge at the west gate entering into Forbury. . . .' Then followed a list of the various fisheries and meadows, including the Great and Little Plummery, and finally the walled-in Forbury 'in which the town doth yearly keep four faires' and which although covering seven acres was worth only 20*s*. annually because of the numerous public paths.

Within two centuries almost all the buildings described above had disappeared and the fine stonework had gone beyond recall. Yet today even if the substance has gone much of the shadow remains. The existing street-plan of central Reading reveals the original abbey-site of 30 acres of dry gravelly soil which stretched from the Kennet and Holy-brook on the south to the present outer Forbury roads on the east and north and to a line formed by High Street and the town hall on the west. Within these limits, the north-western quarter formed a walled outer court, whence an inner gateway led to a larger enclosed court containing the chief gardens and the main monastic buildings. This inner gatehouse survives although much restored about 1869. Dating basically from the second half of the thirteenth century, it consists of a central gateway flanked by narrow, two-storied wings, the whole being surmounted by the large room in which Abbot Hugh Faringdon was condemned. It is now used as the abbey museum.

Of the magnificent abbey within the inner court, mostly erected before 1200, scarcely a shaped stone survives *in situ*. The outlines of the great church, which measured 450 feet by 95 feet, cannot even be traced by the eye. Some of the foundations of the north transept remain but most of it has been covered by the Roman Catholic church of St. James. The south transept walls still stand to a fair height but, as elsewhere in the abbey ruins, only as a crude flint-rubble core, with just one faced stone left to recall its former glory.

Some of the shell of the Chapter house remains and the position of stone-benches round the inside of the walls is visible, while just to the south, a passage bears signs of former wall-arcading with a little herring-bone work still in its original position. The large dorter has vanished except for the bases of two walls whereas the smaller rere-dorter near the Kennet has managed to retain parts of all its four sides.

Three other notable fragments of the abbey buildings survive. The longer side-walls of the original mill over the Holybrook are incorporated into the present mill while two fine late twelfth-century arches still span the stream.

At the far western side of the abbey precincts stood the Hospitium of St. John Baptist and the church of St. Lawrence, both of which grace modern Reading. The existing dormitory of the Hospital of St. John was entirely rebuilt in 1486 when it was transformed into a school. It hides half-ashamedly behind the municipal headquarters and in spite of restorations shows much original work, not least in the square-headed windows.

The church of St. Lawrence arose presumably at the same time as the abbey and was intended for the good of the townsfolk. A round-headed door and window in the south wall may belong to the twelfth-century structure whereas the pointed east windows tell of a slightly later reconstruction of the chancel. Many additions and alterations were made in the next three centuries and resulted in a handsome, dignified church with splendid lengthwise vistas. Even the font pre-dates the dissolution of the abbey, as it was installed in 1522, the stonework costing 31*s.* 8*d.* and the lead a few shillings. Although so much a part of the monastic site,

St. Lawrence gives the impression of a civic church which has grown in stature with the town it served and whose sons it has been pleased to remember.

A far surer contact with monastic ideals seems to linger on in Greyfriars church at the corner of Caversham road. Here, at some distance and distinct from the abbey, the Grey Friars erected a chapel about 1300, which was turned at the dissolution partly into a town hall and partly into almshouses. It had long served as a bridewell and dissolved into a ruin open to rain and sun before it was re-roofed and enlarged about 1863. The ancient masonry includes a chancel arch, a traceried west window and two grand Decorated arcades, which in spite of restoration are quite the finest old stonework in the town.

Little need be said of the fate of the open spaces once enjoyed by the monks of Reading, for these, and especially the Plummeries outside the precincts, have been put to markedly non-ecclesiastical uses. Only the outer court or Forbury has escaped and with its mantle of perennial green remains an oasis in a sea of noise and turmoil. Between flower beds overtopped by a monumental lion and a modest band-stand, paths lead down through a tunnel to the ruins themselves, where a notice tells us that 'Sumer is i-cumen in' was written here. And so on this once-delightful spot, about seven hundred years ago, arose the first known English song to be set to musical notation.

* * * * *

MAYORAL READING

The citizens of Reading were firmly under the thumb of the abbot right from the foundation of the abbey. It is true that the burgesses early showed signs of civic rebellion and quarrelled with the abbot in 1253 but their merchant gild then became virtually under the control of the abbey. The townsfolk, however, continued to benefit from royal visits and frequently obtained from the King privileges much frowned upon by the local abbot. When in 1301 the chief officer of the gild assumed the name of mayor, the abbots steadfastly refused to recognize such a title. And when in 1405, Abbot Richard granted the burgesses the passage of boats on the Kennet adjoining the abbey 'from sun rysing and the sun going downe and not otherwise' he stipulated that no person on 'the said severall waters (was) to make any play, riott or noyse which might turn to the prejudice, damage or disease of the said Abbot and Convent'. A few years after the visit of Henry VI in 1453, the mayor was given the privilege of carrying a mace, whereupon the abbot complained and the right was rescinded. Eventually in 1487 the mayor was actually allowed mace-bearers but his power was in truth insignificant up to the dissolution of the abbey.

After 1538, royal visits to the royal abbey gave the mayor and burgesses opportunities to petition the King. During Henry VIII's visit in 1540 they petitioned him for a new charter of incorporation, which was duly granted two years later. In 1552, Edward VI came here and was welcomed in great style by the corporation all 'in their best apparelles' ready with the customary gift of two yoke of oxen. Queen Mary and Philip were received in a similar manner, while Elizabeth, who stayed several times at the abbey, granted the town a new charter in 1560, and as its revenues were decayed gave it rights, profits and properties enough to restore its finances. The corporation, however, now had to repair the many bridges leading into the town and for this purpose were allowed two hundred loads of freestone from the abbey ruins.

The pillage of the abbey buildings did much to enrich the town's churches as well as its bridges. St. Lawrence's, in which Elizabeth had her own pew, underwent some alterations, especially to the roof timbering and to the nave arcade.

As became the civic church it was soon to acquire the memorials of its mayors, notably Edward Butler, whose brass of 1584 says he was 'fyve times maior of this toune'. The church of St. Mary the Virgin or St. Mary Butts was practically rebuilt in 1551 when the parishioners bought the ceiling of the abbey church and twenty-one loads of other timber. The early Norman doorway and somewhat crude Early-English arcade in St. Mary's almost certainly came from the abbey ruins. Hence the unfettered citizens embellished their secular churches with materials patiently accumulated by the monks.

Already in Elizabethan times, Reading was growing wealthy and five main and several minor companies supervised its various trades. By far the chief was the Company of Clothiers and Cloth-Workers, which also embraced 'dyers, weavers, shearmen, shuttle-makers, and ash-burners'. The benefactions of clothiers soon began to enrich the town and strengthen the corporation, for the mayor and burghal merchants worked in harmony. Nor is it surprising that three of Reading's greatest sons belong to this epoch.

Sir Thomas White, who was born here in 1492 and probably was taught first at the local grammar school in St. John's Hospital, spent most of his early life in London and became lord mayor in 1553. At the end of his term of office he decided to found a college in the same way as a friend had just founded Trinity College at Oxford. On the first of May 1555 he obtained a royal licence to create a college for 'the learning of the sciences of holy divinity, philosophy and good arts', dedicated to the praise and honour of God, the Blessed Virgin Mary and St. John Baptist, the latter being the patron saint of the Merchant Taylor's Company of which Sir Thomas had been a master. Two years later, he gave Reading School two scholarships annually to his new foundation and so began the connexion between Reading and St. John's, Oxford.

This educational ladder was probably used by John Blagrave, a noted Elizabethan mathematician, who went to St. John's but apparently did not take a degree before retiring to Southcote Lodge, Reading, to study mathematics. His four published works dealt mainly with navigation and geometry as one of the titles—*Astrolabium Uranicum Generale: a necessary and pleasaunt solace and recreation for Navigators in their long journeying*—will testify. On his death in 1611 among other legacies to the town he left twenty nobles a year to be competed for by three maid-servants, one being selected by each of the three parishes in Reading. The maids had to be of good character and of five years' service under one master and had to appear in the town hall on Good Friday and cast lots for the money in the presence of the corporation. The same cheerful confounding of mathematics and maidens appears on Blagrave's memorial on the south wall of the nave of St. Lawrence. Here he is shown resplendent in ruff holding a sphere and a quadrant while about him in allegorical elegance are grouped five buxom females bearing labels most ladies would abhor—Icosahedron, Octahedron, Dodecahedron, Tetrahedron and Cubus, the names of the five regular solids of equal and equilateral triangles.

Neither Sir Thomas White nor John Blagrave achieved the fame of William Laud who was born on the seventh day of October 1573 in a house on the north side of Broad Street now marked by Laud Place. The son of a prosperous clothier he went to the borough school and so by scholarship to St. John's, Oxford. In 1611 he was made president of his old college and this office he kept till appointed Bishop of St. David's ten years later. About 1628 he became chancellor of Oxford University and in 1633 was appointed Archbishop of Canterbury. Then for eight years he wielded influence far beyond the sphere normal to an archbishop and at the end of that time was thrown by parliament into the

Tower. The severity he had meted out to others was now shown in full measure to himself and on the tenth of January, 1645, when seventy-two years old, he was beheaded on Tower Hill.

Laud has never caught the popular eye, although he frequently did the right thing—at the wrong time! Of 'unbounded ambition and inflexible severity', he was a relentless reformer who spent all his life doing 'good' to others and never realizing, as Berkshire men say, 'that folk do not like being done good to'. Possessing no sense of humour, he yet invoked an undying pun,. for Archie Armstrong, the court jester, having begged permission to say grace at Whitehall in Laud's presence exclaimed, 'Great praise be given to God, and little laud to the devil!' Yet Laud had likeable traits; he was a lover of learning, a great repairer of buildings, and a hater of disorder or lack of uniformity in anything. At Oxford he drew up statutes, most of which still stand, regulating procedure and practice ranging from the noble art of archery to the election of the most high. He always took an interest in Reading his birthplace and drew up plans, which never materialized, for its improvement. He greatly assisted the obtaining from Charles I of the town's charter of 1638, the same which contains a special clause forbidding the erection of cottages and the cutting up into tenements of large houses. Unfortunately the corporation never enforced this law and the problem of overcrowded tenement dwellings was not solved for nearly three centuries. In 1640, Archbishop Laud endowed the borough with £200 a year, mainly for the portioning of poor girls and the apprenticing of poor boys.

At this time other benefactions poured in to the town from woollen-drapers, hair-merchants, leather-sellers, broadweavers, brewers and 'gentlemen', but the clothiers excelled and especially the Kendricks. John Kendrick, clothier of London, the same who befriended Newbury, left the corporation well over £8,000 in 1624, while William Kendrick of Reading in 1634 bequeathed and endowed five tenements for almshouses. Under such an impetus Reading was flourishing exceedingly when calamity overtook it as surely as it had overtaken Abbot Hugh and Archbishop Laud.

The outbreak of the Civil War found Reading's allegiance nicely divided, most of the neighbouring gentry being for parliament and most of the corporation for the King. The town passed alternately from one to the other and each exercised every known 'species of oppression on the unfortunate inhabitants'. The King held the borough first, whereupon the parliamentarians under Essex marched from London and on April 17th, 1643, began a bombardment with cannon ranging in calibre up to two of the heaviest guns from the Tower. The town surrendered honourably on April 26th, but not until much damage had been done, especially to the abbey and to St. Giles' Church. The parliamentary troops pillaged the houses and the townsfolk suffered many exactions including a thirty weeks' tax for the fortification of Wallingford. In September, the parliamenty army quartered here for a few days after the first battle of Newbury and when they left the Royalists marched in and the householders had to pay, in money or labour, for the rebuilding of their own defences. In May 1644 the King abandoned Reading to the Roundheads, who forced the corporation to pay, among other things, for the re-erection of Caversham bridge. By the end of the Civil War, Reading's cloth trade was ruined, the corporation's property mortgaged and the citizens taxed almost out of existence. Not till the late eighteenth century did the town fully recover its former prosperity.

Yet the townsfolk kept up a brave face and in 1646 a man was appointed to kill the stray dogs, the citizens first being warned to keep their pigs in. When Cromwell came a few years later he was presented with sugar and wine at the Bear Inn; and in August 1663 Charles II was given in person fifty pieces of gold and his queen thirty. In 1668 a small skirmish occurred here when the troops of William of Orange routed an Irish regiment of James, with the assistance, it is said, of the people of Reading who fired at the Irishmen from their attics. Thereafter peace reigned and the various trades and agricultural markets needed no help from gilds or corporation, and as mercantile Reading took command the mayor and corporation for a time slumbered and slipped temporarily into the background.

The seeker of visible signs of mayoral Reading will be disappointed except, of course, with the worthy members in office today. The memorials in St. Lawrence recall a few mayors, while in St. Mary Butts is a coloured stone monument to William Kendrick. The old houses surviving can almost be counted on the fingers of one hand. On the south side of Hosier Street, now forming tenements, are the remains of Lady Vachell's house, a late Elizabethan structure with four tile-hung gables. An early seventeenth-century survival may be seen in the three-storied, half-timbered offices of the Phoenix Assurance Company in the market place. The gabled 'Lynford' in Castle Street, with its characteristic overhanging stories, as well as the building next door and probably the Sun Inn opposite are all of this date. There may be a few others but nothing grand or exciting, for the merchants of eighteenth-century Reading loved brick and took an inordinate pride in re-facing old buildings. And those who know Reading will not need to be told that its people never do things by halves. The loss of barge-boarded gables and picturesque half-timbering is sad

> 'But things like that, you know, must be
> At every famous victory!'

* * * * *

MERCANTILE READING

What John Taylor said of cities in general that 'there is not any, which hath a navigable river at it, that is poore' applies particularly to Reading for it was the improvement of waterways which did so much to revive this Berkshire town. By 1725 the Thames was navigable far above Oxford and the Kennet at least to Newbury; Tyneside coal came up by barge to Reading and vast quantities of malt and corn went downstream. At the same time, the Bath Road, coming here for the bridges over the Kennet, gave the added advantage of long-distance land-traffic.

Fine brick houses began to arise, notably that with moulded cornices facing the watercourse in Mill Lane, and the dignified Holybrook House in Castle Street. But the tempo quickened remarkably towards the end of the century when a canal was completed to Newbury, and Reading also had access by water to the Severn and the Midlands. This was a time of much re-facing and re-building in brick as may be seen so well in Church Street and Castle Street and in the varied architectural styles of the spacious London Street. The decade preceding 1790 witnessed the erection of the 'small town hall' on part of the site of the Hospital of St. John and the construction of the elegant High Bridge over the Kennet in Duke Street. The sail-cloth trade with the navy and East India Company was now famous and the great bleaching grounds off Castle Street caught the west winds before they imbibed the delightful aroma of Cock's sauce-factory and the brewery of Simond's. Within a few years the population exceeded 9,000 and so great was the wealth that when certain parishioners objected to the newly-appointed vicar of St. Giles they founded a new church, St. Mary in Castle Street.

But here we can hardly do better than quote the learned Dr. Mavor who with a partiality passing almost into untruth wrote of Reading in 1808: 'Delightfully situated on a gradual ascent from the Thames, and washed by the Kennet, which flows nearly through its centre in several streams, and falls into the prince of British rivers, a furlong below the town. The houses are chiefly of brick, well-built and commodious; and the streets are spacious and handsomely paved. An air of gentility is thrown over the place; and there is an elegant sociability in the manners of the inhabitants which is irresistibly attractive to strangers. Hence villas are constantly rising in its vicinity; nor is this to be wondered at, as there is not a country town in the kingdom that unites so many charms and advantages to persons of independent fortune and cultivated minds.' Mavor goes on to enumerate the manufactures of malt, beer, flour, pins, silk, sacking and sail-cloth and the markets, one of which on Saturdays sold 100 loads of wheat.

Yet further opportunities lay ahead, for in 1810 the final opening of the Kennet and Avon canal allowed Bath free-stone and Somerset coal to pour into the town. Reading soon reflected the cheapness of a superb building stone and the smooth façade of Queen's Crescent and many commodious dwellings in various fanciful styles in Kings Road, Elden Square, Castle Hill and elsewhere are faced or cornered with limestone. The most striking building, however, is the central block of the Royal Berkshire Hospital, with its stately portico built in 1839 by Henry Briant and flanked in 1862 by wings and colonnades. The vast castellated gaol built in red brick in 1833 on the riverine side of the abbey site attracts for other reasons as it has shattered the skyline ever since.

In early Victorian times Reading still clung to the tips of the twin gravel terraces nearest the Kennet where the streets, as today, are quite flat except where they decline to the river itself. Miss Mitford, whose parents once lived in a verandahed Georgian house in London Road, minutely describes the town and its residents about 1835 under the name of Belford Regis. The approach from the south to the top of the hill leading down to the old home of the Mitfords was truly rural but from it 'we see at once the history of the place, that it is an antique borough town, which has recently been extended to nearly double its former size; so that it unites in no common degree the old romantic, irregular structures in which our ancestors delighted, with the handsome and uniform buildings which are the fashion now-a-days. I suppose that people are right in their taste, and that the modern houses are pleasantest to live in, but, beyond all question, those antique streets are the prettiest to look at. The occasional blending too is good. Witness the striking piece of street scenery which was once accidentally forced upon my attention as I took shelter from a shower of rain in a shop about ten doors up the right-hand side of Friar Street—the old vicarage house embowered in greens, the lofty town-hall and the handsome modern house of my friend Mr. Beauchamp, the fine church tower [of St. Lawrence], the picturesque piazza underneath, the jutting corner of Friar Street, the old irregular shops in the market place, and the trees of the Forbury just peeping between, with all their varieties of light and shadow. I went to the door to see if the shower was over, was caught by its beauty, and stood looking at it in the sunshine long after the rain had ceased.'

Within a single generation of Miss Mitford's description Reading had again more than doubled itself and so the growth went on until the population of 9,000 in 1800 had increased eightfold within the century. Two famous firms greatly assisted this expansion: Sutton's, founded in 1806 by Martin Hope Sutton an enthusiastic botanist, did much to relieve the Irish famine of 1847 by supplying to distressed areas, seeds of quick-growing vegetables. Thereafter the firm expanded rapidly and today employs at Reading alone six hundred persons on the intensive cultivation of nearly 100 acres. They give to the western end of the town a patchwork of colours of exhilarating brilliance and stretches of green sward as smooth and faultless as billiard cloths.

The firm of Huntley & Palmers was founded by Joseph Huntley in 1826 for the making of 'captain's biscuits'. In 1841, George Palmer joined the business and later invented a machine for cutting and stamping, which together with new varieties of biscuits, caused a great rise in output and an increase in workers from about 200 in 1850 to 3,000 in 1880. Today, in spite of restrictions, over 3,000 people are engaged and Reading is world famous for biscuits as well as for seeds. For a county notably lacking in gastronomic tit-bits other than sauce and beer, Huntley & Palmers makes full amends, for the ambrosial smell of biscuits straight from the baking racks is quite inescapable, and, like the first sight of the 'fancy department', haunts one for life whenever coffee is served or lunch is belated.

Other firms and the railway also materially fostered the growth of Victorian Reading, and the city now overspread its original site, going down in places towards the Thames and, more commonly, in other directions up the slope to a higher terrace. New assize courts were built, most of the churches were severely restored and three new churches arose, not to mention the new Town Hall, largely the work of Alfred Waterhouse. The museum had by now acquired a wealth of treasures, for to objects found in the neighbourhood of Reading, were added most of those unearthed in the great Roman city of Silchester. The whole is a feast of delight which can hardly be too often visited, while for those interested in needlework, the exact copy of the Bayeux Tapestry in the Art Gallery will come as a pleasant surprise.

There may have dwelt in Victorian and Edwardian Reading many a genius yet unsung but its major known contact with the literary world came ironically enough through its gaol. Here from May 1895 to May 1897 Oscar Wilde struggled day by day with 'hard labour' and his *De Profundis* which was not published in full until 1949. It is concerned mainly with castigating Lord Alfred Douglas, against whose father Wilde had brought a libel charge which ended in his own imprisonment, barely three months after the successful appearance of *The Importance of Being Earnest*. Nor did Wilde forget his stay in the town for his very last work was *The Ballad of Reading Gaol*, the story of the last six weeks of 'C. T. W., sometime trooper of the Royal Horse Guards' who was hanged at the prison for murder in July 1896. On the long night before the execution the 'crooked shapes of Terror' haunted the other prisoners, Wilde among them.

'They glided past, they glided fast,
  Like travellers through a mist:
They mocked the moon in a rigadoon
  Of delicate turn and twist,
And with formal pace and loathsome grace
  The phantoms kept their tryst.

'With mop and mow, we saw them go,
  Slim shadows hand in hand:
About, about, in ghostly rout
  They trod a saraband:
And the damned grotesques made arabesques,
  Like the wind upon the sand!

'With the pirouettes of marionettes,
  They tripped on pointed tread:
But with flutes of Fear they filled the ear,
  As their grisly masque they led,
And loud they sang, and long they sang,
  For they sang to wake the dead.'

After the stroke of eight, the fearless trooper was hanged 'as a beast is hanged', while the other convicts suffered untold mental agonies. The ballad ends thus:

'In Reading gaol by Reading town
  There is a pit of shame,
And in it lies a wretched man
  Eaten by teeth of flame,
In a burning winding-sheet he lies,
  And his grave has got no name.

'And there, till Christ call forth the dead,
  In silence let him lie:
No need to waste the foolish tear,
  Or heave the windy sigh:
The man had killed the thing he loved,
  And so he had to die.

'And all men kill the thing they love,
  By all let this be heard,
Some do it with a bitter look,
  Some with a flattering word,
The coward does it with a kiss,
  The brave man with a sword!'

C.3.3

* * * * *

MAGISTRAL READING

The early education of Reading folk is cloaked in controversy and mystery. The oft-repeated story of the mass migration of a few thousand students and masters from Oxford to Reading in 1213 'to the great emolument, and advantage of the town' may be kindly dismissed as arrant nonsense. The foundation of the local grammar school may be of great age and may even precede the abbey but a doubt is there and it is pleasant to step to the certainty of the foundation or re-foundation of Reading school at the Hospital of St. John in 1486. Here the school flourished till about 1870 when it moved to palatial premises on the hill near Whiteknights Park.

Twelve years later an important venture in adult education began in Valpy Street, where classes in art and science were started within part of the municipal buildings. In 1892 the newly-formed Reading Extension College, under the aegis of Oxford University, took over these premises and soon also acquired the vicarage of St. Lawrence. To quote from W. M. Childs' book, *Making a University*: 'The Vicarage had an old-fashioned front looking forth upon the time-worn stones and gracious trees of the churchyard. . . . The building devoted to science and administration was of another order. It had once formed part of the great Abbey of Reading, and was a massive structure in flint, stone, and brick, most of it fifteenth-century work, resting, it seemed, on Norman foundations. The fragment in our occupation had originally been part of the vanished Hospital of St. John, and had served as a dormitory for wayfarers.'

In 1895 the Aylesbury Institute of the British Dairy Farmers' Association, also newly established at Reading, began working in close co-operation with the college and soon afterwards, as a separate venture, a hostel arose for young women who wished to study 'the lighter branches of agriculture'. So commenced the interest in dairying and horticulture which has borne such good fruit ever since. A great step forward was made in 1904 when it was decided to leave Valpy Street, which was inconveniently confined, as it were, by the overshadowing wings of assize court, police station and county gaol. A level, spacious site was acquired on the London Road, including the 'Acacias', an early-nineteenth-century stone villa enlarged and altered by George

Palmer, and a stately row of five Georgian brick houses. Both survive; the 'Acacias' unaltered as a gracious reminder of the generosity of the Palmers, and the Georgian terrace as a companion to a larger terrace of similar age since purchased on the other side of the road. Upon the flat lawns, rich in trees and flowering shrubs, a new college took shape after the fashion described so well by its prime creator. 'Beautiful and stately architecture was beyond our reach; but beauty itself was not, for it was all about us. With the reconciling touch of time our prosaic buildings would be subdued by this beauty, and absorbed into it. We took nature, even the English climate, as an ally. These broad spaces and wind-swept arcades might not always be sunlit, but often they would be; and they would be bracingly different from closed corridors and lobbies. Lawns and flowers would end the vistas of the cloisters; roses would climb about their pillars. Gardens would be seen through laboratory windows, birds would go about their business unafraid, and there would be the companionship of many trees.'

The venture succeeded in spite of financial worries and was greatly strengthened in 1905 when George William Palmer endowed it—then University College, Reading—with £50,000, and in the following year Lady Wantage provided a hall for men students. This hall was named after its founder, who personally opened it in October 1908; a well-built Tudor style structure, its amenities are simple and dignified with an economy of space and quite remarkable convenience.

In 1911 the University College was endowed with £50,000 from Lady Wantage and £150,000 from the Palmer family, with a view to extending later into full University status. Within a few years five halls of residence were open, three of them for women, and all blessed with tree-clad sites near Redlands Road, while a mile or so beyond stretched the large farm of the National Institute for Research in Dairying and an extensive horticultural estate. Nor were the lecturing needs neglected, for in 1923 a new library was opened; facing across green lawns, it can show brickwork of a quality never excelled in Berkshire.

Finally, in January 1925, the University was incorporated by royal charter, with W. M. Childs its first vice-chancellor. It was an achievement of which Reading might well be proud, for the foundation of a University proper in a city of less than 100,000 inhabitants has no parallel in modern Britain. Today Whiteknights Park has been bought for future extensions and a dozen hostels overbrim with wisdom. The pleasant balance of sexes continues and the three scallop shells of gold on an azure ground, although unfrocked when the abbey fell, is carried once more as a residential crest. The town, now robed and gowned, takes on an air of learning but lest any should think the process has reached perfection let them read the shop-sign of a Berkshire son who was born long before the University was thought of.

'ISAAC FACTOTEM

Barber, Periwig Maker, Surgeon, Parish Clerk. Schoolmaster, Blacksmith and man midwife.
Shaves for a penne, cuts hare for too pense, and oyld and powdird into the bargin. Young Ladys genteely edicated. Lamps lited by the year or quarter. Young Gentlemen also taught the Grammar Language in the neetest maner and grate keer takin of their morels and spelin. Likewise makes and mends all sorts of Butes and shoes. Teches the Hoboy and Jewsharp. Cuts corns, bledes and blisters on the lowest Terms. Cowtillions and other dances taut at home and abrode. Also deals holesale and retale perfumery in all its branchis. Sells all sorts of stationary wair, together with blackin balls, red herrins, gingerbred, coles, scrubbin brushes, treycle, mouce traps and other sweet metes. Likewise Godfathers cordiel, red rutes, Tatoes, Sassages, and all other

garden stuff. N.B. I teches joggraphy and those outlandish kind of things. A Bawl on Wensdays and Frydays. All performed, God willin. By me.

Isac Factotum.'

Here indeed was a liberal education!

CHAPTER XIII: The Loddon Country

The Kennet swift, for silver eels renown'd
The Loddon slow, with verdant alders crown'd.

ALEXANDER POPE

THE Loddon rises near Basingstoke and entering Berkshire at Stratfield Saye Park flows determinedly north-eastward to the Thames at Shiplake. Its course lies mainly over the so-called London Clay and is a leisurely traverse of flat meadows between banks fringed with willow, poplar and many-trunked alders. The gentle current and succession of secretive bowers and resting-places, the reflexions of trees and absence of buildings, form an ideal boating river liked by all and not least by Miss Mitford.

'Is it not a beautiful river? Rising level with its banks, so clear and smooth and peaceful, giving back the verdant landscape and the clear blue sky, and bearing on its pellucid stream the snowy water-lily, the purest of flowers, like the lady in *Comus*. That queenly flower becomes the water and so do the stately swans who are sailing so majestically down the stream, like those who—

'"On St. Mary's lake
Float double, swan and shadow."'

The 'snowy water-lily' is the lovely white water-lily (*Nymphaea alba*) which is less common than its yellow-headed companion. The Loddon has other botanic delights: the pondweeds include one species (*Potamogeton Drucei*) quite peculiar to this river, while the lower riverine fields bear the waterdropwort, the graceful drooping snakeshead fritillary, and, above all, the Loddon lily or summer snowflake (*Leucojum Aestivum*) which beautifies the banks and osiers of the sluggish stream in a massed profusion unknown elsewhere in England.

Away from the alluvial fringe of the watercourses the wide flat clay vale carries rivulets along every hedge and along each road for mile after mile oak succeeds oak, nicely spaced as if part and parcel of adjacent parkland. Only at the outermost fringe of the Loddon drainage does the ground rise to hills capped with Bagshot sands and here firs take over and a ragged growth of gorse with a treacherous entanglement of bramble and bracken. But amid the oak and the elm of the Loddon plain the conifer has an alien look just as the lovely weeping willow stands aloof amid the pollarded trees of the fast-flowing Kennet. At intervals villages appear along the tree-lined byways, their houses ranging from mellowed red-brick to twentieth-century plaster and lying in dispersed fashion or occasionally in brief rows. Here and there a more palatial structure stands on a slight hillock or hides behind tall hedgerows, and marks the home of a county magnate or of a farmer or—as is so common today—the abode of the blind, or the sick, or the fatherless. The whole is a quiet, clean countryside, which charms by the pleasant balance between man and nature, for the house-plots are cut from the woodland, and the woodland is neither compact nor continuous.

Stratfield Mortimer is typical enough of these Loddon villages which have suddenly taken on a new life and impetus in the last twenty years. It lies three miles west of the river where oak and elm begin to give way to vast stretches of pine and fir. Villas and shops stretch at wide intervals to Mortimer common but only Stratfield Mortimer itself has accumulated a fair aspect of late-Georgian and early-Victorian dwellings, softened by long-established gardens and shrubberies. The church was wholly rebuilt in stone in the 1860's yet retains the old style and a spire of goodly proportions. During the rebuilding a Saxon tomb-cover was found beneath the tower and has now been set upright in the south wall of the chancel so that the marginal inscription may be read. It runs:

> VIII. KL' OCTB. FUIT POSITUS AEGELPARDUS FILUS KYPPINGUS IN ISTO LOCO. BEATUS SIT OMO QUI ORAT PRO ANIMA EIUS.—TOKI ME SCRIPSIT.

Or in simple English, 'On the 8th before the Kalends of October (September 24th) Aegelward son of Kypping was laid in this place. Blessed be the man who prays for his soul. Toki wrote this.' This tomb, by far the oldest in Berkshire, is thought to be that of Aedelward, a Hampshire ealdorman mentioned in the Saxon Chronicle in the year 994. A Kypping or Cheping held the manor of Stratfield in the reign of Edward the Confessor while Toki is known to have been a prominent courtier of King Canute. Nearby are two fifteenth-century brasses, one of which shows Richard Trevet in plate armour, but of more interest is the old glass in a window behind the organ. Among the bewildering mosaic of varying age and quality is a portrait, probably of the early-seventeenth century, of William of Wykeham with his motto 'Manners maketh man'. William had much to do with south Berkshire as in 1356 he became clerk of the royal works at Henley and Easthampstead and shortly after, surveyor of the works at Windsor. Yet his only connexion with this remote corner of the county was that at one time he was a tenant of the Earl of Mortimer, and the Stratfield Mortimer people have not been slow in catching at the skirts of greatness. In fact, William of Wykeham flung his munificence outside Berkshire creating to the south the school at Winchester and to the north New College at Oxford.

No matter what route is taken eastward from Stratfield Mortimer it soon enters Miss Mitford's country. Today Reading, or 'Belford Regis', has stretched its tentacles southward until it almost rubs shoulders with Three Mile Cross, the scene of *Our Village*. A pleasant cluster of dwellings remains on a by-road and among the huddle of houses is a shop or two, a village hall and a library with an adjoining small, creeper-clad cottage where Miss Mitford lived. It was 'a series of closets, the largest of which may be about eight feet square', yet to her it soon blossomed into 'a miniature house with many additions, little odds and ends of places, pantries and what not; all angles, and of a charming in-and-outness; a little bricked court before one half, and a little flower-yard before the other; the walls old and weather-stained, covered with hollyhocks, roses, honeysuckle, and a great apricot tree.' Her well-beloved garden with 'its pinks, and stocks, and carnations, and its arbour of privet, not unlike a sentry box' has, however, been partly built upon.

Miss Mitford came to the humble cottage at Three Mile Cross largely because of the reckless extravagance of her father whom she never ceased to adore. Mr. Mitford was a physician who married a well-endowed wife and soon ran through her fortune. He then enjoyed a most remarkable windfall. His little daughter, then ten years old, drew a ticket in a lottery and insisted on taking the number 2,224 as it added up to her age. This particular number had already been divided into shares but Dr. Mitford, by paying a little extra, managed to secure the ticket his daughter wanted, and so won a prize of £20,000. Soon after this the Mitfords left London Road, Reading, and bought an estate nearby at Grazely where what with fanciful re-building and his former extravagances the father by 1820 had reduced the family to a penniless condition. They then moved to Three Mile Cross to the cottage between a public house and the village shop, whither Mrs. Barratt Browning and Mrs. Trollope and so many others found their way. Here Miss Mitford kept her parents mainly by writing plays and sketches of country life. Here, too, both her parents died, and were buried in Shinfield church, Mrs. Mitford in 1829 and Dr. Mitford in 1842, when he left debts which were paid off by the help of admirers, Queen Victoria among them.

Of Mary Russell Mitford's numerous writings the sketches contained in *Our Village* stand supreme. She loved every inch of the locality and delighted not only in the changing scenes and seasons but also in her homely neighbours who were to her individuals beyond price, personalities beyond praise, indeed the crown of creation. She has had many imitators but none has excelled her in intimacy of house and home. 'No prettier scenery could be found anywhere than the shady, yet sunny Berkshire, where the scenery, without rising into grandeur or breaking into wildness, is so peaceful, so cheerful, so varied and yet so thoroughly English.' In such a landscape stood 'my beloved village . . . the long straggling street, gay, bright, full of implements of dirt and noise, busy merry stirring little world . . . the winding up-hill road with its borders of turf and its primrosy hedgerows . . . the breezy common and its fragrant gorse'. In 'the prettiest cottage on our village green' used to live John Wilson, a handy fellow who 'could do any sort of work; was thatcher, carpenter, bricklayer, painter, gardener, gamekeeper, everything by turns, and nothing long'. No job came amiss to him. He killed pigs, mended shoes, cleaned clocks, doctored cows, dogs and horses, and even went as far as bleeding and drawing teeth in his experiments on the human subject. 'In addition to these multifarious talents, he was ready, obliging, and unfearing; jovial withal, and fond of good fellowship; and endowed with a promptness of resource which made him the general advisor of the stupid, the puzzled, and the timid. He was universally admitted to be the cleverest man in the parish; and his death made quite a gap in our village commonwealth'. There was too that notable cricketer Farmer Thackum of Beech Hill, who upset the local team by his 'remarkable manner of bowling, which is circular, so to say, that is, after taking aim he makes a sort of *chassé* on one side before he delivers his ball, which pantomimic motion had a great effect on the nerves of our eleven, unused to such quadrilling'.

By the time Miss Mitford left Three Mile Cross in 1851 almost every house had become famous and, on leaving, she assured her readers that it was still 'the same long straggling street of pretty cottages, divided by pretty gardens, wholly unchanged in size or appearance, unincreased and undiminished by a single brick. To be sure, yesterday evening a slight misfortune happened to our goodly tenement, occasioned by the unlucky diligence mentioned in my first notice, which, under the conduct of a sleepy coachman and a restive horse, contrived to knock down and demolish the wall of our court, and fairly to drive through the front garden, thereby destroying sundry curious stocks, carnations and geraniums. It is a mercy that the unruly steed was content with battering the wall; for the messuage itself would come about our ears at the touch of a finger, and really there is one little end parlour, an afterthought of the original builder, which stands so temptingly in the way that I wonder the sagacious quadruped missed it.'

She moved only to Swallowfield, where her friends the Russells lived. To use her own words: 'I walked from one cottage to the other on an autumn evening when the autumn birds . . . were circling over my head, and I repeated to myself the pathetic lines of Hayley, as he saw those same birds gathering under his roof during his last illness:

' "Ye gentle birds that perch aloof
And smooth your pinions on my roof
Prepare for your departure hence
Ere winter's angry threats commence;
Like you, my soul would smooth her plume
For longer flights beyond the tomb." '

Here Charles Kingsley found her 'packed round with

books up to the ceiling, on to the floor' and came away impressed with her beautiful speech, her glowing eyes and her 'great globular brow'.

Four years later, on 18 January 1855, she was buried beneath a plain granite cross erected by a few of her oldest friends. She lies at the side of the churchyard nearest the park, overlooked by a great decrepit elm and at one end of an avenue of gigantic trees leading to Swallowfield Court. Near her are tombs of the Russells with memories of Thackeray and Dickens and all about are country sounds, the noise of trees, cawing of rooks and the tumbling of the Blackwater into the placid Loddon.

The little railed churchyard stands on the southern extremity of Swallowfield Park overlooking the Blackwater, and surrounds with mathematical nicety a small flint church built by John le Despenser in 1256 on the site of an earlier chapel, of which he incorporated the Norman north and south doorways and most of the nave. He received a licence from the Pope for this purpose because of constant flood and danger from robbers on the journey to Shinfield. The building was much restored in the nineteenth century and the Russell chapel was added. Its interesting features include two old brasses, a strongly-bound chest with a domed lid, and two large seventeenth-century mural monuments in marble to the Backhouse family, both in a goodly classic design. The church would be a delight if all the windows allowed the sunlight and shapes of trees to brighten its interior. It was, moreover, the cause of at least one notable letter, for Sir Charles Russell when restoring it in 1870 wrote to the Duke of Wellington for a donation, and received the reply—'Dear Sir Charles . . . I too am restoring a church, and if we both agree to give the same amount no money need pass between us. Yours Wellington.'

Swallowfield Court, the home of the Russells, is a two-storied classic structure, built about 1820 round a quadrangle, parts of which had existed since 1689. A finely-carved stone gateway of the older house now leads into the gardens, which have always been fine and were said by John Evelyn in 1685 to abound 'in the delicious and rarest fruit . . . There is one orchard of 1000 golden and other cider pippins; walks and groves of elms, limes, oaks and other trees. The garden is so beset with all manner of sweete shrubbs that it perfumes the aire.' Evelyn probably supervised the planting of the yew hedges, the cedars and the mulberries.

Swallowfield, like all Berkshire manors, was skittish and often cast its owners. From the Despensers it passed through a host of noble families to the queens of England and so through the Backhouses, a respectable family grown rich in trade, to the Clarendons by marriage. In 1677, Lady Clarendon was chosen as governess for Princess Anne whose favourite companion at that time was Sarah Churchill with whom she gambled at cards even on Sundays to her ladyship's disgust. The Clarendon's greatly enlarged and improved Swallowfield Court but eventually in 1719 it was sold to Governor Thomas Pitt who had made a large fortune in trade in the East, and who after 1702, when he bought the Regent diamond, was always known as 'Diamond Pitt'. The rough stone cost £24,000 and took two years to cut, the clearage and dust alone being valued at over £7,000. Pitt sold the diamond in 1717 to the French Crown for £130,000, although he never received all the purchase money. As large as a plum and flawless, it adorned the crown worn by Louis XV at his Coronation, was worn by Napoleon in the handle of his coronation sword and is now in a special case in the Louvre. Swallowfield had connexions with less friendly dealings with France for 'Diamond' Pitt's grandson was the Earl of Chatham and his great-grandson the famous Pitt.

After various changes, Swallowfield passed in 1820 into the Russell family, who entertained here among others Wilkie

Collins whose story *The Moonstone* probably arose from tales of 'Diamond' Pitt. The Russells built the present house and did much for the village. Sir George Russell was an intimate friend of Kingsley, Thackeray and Dickens and knew well Longfellow and most other contemporary writers. He especially liked Dickens whom he first met in 1853—as a charming companion he never knew his equal—and on Dickens' death his case of pistols went to Sir George Russell and his revolver to Sir Charles as well as his dog 'Bumble' which lived 'for many years, prized and petted by Swallowfield and its owners'.

From the vicinity of Swallowfield Park a rural, tree-lined by-way leads straight to Arborfield Cross and Hurst. Arborfield itself lies to the west of the road a few furlongs nearer the Loddon. The Hall, near the banks of the river, was originally Jacobean but of this structure only the stables and some outbuildings remain. The ruins were described by Miss Mitford:

'The splendid chambers, with their carving and gilding, are exposed to the wind and rain—sad memorials of past grandeur. The grounds have been left in merciful neglect; the park, indeed, is broken up, the lawn is mown twice a year like a common hay-field, the grotto mouldering into ruin, and the fish-ponds choked with rushes and aquatic plants; but the shrubs and the flowering trees are undestroyed, and have grown into a magnificence of size and wildness of beauty such as we may imagine them to attain in their native forests. Nothing can exceed their luxuriance, especially in the spring, when the lilac, the laburnum, and double-cherry put forth their glorious blossoms. There is a sweet sadness in the sight of such floweriness amidst such desolation; it seems the triumph of nature over the destructive power of men. What a fragrance is in the air from the balmy fir-trees and the blossomed limes! What an intensity of odour! And what a murmur of bees in the lime-trees! What a coil those little winged people make over our heads! And what a pleasant sound it is.'

In Victorian times the house was rebuilt but has once more fallen into decay, and close beside is the ruined choir of the church of St. Bartholomew, which was stripped of its roof in 1863 when a new church was built nearer the village. Some parts of the old church were incorporated in a mortuary chapel which contains a fine marble tomb and several other monuments. On the floor of the chancel is an epitaph to the wife of a former vicar that might well be applied to the whole edifice:

> 'A sigh the absent claims, the dead a tear;
> Forgive the wish that would have kept you here.'

The five miles from Arborfield to Hurst crosses typical Loddon country, except at Bearwood where a deposit of peat encourages rhododendrons which give a brilliant fringe to a large, shallow lake. The farmsteads are tucked away behind treegrowth and the district seems to have been divided into sizeable estates, each with its considerable dwelling. Many of these larger buildings were founded in Tudor times but almost all were rebuilt in the eighteenth or nineteenth centuries. Hurst House, just east of the church, incorporates fragments of a Tudor structure, including fine carved panelling and massive moulded doorways; Haines Hill has a long gallery of late-Elizabethan or early-Jacobean age; while parts of Hurst Lodge and Hinton House may also date back to this time. But Hurst, like all Loddon villages, is so scattered that the visitor despairs of ever finding it all until the nucleation near the church precludes further search. Here on a slight hillock are grouped Hurst House, the church, the almshouses and the Castle Inn. The latter was formerly the Church House and has a sixteenth-century origin, being presumably intended for social functions with an ecclesiastic bias or, as the villagers say, for 'holy fun'. It keeps its very fine bowling green in constant use. Nearby are the mellowed-brick almshouses founded in 1644 by William Barker of the county of Wilts, to which shire this patch of land was then attached. On the other side of the road rises the early-seventeenth-century brick-tower of the church of St. Nicholas. The oldest parts of the church are the north aisle arcade and carved grotesque corbels, of the late twelfth century, and three deeply recessed lancets which like the north door are Early English. Restorations have not removed the great interest of the furnishings of this pleasant building. Near the painted Jacobean pulpit is a curious hour-glass—a wonder of flowing lines and continuity—while the pillar beside it bears a scroll:

'As this glasse runneth,
So man's life passeth.'

The delicate painted screen adorned with the royal arms of the Stuarts above and with Tudor symbols beneath, gains in effect by being extended across the north aisle. The monuments are many and handsome. The most imposing, that to Lady Margaret Savile (*ob.* 1631), fits with uncommon cunning into its wall-space. It shows her kneeling at a desk facing her husband, with other figures within the recess, which is framed in looped curtains held back by ladies and cherubim. Nearby is an altar tomb, with brasses set in the stone canopy, to Richard Ward, cofferer to the last four Tudor monarchs, and to Colubra his wife and their numerous sons and daughters. Farther west is a brass to their eldest daughter Alse, who as if tired of her mother's rigid back, has taken to a four-poster bed. A second small brass recalls Richard Kippax, an examiner in the Star Chamber, who died in 1625. On the opposite wall is an ambitious marble monument to Sir Richard Harrison and his wife but it is less happy than that on the wall of the chancel to Henry Barker (*ob.* 1651), whose reclining effigy has at its feet a skeleton with an

The Leaning Market Cross House, Windsor

Hurley's "Ye Olde Bell" Inn, 15th-century

hour glass and at its head the bonniest babe in all monumental Berkshire.

The country near Hurst is dominated economically either by Reading or Wokingham. The latter today has an ever-widening fringe of new houses which forms a foil to the many old half-timbered dwellings with overhanging stories in the streets near the church. Rose Street in particular has some pleasant half-timber and brick, but the original Rose Inn, where Gay, Pope and Swift beguiled a very wet day by composing verses to 'sweet Molly Mog' the innkeeper's lovely daughter, no longer remains. The market-place is softened somewhat by the mulberry trees planted in the seventeenth century to assist the local silk industry, but the Town Hall cannot be hid. An eccentric fabrication of red and black brick and cast iron, it defies pure classification and is perhaps best regarded as intensely individual. The old church has been much restored but the interior shows two lofty and dignified Perpendicular arcades and fine roof-timbering on corbel heads. The font also is Perpendicular, having cabled moulding round its edge with a pattern of Tudor roses and foliated crosses. Yet Wokingham's most charming structure is undoubtedly the Lucas Hospital, one mile to the south in the suburb of Luckley. Built just before 1670 in good red brick, it consists of a main block with two wings, that on the east being the chapel and that on the west the chaplain's lodging. A window in each of these wings has a little original armorial glass. The hospital is managed by the Drapers' Company, whose master visits the inhabitants annually and sees that the structure is kept in a perfect state of repair.

At Wokingham the forests of south Berkshire are already at one's doorstep but of the nearby villages Binfield at least remains transitional between Loddon plain and the Windsor woodlands. This is a scattered settlement with a wealth of trim cottages and quite a number of commodious and even palatial dwellings, all graced and coloured with a variety of trees. The church stands between the parks of Binfield House and Billingbear and is readily distinguished by its old squat tower built of 'pudding stone' patiently collected when the 'iron-pan' of the nearby heaths was being broken up. The church is entered on the south by a beautiful weather-beaten porch, with feathered and traceried bays of carved oak of the fifteenth century. The tower and nave arcades and a window or two are also probably of this date or even a century earlier. In spite of much restoration, the church holds many interesting features. A small brass—the oldest in Berkshire—shows a vested priest who was rector here in 1361 and bears an inscription in Norman French:

'Water de Annefordhe gist icy dieu de sa aime eit mercy.'

Another brass is a palimpsest commemorating Richard Turner and his wife Katherine, of the mid-sixteenth century on the one side and on the other an abbot in full canonicals of about 1400. Close to the Jacobean pulpit is an intricate wrought-iron hour-glass stand with vine leaves and grapes, oak leaves and acorns and various armorial bearings, including the three horseshoes of the Farriers' Company. The stained glass includes several panels of fifteenth-century workmanship, such as the figures of St. George and the dragon, which are well worth the seeing. The church too abounds in black marble tombstones with carved coats of arms, and in mural tablets, among them some to the Dancastle family through whom Alexander Pope, father of the poet, came to live at Binfield.

The senior Alexander Pope was a linen-draper who retired to an estate of twenty acres in Binfield in 1700 when his son Alexander was twelve years old. The tenement—

'A little house with trees a-row
And like its master very low'—

used to be called Popeswood but has latterly formed part of the residence known as Arthurstone. Here John Dancastle and the elder Pope had tastes in common of which the chief was gardening and the poetic son describes how his father

'Plants cauliflowers and boasts to rear
The earliest melons of the year.'

The poet was an only child so that his studies were mostly of his own choosing and pursued with more than ordinary concentration. As he said years later

'True ease in writing comes from art, not chance,
As those move easiest who have learnt to dance.'

He is supposed to have loved wandering in Windsor Forest and there is a group of beech trees near his home which he specially favoured when he tried to write verse. To one of these trees a brass plate is now fixed with an inscription ending with the words

'His shade these haunts, his name the world doth fill.'

In these solitudes Pope trained himself to be a poet with a severity which undermined his health and eventually led to the famous Dr. Radcliffe of Oxford prescribing for him a strict diet, less study and a daily ride in the open air. On one of these rides he met a neighbour, Sir William Trumbull of Easthampstead Park, a charming old man with a fine collection of books and pictures and a liking for literature. Pope in a letter describes the rest of his neighbours:

'I assure you I am looked upon in the neighbourhood for a very sober and well disposed person, no great hunter indeed, but a great esteemer of that noble sport, and only unhappy in my want of constitution for that and drinking. They all say 'tis pity I am so sickly, and I think 'tis pity they are so healthy; but I say nothing that may destroy their good opinion of me.'

In 1713 he published *Windsor Forest* and in the following year *The Rape of the Lock*. Later at Trumbull's suggestion he began to translate the Iliad into English verse, or rather to versify other people's translations. This proved so successful financially that the poet was able to leave Binfield.—'I parted from honest Mr. Dancastle with tenderness, and from Sir William Trumbull as from a venerable prophet.' Pope craved intellectual human companionship, and it is doubtful if he were ever really happy at Binfield, though he could appreciate and even envy a mind which could find complete contentment in such a locality.

'Happy the man, whose wish and care
A few paternal acres bound,
Content to breathe his native air
In his own ground

'Blessed, who can unconcern'dly find
Hours, days and years slide soft away,
In health of body, peace of mind,
Quiet by day.

'Thus let me live, unseen, unknown,
Thus unlamented let me die,
Steal from the world, and not a stone
Tell where I lie.'

CHAPTER XIV: The Sporting Thames

I care not, I, to fish in seas—
Fresh rivers best my mind do please,
Whose sweet calm course I contemplate,
And seek in life to imitate:
In civil bounds I fain would keep,
And for my past offences weep.

IZAAK WALTON

IF, as the Arabs say, three things ease the heart from sorrow—water, green grass, and the beauty of women—the Thames is a great comforter. It is true that female forms have enlivened its waters only since Victorian times but men can claim with sincerity to have been always 'by it, and on it, and in it'. Apart from the seasonal warm weather dabblers, the male frequenters of the Thames fall into boatmen, oarsmen and fishermen, the order being commensurate with the disturbance they cause on the face of the waters.

The Thames bargee had a flavour and language quite his own which had been growing upon him for several centuries. He was already old when King John in 1205 gave William FitzAndrew permission to ply one vessel between Oxford and London without let or hindrance on the part of the bailiffs of Wallingford and Windsor. As boats grew larger the navigation upstream became more difficult and considerable improvements had to be made to the watercourse before Oxford could be reached in safety in the early-seventeenth century. Even in 1677 the navigation was such that 'in dry times barges do sometimes lie aground three weeks or a month or more'. The system of flashing was now in full force, water being impounded above shallows and then suddenly released, the flood carrying barges downstream over the shoals. Upstream, barges were hauled over shallows mainly by means of capstans and horses. In 1772, the river was greatly improved and twenty-six pond—or pound—locks constructed as well as an almost continuous tow-path. Most of the barges working between Oxford and Windsor now became 'Newbury sized' or 109 feet long by 17 feet wide, about 110 to 128 tons burthen and 4 feet in draught. The steersman was helped by bargemen, each with an ashen pole several yards long; upstream eight to fourteen horses were needed but downstream one horse would keep up a good pace. Cheese, corn, and beechwood were among the main cargoes going down while coal was important coming up. Not till Victorian times did railways begin to kill this traffic, and then river-steamers came in, and still today in summer the river may be threaded in calm, quiet ease from Oxford to Kingston Bridge pier, there being two steamer-services each way daily.

The oarsmen of the Thames have grown in numbers rapidly since the decline of barge traffic. The 'wet-bobs' of Radley and Eton and the regattas at Henley, Marlow and elsewhere, although for the most part not primarily concerned with the Berkshire bank, bring much animation to it. Competitive rowing became common and popular on the 'take-twenty-eggs' and beef-steak diet of the mid-nineteenth century. Henley forestalled Maidenhead as the chief centre partly because the first Oxford and Cambridge race in 1829 and that of 1837 were held from Hambleden Lock to Henley Bridge. But Berkshire has some consolations, for the Leander Club live at Remenham, and one of the toughest feats of oarsmanship was performed by local men. On Thursday 15th August 1822, for a large wager, Viscount Newry and five of his servants, all Maidenhead or Cookham men 'not accustomed to the work, rowed from Oxford to London in eighteen hours. Precisely as Great Tom struck the hour of three in the morning, the boat left Oxford and at 8 hr.

58 min. 30 sec. p.m. arrived at . . . Westminster Bridge, winning the bet with just one minute and a half to spare.'

The very antithesis of the oarsman is the fisherman, the oldest and most devoted frequenter of the Thames. Today, a lovable silent figure perched on a little stool, he sits singly in discreet detachment, with his rod protruding over the water-face, with never an audible song or joyful gesture until darkness calls him home. He disappears as obsequiously as he came, oft leaving the river as full as he found it, but hope deferred does not make his heart sick for every day he recalls how trout of fifteen pounds have been caught in the Thames and Kennet, and how the river abounds also 'in barbel, pike, eels of excellent quality, gudgeon, dace and various other common fish'. He alone knows the meaning of 'common'!

The Thames has uses and users other than these. It has long driven water wheels, as at Temple Mills, and has long been used by fishers of men. The ancient priory at Hurley and the abbey on the other bank together signify a connexion between the river and church which began in Saxon times. Hurley church is traditionally the burial-place of Edith, sister of Edward the Confessor. Shortly after the Conquest the manor and church were given to the monastery at Westminster to form a cell of Benedictine monks, and as such the buildings were dedicated in 1086 by Bishop Osmund. The church now became an integral part of the priory and formed, as it were, most of its southern side. The present round-headed, deeply-splayed windows, although much restored, show an early Norman origin, while the south and west doorway and west window are twelfth-century additions, the latter with its rich chevron moulding being particularly pleasing. The main alterations to the Norman building were the cutting of a priest's doorway and of a fine Decorated window, and the erection, in the early-fifteenth century, of a wooden bell-turret and a panelled, tub-shaped font. Recent excavations have shown that the monastic church was longer than the present structure and probably had aisles and a gallery entered high up on the north side. The church furniture includes two mediaeval pews, beautifully carved but now pushed away at the west end of the nave.

The other surviving fragments of the monastery lie north of the church. Here, an old stone archway surmounted by a quaintly-tiled niche, leads into a quadrangle, the private grounds of 'Lady Place'. The east and west sides of this square, although picturesque, are fairly modern reconstructions of old materials, including an Elizabethan window and well-weathered timbering. The south side is formed by the church, and the north by the former monastic refectory. The far section of these sides, from and beyond the Norman doorway in each, would appear to have been cloistered. In the church wall, for example, about nine feet above ground-level are sawn-off beam-ends that could have formerly been connected with the roof of a cloister. These cloisters probably ran round the whole of the eastern half of the present quadrangle. The refectory itself is now a long barn-like building, with round-headed Norman work below and trefoiled pointed lights of early Decorated style above.

The modern 'Lady Place' replaced a house built on the site of the monastery by John Lovelace (*ob.* 1558) whose tomb may be seen in the church. Two sides of the moat and the former fishponds adorn the gardens while the crypt of Lovelace's mansion remains, where, under the pavement, three bodies in Benedictine habits were once found. Of its many owners the one who made the most stir was John, Lord Lovelace (*ob.* 1693), who worshipped Whiggism and strongly favoured the coming of the Prince of Orange. A tablet on the walls of the vault, later visited by George III, tells how plans and arrangements were made here for inviting the Prince to England. Macaulay elegantly describes it:

'This mansion, built by his ancestors out of the spoils from the Spanish galleons from the Indies, rose on the ruins of a house of Our Lady in this beautiful valley through which the Thames, not yet defiled by the precincts of a great capital . . . rolls under the woods of beech round the gentle hills of Berkshire. Beneath the stately saloon, adorned by Italian pencils, was a subterranean vault, in which the bodies of ancient monks had sometimes been found. In this dark chamber some zealous and daring opponents of the Government held many midnight conferences, during that anxious time when England was impatiently expecting the protestant wind.'

The picturesque grouping about Hurley priory is much enhanced by two large barns and a circular dovecote. The fine tiled barn lying in the field west of the church is splendidly built but although called a 'tithe-barn' can hardly be earlier than late Elizabethan. The dovecote seems older and more in need of repair. Alongside the road to the church is a smaller barn, constructed of shaped chalk blocks and flint, with a fine moulded cornice which has the antiquity expected of a monastic tithe-barn. This cluster of barns and ecclesiastic buildings is fended on one side by a tall mellow brick-wall which adds much to its charm. Yet the approaches have need of a fairy godmother—the mire-fouled fringes of the little green, the rank growth round the dovecote, the inelegant advertisements in so small a street, should be tidied and sweetened.

By way of contrast that part of Hurley away from the meadows of the river-end has a quite remarkable tidiness. Some of the half-timber brick houses near the main road have mellowed with the centuries into delightful dwellings while the Bell Inn still retains original fifteenth-century work. It was presumably the guest house of the old priory, to which, rumour says, it was linked by an underground tunnel. Its upper story is overhanging, and with its timber-porch, entrance doorway and oriel window forms a picturesque asset to the pleasant village street.

The two-mile trip along the Thames from Hurley to Bisham could hardly be bettered, for the tree-dotted meadows of Temple Park are backed by the beech-hung cliffs of the chalk hills, and when Temple Park ceases the grounds of Bisham Abbey make full amends. The abbey dates from 1337 when it was built by William Montacute, Earl of Salisbury, for the Austin canons. Here most of the illustrious members of the founder's family were buried:

'William, Earl of Salisbury, son of the founder, who distinguished himself at the battle of Poitiers; John, Earl of Salisbury, who confederating against Henry IV was slain at Cirencester in 1401; Thomas, Earl of Salisbury, the famed hero of Henry the Fifth's reign, who lost his life at the siege of Orleans in 1428; Richard Neville, Earl of Salisbury and Warwick, who was beheaded at York, in 1460 . . .; Richard Neville, the King-Maker, who fell at the battle of Barnet, 1470; and the unfortunate Edward Plantagenet, son of the Duke of Clarence, who, bred up from his cradle in prison, was beheaded in 1499 for attempting to taste the sweets of liberty. Most of the above-mentioned illustrious characters had splendid monuments in the conventual church, but these were all destroyed after the destruction of the abbey.'

Shortly after the dissolution, the abbey-site was granted to Anne of Cleves and eventually it passed to Sir Philip Hoby, who built an Elizabethan mansion on to the scanty remains of the old abbey. Apart from the moat, the fourteenth-century fragments that survive are a fine Decorated porch with the original oak door; a part of the massive wall of the chapel with one geometrical window and two arched openings; and the great hall, where however the original windows have been altered or blocked and a minstrels' gallery added.

The fine mansion built by the Hobys in the years 1557 to

1561 included a 'council chamber' with a fine oriel window above a raised alcove, a panelled dining-room with mullioned windows, a panelled study, and a tall tower. Today after small additions in later centuries, the house shows almost all forms of building metals—from finely-cut chalk with some flint diapering of the abbey, to mellow red-brick of Tudor age, with stone mullions and well-weathered plastering. It gives a succession of surprises at angles and corners while the whole rises above English lawns amid a sprinkling of trees that tantalizingly truncates the view from the Thames. The interior features are characteristic of the Hobys, who were cultured and fond of colourful decoration. The tapestries are of the early sixteenth century while much of the woodwork, some of the plasterwork and the heraldic glass are Jacobean. At Bisham Abbey the sporting Thames comes into its own for the building now inspires the National Recreational Council, although men such as the Nevilles and Salisburys—who presumably lie hereabout—will not be unduly disturbed by the rhythmic pastimes of their modern successors.

The parish church of All Saints stands on the bank of the Thames a few hundred yards downstream, and the churchyard wall has landing steps for river craft. To go by Thames to worship is, unfortunately, less common today than a generation ago but Bisham church has lost none of its charm and surely the boats on summer Sundays will converge again on the sound of its bells. The tower overlooking the river dates from 1150 and is built of hard chalk surmounted by brick battlements of Tudor age. The remainder of the church has been much restored but the Hoby chapel, with its three painted marble tombs, is a great delight. The monument to Sir Philip and Sir Thomas Hoby shows them reclining in full mail armour, which is exquisitely executed so that every buckle and rivet is visible. Sir Philip lies nearest the wall. The first of the line to hold Bisham, he was a zealous protestant reformer, while Sir Thomas was ambassador in Paris where he died in 1566. The latter's widow, who executed the costly tomb and wrote the epitaphs, found much solace in these compositions and in ordering pompous funerals. She wrote a long elegy for her second husband, Lord Russell, who was buried in Westminster Abbey, nor did she forget herself. Just before her own death at the age of 81 she wrote to the Garter King of Arms inquiring 'what number of mourners were due to her calling . . . the manner of the hearse, of the heralds and church?' In 1609 she duly left to Bisham a treasure in painted marble, which centres upon herself—a beautiful creature, goffered superbly, in coronet, coif and ruff, much as depicted by Holbein in her portrait in Bisham Abbey. At Lady Elizabeth's knees is a tiny babe who died in infancy; facing her across the prayer-desk is her daughter Anne Russell, Countess Herbert, who survived her, and behind her are the three daughters whom she outlived—Elizabeth Russell, and the two Hobys who died when children. Outside the canopy kneel her two surviving sons, Sir Edward Hoby and Sir Thomas Posthumus Hoby, the latter being born after his father's death. The whole monument is a feast of heraldry, precise and immaculate in content and colouring.

Sir Edward Hoby, who succeeded at Bisham, entertained Queen Elizabeth here and was often visited by James I, probably because of a mutual interest in theology. Hoby even went so far as to publish pamphlets entitled *A Counter-Snarle*, and *A Curry Combe for a Coxe Combe*. He married a cousin of Queen Elizabeth, named Margaret Cary, who is remembered here by a pyramid surmounted by a flaming heart and adorned at its foot by four stately swans, the family crest of the Carys. Sir Edward was succeeded by Peregrine Hoby, a natural son somewhat unexpected of a religious tractarian.

The Hoby chapel is lighted by a large Tudor window

filled with enamelled glass of fine workmanship wherein the armorial bearings of the family up to the year 1609 are accurately shown.

The church contains other interesting memorials: two figured sixteenth-century brasses, one to a merchant adventurer and the other to 'Thomas Trekett, sometyme fyssmonger of London'; a monument to an Eton schoolboy and his dog; a Perpendicular altar-tomb brought from Anglesey; and in the sanctuary a shot-riddled pennant taken by Lieutenant Paul Eddis from his submarine E.13 sunk off Denmark, and eventually brought home by its rescuer who escaped from internment by being nailed into a barrel.

Beyond Bisham the Thames proceeds through the chalk hills and circumvents the great bastion of chalk about Cookham Dean and that superb viewpoint Winter Hill. Afoot this is a pleasant country with twisting roads shaded by tier upon tier of beech and bright with patches of willow-herb. Afloat the leisurely traveller sees the same wooded slopes as a green bluff, from which a thin smoke column from an isolated mansion alone betrays life. He sees too the 'eights' and sailing-boats and the weirs and willowed eyots which break the current, making the light and shade dance on the waters. The Thames is scrupulously impartial; below Marlow bridge it cuts into the Berkshire cliffs about Quarry Wood and then at Cookham moves over to the other side of its valley and cuts into the wooded precipices of Hedsor and Cliveden, leaving, as is the custom of biggish rivers, a wide flat plain on the opposing bank. On this flat patch stand the older parts of Cookham.

The manor of Cookham by Saxon times had fallen to the Crown who kept it until 1818. Today it is flowing with inns and eating-houses as becomes a favourite riverside resort which has managed to preserve much of its old-world character. The main part lies near the river, where the church and church gate-house and an imposing Georgian dwelling form an inviting entry. Thence a quaint medley of buildings stretches to the Moor, a large watery green with a big brick bridge spanning a disused watercourse. Beyond the houses begin again and lead up to Cookham Dean where villas are grandly dispersed amid orchards and trees.

The church of Holy Trinity has an undeniable spaciousness and dignity in spite of restorations and over-darkened windows. These qualities partly arise from the extensive use of chalk, which was presumably dug from an old mine in Bisham Woods. Of the original Norman church, the north-west wall with one round-headed window are the chief survivals while of later additions the early-thirteenth-century chapel of St. Catherine, because of its lancet windows, doorway and piscina, is by far the finest. The many interesting memorials and furnishings include several brasses, an elaborate monument to Arthur Babham (*ob.* 1561) and family, and a sensitive marble by Flaxman to Sir Isaac Pococke (*ob.* 1835), the painter of historical scenes and dramatizer of the *Waverley Novels*, who, as the carving shows, died suddenly 'whilst on the Thames near his own home'. A medallion here recalls Frederick Walker, one of the many artists who have made Cookham their home. It does not however, need the eye of an artist to appreciate the loveliness of the churchyard, with its virginia creeper against chalk and flint, and the standard roses grouped among well-kept tombstones.

Near the church and bridge at Cookham the Thames branches into three channels which soon unite into the noted boating reach which stretches two miles to Boulter's lock, so named from a bolter or miller of corn. Thence another mile leads to Maidenhead bridge, a handsome stone structure opened in 1777 and designed by the same Robert Taylor who founded the Taylorian at Oxford. Maidenhead makes a fascinating study of the effect of routes on the rise of a township. Its growth began about 1280 when a crude bridge replaced the ford and attracted to it the main road from London to the West which formerly crossed the Thames at Babham End near Cookham. The hamlet of South Elington, as it was then called, became in this century Maydenhethe, from which its present name is derived. The bridge needed constant repairs and the Crown frequently made grants for that purpose; in 1337, Edward III granted the 'bailiffs and goodmen of Maidenhithe' one penny toll on every cartload of goods going over the bridge and one penny on every boatload going under it. James I added the gift of three oaks yearly from the nearby woods.

The traffic by road and river early became important as the village seemed just the right distance from London to be a stopping stage for horses, carriages, boats and even pedestrians. It was soon full of inns. At the Greyhound—since burnt down—Charles I met his children for the last time. Most later monarchs dined in the town more than once. Here in 1811 the Duke of Clarence dismissed for ever the devoted Mrs. Jordans who had borne him a mere ten children. Hither to Marsh's Inn came the rebellious upper forms of Eton on November 2nd 1768, their bill upon leaving on the following day being:

	£.	*s.*	*d.*
Beer for supper and dinner	2.	1.	od
Wine and punch etc.	12.	13.	3d
Dinners, suppers & breakfast for 160	40.	0.	od
Fires	1.	0.	od
Cards		4.	od
	55.	18.	3d

Yet the visitor looking for old buildings in Maidenhead will not find them even in the inns and the only structure of any antiquity is Smith's almshouses in the Bath Road. A quaint building of mellow, moulded brick with a long low roof, it bears over the central archway the inscription: 'Theis Almshouses were erected and built at ye sole and proper cost and charges of James Smith Esquior, citizen and salter of London in the yeare of our Lord 1659'. Next door is the ornate Haven of Rest founded in 1895 by George Herring whose cremated ashes lie beneath the sundial on the front lawn.

A few pleasant Georgian houses remain but nineteenth-century Maidenhead was a small township half in the parish of Bray and half in Cookham. Its corporate life had, it is true, awakened on the foundation of the Guild of St. Andrew and St. Mary Magdalen in 1451 but the town was never incorporated by royal charter till 1581 and had no mayor till the reign of James II. As late as 1821 only 950 persons lived in the town, yet by 1841, when the railway had arrived over the red-brick bridge designed by Brunel, the number had increased to 3,315. This bridge, together with Skindle's Hotel which is sufficiently in Berkshire to allow the boundary beaters to take the mace through the front door and out of a side window, was immortalized in Turner's superb landscape 'Rain, Steam and Speed'.

In the 'sixties a tremendous wave of popularity for the river doubled the town's size and re-doubled it before the end of Victoria's reign. The cream of fashion frequented Maidenhead, forcefully led by the Brigade of Guards. The town was made a parish or borough of its own and, as such, has never looked back for when boating suffered a temporary decline the motor-car took over.

Today the twenty thousand inhabitants are as sands on the seashore to the hordes of visitors, whom they feed and amuse. Now, as formerly, the western outskirts are adorned by Maidenhead thicket, a mixture of rough pasture and thorny browsage once the haunt of highwaymen. *Jackson's Oxford Journal* for November 1st 1755 tells of a typical hold-up:

St. George's, Windsor: The Choir

A Guardsman at Windsor Castle

'Last Tuesday about twelve o'clock at Noon, the Oxford Machine in which were three Gentlemen, was stopped by a single Highwayman well-mounted, with a black Mask, in Maidenhead Thicket. Upon demanding their money, the Passengers gave him about twelve Guineas; he then demanded their Watches, which two of the Gentlemen delivered, but one of them desiring he would return the seal, on which was his Coat of Arms, the Highwayman observing that the watch was only Pinchbeck, said it would be of little service to him, and returned it. He then made off into the Thicket.'

In Georgian and Victorian days Maidenhead was well known in sports other than highway-robbery. In 1787 George III and all his family attended the horse-races here; at football in 1871–2 the newly-formed club lost only one match—that against Crystal Palace in the second round of the Association Cup; at cricket on 24th June 1793 a grand match was played 'in Lord's Cricket Ground, Marybone, between nine gentlemen of the Marybone Club and two of Middlesex against eleven of the Maidenhead Club for 500 guineas a side . . .' The Marybone eleven included players such as T. Lord, who owned the famous ground named after him, but Maidenhead gained a convincing victory.

The local cricket pitch then was in Bray parish so that some credit for these early feats goes rightly to Bray which is so often called 'Maidenhead's mother'. The ancient riverside village lies a mile to the south at the end of a gravel-floored reach of the Thames noted for its punting. The Perpendicular tower of St. Michael's rises picturesquely above the plain with its riverine fringe of sunlit bungalows and pretty gardens. The habitations of Bray parish are a delightful assembly of young and old, of quaint half-timbering and post-Georgian fancies, of large mansions and small dwellings. It is, however, the river that makes it, for the flat featureless plain lacks the vivacity of the chalk country near

Cookham. The river has fostered the several old inns which lie, as the sartorially minded will notice, in the foraging ground of Eton. Yet Bray has a charm of its own.

The original church was replaced in the late thirteenth century by an Early-English structure of which the nave arches, the west end, and parts of the north wall and upper chancel survive. The chapel of St. Nicholas was built before 1467 when John Norreys of Ockwells left money for its re-furbishing, but was probably reconstructed in the next century. As seen from the west doorway, the church forms an entrancing vista of pillars and corbels reminiscent of a cathedral. There are many quaint epitaphs. That to John Rixman, who died in 1620, recalls the triumph of true-love over the delights of a senior common room.

'When Oxford gave thee two degrees in art,
And love possest thee master of my heart
Thy colledge fellowshipp thou lef'st for mine
And nought but deathe could seprate me from thine . . .'

Equally blessed in his womenfolk was Sir John Foxley (*ob.* 1378) who is depicted by an attractive brass, in which a very alert fox supports a column that branches to carry in its turn Sir John and his two wives. The knight wears chain mail while the ladies seem clothed in a form of armorial dress. Connubial bliss is also maintained in a life-sized painted marble monument to William Goddard (*ob.* 1609), the founder of Jesus Hospital, and to Joyce Maimsell his wife.

North of the spacious churchyard stands the small chantry chapel of St. Mary the Virgin which in part dates back to the thirteenth century and has some fine flint-work and a vigorous carving of a horse. On the opposite side is the half-timber gatehouse which bears the date 1448 on one of its roof-beams and retains much of its original structure. This part of Bray should be seen on a Sunday afternoon when the

world is alive with youngsters and the church's towered doorway seems like the hole in the mountain into which the pied piper is leading the children of Hamelin.

Bray parish has at least three other architectural attractions. On Monkey Island are the remnants of two banqueting pavilions built by the Duke of Marlborough: one, now an hotel, has a room painted with sporting Monkeys; the other, now a private residence, has a main upper room with a fine stucco ceiling resplendent with naiads and shells and mermaids.

The picturesque old almshouse called Jesus Hospital was founded by William Goddard in 1627 and is, as the coats-of-arms indicate, under the aegis of the Fishmongers' Company. Its forty occupants share a chapel and a communal kitchen and bakehouse while each has a dwelling facing a quadrangle divided into forty gardens. This quadrangle is entered by a gabled brick porch with stone mullioned windows and adorned with a statue of the founder. The whole is much beautified by topiary work and flowers, and acquired a national fame from its use as a background to Frederick Walker's painting 'The Harbour of Refuge'.

The other treasure is Ockwells Manor, nearly two miles west of Bray, built by Sir John Norreys between 1446 and 1466. A fine example of domestic architecture of that period, its half-timbered, brick-filled façades are grouped around a small central courtyard. The east front with fine barge-boarded gables is particularly lovely and its panelled windows contain contemporary heraldic glass in which are set forth the shields and arms of Sir John Norreys, his sovereign Henry VI, and sixteen of his dearest kinsfolk. Each shield is in a separate light and richly set in a delicate, decorative background with frequent use of the motto *ffeyth-fully serve*.

Such a motto is unexpected in Bray which is always known for its weathercock vicar. This gentleman appears in Thomas Fuller's *Worthies of England* (1662) under

'Barkshire. . . . first we will dispatch that sole proverb of this country, *viz.*

'The Vicar of Bray will be Vicar of Bray still.

'The vivacious Vicar hereof living under King Henry the Eighth, King Edward the Sixth, Queen Mary and Queen Elizabeth, was first a papist, then a protestant, then a papist, then a protestant again. He had seen some martyrs burnt (two miles off) at Windsor and found this fire too hot for his tender temper. This Vicar being taxed by one for being a *Turn-coat* and an unconstant Changeling, "Not so," said he, "for I always kept my principle, which is this, to live and die the Vicar of Bray." Such many now adayes, who though they cannot turn the wind, will turn their mills, and set them so, that wheresoever it bloweth, their grist shall certainly be grinded.'

Although Fuller mentions no name, the accusation of being the turncoat vicar has been rather flung at Simon Alleyn who became vicar of Bray in 1551 and held this living and the one at Cookham and a canon's stall at Windsor until he died fourteen years later. This period of time touches on the reigns of Edward VI, Mary and Elizabeth, and as Charles Harper shows so delightfully 'there was thus supposing him to have been originally instituted as a Protestant, only one violation of conscience necessary to his retaining his post: a small matter!' Fuller, however, is quite unreliable, and Simon Symonds and others also compete for the honour. But the truth seems to be that Fuller's account and the song are two different things, and that Francis Carswell, who held the curacy here from the reign of Charles II to William III, might also be the famous vicar. The original song can be traced back to the early-eighteenth century and, as 'The Religious Turncoat . . .' mentions no place by name. The most popular version, with the title 'The Vicar of Bray', was written in the time of George I by an army officer who ascribed the change-overs to the reigns ranging from Charles II to George I. Of course, the word Bray only enters the chorus and there becomes almost a necessity to fit the rollicking rhyme. Later generations of sticklers for accuracy have tried to find a real vicar as well as a real place to excuse what may after all be only a poet's licence. There is in fact very little certainty about it historically, apart from the good vicar's determination:

'And this is law I will maintain
Until my dying day, sir,
That whatsoever King shall reign
I'll be the Vicar of Bray, sir.'

Once at Ockwells, even the lure of the Hotel de Paris at Bray or the call of the chef at The Bell at Hurley should not distract lovers of little places from making an inland journey of three miles to Shottesbrooke. Here an irregular-shaped parish hinges upon a large park and a manor-house and the whole is beset with trees as becomes a domain carved from the forest. The manor-house dates in part back to Tudor-times but was Gothicized in the early-nineteenth century and given façades of patterned brick with turrets and battlements.

The dominant feature of the landscape is the tall, ribbed spire of the church of St. John the Baptist which rises high above the trees of the park. Traditionally it is said to owe its existence to the unexpected recovery of Sir William Trussell, the owner of the estate, who had drunk himself to to edge of the grave. Sir William in 1337 also founded a chantry or college, with a warden, five priests and two clerks, to serve the church. But the present structure is certainly of about 1370, so it appears that the older church and no doubt the college were destroyed by fire and re-built at this time. A legend of the erection of the spire tells how the architect, on fixing the weathercock, called for wine to drink a health, and after drinking crashed to the ground. He only uttered 'O! O!' before dying and his last words were carved on his tomb on the spot where he fell.

The church is a lovely building soaring upwards like a small cathedral, the slender spire appearing to take the steeply-pitched roofs aloft with it. The walls of shaped flints with stone dressings, add to the dignity of the simple cruciform plan and the nicely-proportioned design: All the windows have deeply-moulded curvilinear tracery while a few small lights retain their original coloured glass. These and the sedilia, the font, and the delicately carved 'founder's tomb', or, for that matter, almost all the building, date from the late-fourteenth century. Shottesbrooke shows late-Decorated at its best in a parish church, and Berkshire has no other of the time to equal it.

During the centuries the building has acquired many interesting memorials. The finest brass shows, by deep, artistic incisions, two men, the one a layman with a forked beard, long habit and short sword, and the other a vested priest. Generally assigned to about 1370, this brass may well be to Sir William Trussell and his brother. Another brass remembers Richard Gyll, Sergeant of the Bakehouse to Henry VII and Henry VIII, and yet another recalls 'Thomas Noke, who for his great age and vertuous lief was reverenced of all men, and comenly called Father Noke, created Esquier by Henry the VIII'. He was, so the brass proceeds, tall and comely, a wonderful artillery man, lived to be eighty-seven, and 'had in his lief three Wifes, and by every of them som Fruyte and ofsprynge'. There is, too, an 'interrupted' effigy to William Throckmorton of diminutive size, a brass occupying the place where his middle should be. The Vansittarts, who lived at the manor, added their share of memorials, including a tablet of a naval battle in 1747 to a young midshipman killed while serving with Admiral Hawke off Cape Finisterre.

Of the college, nothing but memories are left. It went

the way of other chantries in 1548 and for long its chief reminder was an orchard with trees trimmed in the form of crosses. But Shottesbrooke did not so easily slip out of history, for Francis Cherry turned the manor house into a refuge for the non-jurors, or people who would not take the oath of allegiance to William of Orange. He was allowed by his father £2,500 a year partly to relieve the distressed, and he it was who discovered the talents of William Hearne, the son of the parish clerk of White Waltham, whose expenses he paid until Hearne had graduated at Oxford. Cherry was a fearless rider and is said once on noticing how closely William III kept to him when stag-hunting, to have leaped his horse down a dangerous drop into the Thames in the hope that the King would follow and break his neck. The effort, however, was wasted. On the death of his father, Cherry took over debts amounting to £30,000 and once passed a few days in Reading gaol, but like a true gentleman spent £100 in entertaining the gentry who visited him there.

CHAPTER XV: Royal Windsor

Straight mine eye hath caught new pleasures,
Whilst the landskip round it measures;
Russet lawns and fallows gray,
Where the nibbling flocks do stray;
Meadows trim, with daisies pied;
Shallow brooks and rivers wide;
Towers and battlements it sees,
Bosomed high in tufted trees.

MILTON, *L'Allegro*, written at Horton, three miles east of Windsor

THE CASTLE

GEOGRAPHY holds the key to Windsor's greatness. Here a detached hillock of chalk rises 100 feet above the surrounding plain and lies safely within a sharp loop of the Thames. In past geological ages the river undercut this hillock, forming steep cliffs on all its sides except the south where it grades imperceptibly into the clayey lowland. So nature contrived a fortress-site, commanding a wide territory.

Strategically the knoll sat prettily astride routes to London from the upper Thames and Kennet. But the site also combined a strategic location with possibilities of pleasure and remoteness from urban plagues. Its porous rock gave a deep, pure water-supply; it was just a day's march from Westminster; it had the river for transport and the forest for hawking and hunting.

The earliest royal residence in this vicinity was at Old Windsor on the flat wooded lowland two miles to the south-east, a place which soon attracted William the Conquerer who 'loved the tall stags as if he were their father'. When William began to build a chain of fortresses around

London, the chalk crag near Old Windsor fell inevitably into this defensive ring. Upon it, soon after 1070, the King had constructed a series of earthworks consisting of three wards, each with a ditch and rampart crowned with timber palisades. The plan was shaped like an hour-glass, the middle ward being the smallest and strongest, for here was an artificial mound nearly fifty feet high, girded by a deep ditch and crowned with a wooden fortress. The site covered thirteen acres and stretched lengthwise for over 500 yards as does the present castle.

This wooden fortification was probably not deemed habitable by the King until the reign of Henry I, nor was it until the next significant reign that the first stone buildings graced the site. Then Henry II constructed royal lodgings and a round tower as well as strong outer walls on all but the steep western flank of the hillock. The stone for facing the walls came from Bagshot Heath and may still be distinguished along the lower parts of, for example, the east front of the upper ward. Among other surviving fragments of Henry II's castle are two sally-ports from the upper bailey into the castle-ditch, that on the south being almost perfect.

Although Henry III did not look upon Windsor as a favourite residence, the castle, as Tighe and Davis say, 'benefited by his taste for architecture in a degree which totally changed the aspect of at least the lower ward, where his works may still be traced to a considerable extent'. Henry extended the domestic lodgings and built the first chapel, of which the north wall survives as the graceful arcading on the southern flank of the Dean's Cloister. Of its original frescoes, only the head of a white-haired, bearded monarch remains although another contemporary fresco—also probably of Edward the Confessor—appears above the doorway to the nearby vaulted passage. Henry III's additions, however, are best remembered by the west wall with its semi-circular towers all of which date mainly from 1220 to 1230. Clewer or Curfew Tower, which guards the north-western corner, is, apart from some new stone-facing and the conical roof, almost in its original state. Its lower walls are nearly thirteen feet thick and contain within their thickness a sally-port that descends to a point now nearly half-way across the present street and formerly in the old ditch.

The next notable royal builder at Windsor was Edward III, who was born in the castle on 23 November 1312 'at forty minutes after five in the morning'. Of his many alterations to the upper ward, the chief survivals are the stone-vaulted Grand Entrance—where the Old Master drawings are now exhibited—and the Inner Gatehouse, which with its narrow arch and portcullis and two fine drum towers dates from 1359. Masons and artificers were collected from all English counties, and from 1356 to 1362 William of Wykeham was surveyor of works. The lovely canon's cloister and the elaborate vaulted porch under the treasury of St. George's Chapel were finished just before Wykeham took charge but the upper range of the lodgings of the Military Knights arose in his time. Tradition has it that the inscription *Hoc fecit Wykeham* was cut in the stonework, a presumption which offended the King until the surveyor explained that it meant not that Wykeham made the building but that the building made Wykeham. There was, however, no sign of such an inscription when Sir Jeffrey Wyatville perpetuated the story by cutting *Hoc fecit Wykeham Anno Domini 1356* on the north face of Winchester Tower.

Edward III also founded the Order of the Garter and a college of deans, canons, choristers and Military Knights to serve it. The origins of the Order are very obscure. Early in the year 1344, the King held a Round Table at Windsor. 'At the costly banquets were the most alluring of drinks in plenty, enough and to spare. The lords and ladies failed not to dance, mingling kisses with embraces. Among the knights jousting was practised for three days together. Many entertainers made the most charming melody and sundry other diversions. Some received changes of raiment, some gifts in abundance, some much gold and silver. On the fourth day the King began the Round Table; which done, trumpets and kettle-drums sounded, and the guests hastened to a feast, complete with wealth of foods, variety of courses, and overflowing quantities of drink. The joy was unspeakable, the comfort inestimable, the pleasure without murmuring, the hilarity without care.' In the next and some following years, jousts and masques were held during which the participants wore fine apparel and carried symbols or badges. Early in 1348, the records mention a white streamer 'Powdered with blue garters', containing this motto: '*hony soit q' mal y pense*'. This symbol and motto seems already to have become popular and the King seems already to have given up the idea of a Round Table in favour of a smaller order, when a great meeting was held at Windsor in May 1348 to celebrate the birth of a fourth prince. Shortly after this meeting the Order of the Garter was founded and the old chapel (on the site of the Albert Memorial Chapel) was fitted out splendidly for its services. Edward conferred many privileges upon the college serving the chapel and on April 1st 1352 the burghers of Yarmouth endowed it with 13,200 red herrings a year for ever. Today its founder's sword, a two-handed weapon nearly seven feet long, hangs at the back of the high altar in St. George's Chapel.

Edward's immediate successors made no outstanding additions to his work and although Henry VI spent much time here his energies are reflected mainly at Cambridge and Eton. He was, however, the cause of one delightful rumour. Not two years old but already king he was being taken by his mother to London to open parliament, and on the journey the first night, a Saturday, was spent at Staines. The following morning the baby king refused to travel on the sabbath—he 'schriked and cryed and sprang' and had to be carried back into the inn. On Monday, he showed his royal approval and when borne out to his mother's litter was 'gladde and merye and chered'.

Edward IV has two main claims to fame at Windsor. In 1475 he began building St. George's Chapel, and had on his death eight years later finished and roofed the choir and its aisles. For the priests of the chapel he built the Horseshoe Cloister which in spite of much restoration has some original timber and brick in its lower parts.

The Tudors completed St. George's Chapel. Henry VII had built and roofed the nave by 1496 and had vaulted the choir by 1505, but the magnificent ceiling of the nave was not completed until 1528, or half-way through the reign of Henry VIII. This Henry, however, is better known for the main entrance gateway which bears the pomegranate badge of Catherine of Aragon. The two Henrys were involved in a less-fortunate venture. Henry VII began the rebuilding of the old castle chapel as a lady-chapel to St. George's and as a burial-place for himself and the venerable Henry VI. As he died before it was finished, Thomas Wolsey secured its completion and erected in it a sumptuous tomb to himself. When Wolsey fell from grace in 1529, Henry VIII appropriated the lady-chapel and tomb for his own use. Yet all were destined to lie elsewhere; the chapel became ruinous; the rich metalwork of Wolsey's tomb was sold for £600 in 1646 and the marble base was placed in 1808 over Nelson's grave in St. Paul's.

Both Tudor queens left concrete memorials at Windsor. Under Mary the lower range of lodgings of the Military knights was constructed but her arms and those of Philip of Spain adorn an adjacent tower that was built by William of Wykeham. Queen Elizabeth added the noble gallery (1583) which joins the Inner Gatehouse to the state apartments. Under her, also, the north terrace, built of wood by her father, was reconstructed in stone and along it she took a daily walk whatever the state of the weather.

Of the early Stuarts and Cromwell little need be said here. The New Model Army was trained by Fairfax in the Great Park and to Windsor on February 8th 1649 Charles I's body was brought for burial in Henry VIII's vault beneath the centre of St. George's choir. According to Harrison Ainsworth, Cromwell 'often took a moody and distrustful walk upon the terrace' while 'on the Restoration . . . the velvet sod of the Home Park was as often pressed by the foot of frolic beauty as by that of the tripping deer'. These distractions absorbed a mere fraction of Charles II's energy, for at his command a tempest of French culture swept through Tudor Windsor. Most of the lodgings in the upper ward were replaced by the present range of state apartments designed by Hugh May. Dull as ditchwater without, they shone within like a tropical lagoon. Nor was this all, for Charles had the north terrace widened and had it extended right round the upper ward.

No great structural changes were made to the castle for another century. William and Mary preferred Hampton Court while Queen Anne, although fond of Windsor, left relatively few visible remembrances and on her death the castle fell from royal grace and was actually let out to private persons. George III at first stayed at a lodge in the park but in 1778 decided that Windsor was the right place for his family and proceeded to make the castle more habitable. He soon adored it and Eton its neighbour, and would ride to London and back in the same day rather than stay a night in the capital. Under him, James Wyatt began to convert the barrack-like exterior of the upper ward into the Gothic style. He also removed Wolsey's tomb from the Lady Chapel and constructed there a vault in which lie the remains of himself and most members of his family including George IV and William IV.

These structural schemes were dwarfed by those of George IV who in ten years (1820–30) made grandiose changes under the guidance of Sir Jeffrey Wyatt or Wyatville. On October 1st, 1823, the King made a triumphal entry into Windsor, knighted the mayor and recorder, donated large sums to local charities and gave the good citizens cause to get drunk on more than excitement. In the castle the royal family found much disrepair and inconvenience. There were too, of course, those alterations by Charles II 'who brought the vices and fashions of France to disgrace his native soil', and which 'were in the worst possible taste, and the State Apartments themselves finished in the same wretched style'. Sir Jeffrey Wyatville, at a cost of nearly one million pounds, soon transformed the whole aspect of the upper ward. Ceilings by Verrio and carvings by Grinling Gibbons were scattered by the new wind, and the Round Tower was heightened to improve its proportions. The 'toy-fort' architecture of Wyatville has been severely criticized but as the indispensable *Official Guide* says, he contrived 'out of a primitive stronghold a well-ordered and comfortable residence for the Sovereign'. Since his time little has been needed except repairs and upkeep.

Queen Victoria during the first twenty years of her reign, before the purchase of Osborne and Balmoral, spent many months at Windsor each year as she strongly disliked 'the extreme weight and thickness' of the atmosphere in London. During her reign parts of the lower ward were restored but architecturally she is here best remembered for the Albert Memorial chapel which was reconstructed in memory of the Prince Consort.

Subsequent kings also favoured Windsor and here in December 1949 their Majesties King George VI and Queen Elizabeth held court, so reviving—to the joy of all Berkshire folk—a custom which had lapsed for several decades. It is no wonder that Windsor stands supreme in the affection and loyalties of the British Commonwealth. It is the royal symbol of a democracy in which every man's home is *his* castle, except perhaps the King's!

* * * * *

THE CASTLE TREASURES

It is surprising what touches most the imagination—of others!—at Windsor. An old villager of the Vale of White Horse used merely to watch the sentry-guard and to return home well content. The perfection of it—or the hope of the slightest imperfection—filled the small unsettled corner of his mind for the rest of the year and supplied the beginning and end of all his politer conversation. Others look for and find the sterner side of life, as was known to a guide to the Tower of London, who on being criticized for describing the narrow Norman slits as 'sluices for blood', retorted 'They've come for blood and I give them BLOOD!' Unfortunately for these, in 1949 the popular tales of Windsor were officially degraded to the level of historical facts and, to quote a milk-and-water example, Henry VIII no longer first glimpses Anne Boleyn from a window in Dean's Cloister. Again, to some folk architectural plainness is abhorrent while to others elaborate stonework in chapels is what it was to John Evelyn—'lame statues, lace and other cut-work and crinkle-crankle'. Yet Windsor can meet all tastes and the man who finds here nothing to delight his soul is 'fit only for alarms and stratagems'.

The greatest architectural attraction is St. George's Chapel. Its graceful exterior with rows of flying buttresses, capped with tall square pedestals and newly-added 'King's beasts', heralds a fine interior where lissome pillars and storied windows give a sense of light and space peculiar to the mature Perpendicular style. The elaborate stonework of the ceiling bosses cries out for closer examination but no more so than the angel cornice below the clerestory and the carvings on the moulding of the north aisle. The ceiling of the aisles and central compartment of the body of the building is true fan-vaulting, while that of the nave and choir is 'waggon-headed vaulting, broken by Welsh groins; that is to say, groins which cut into the main arch below the apex'.

The great west window has evoked praise and dismay. Of its seventy-five figures no less than fifty-one are original but the glass panels have been so much re-arranged since 1509 that most of the window's antiquarian interest has been lost. It is certain that some of the panels were collected about 1767 from other windows in the chapel.

The choir of St. George's has the same numerical abundance and burgeons with an overwhelming richness. There are three tiers of carved stalls, the upper being for Knights of the Garter, and deans and canons. At the back of each knight's stall is an enamelled shield of the arms of each knight who has sat there and above is the present holder's banner and helm with crest. The shields begin with Lord Basset, who died in 1390, and continue to form the finest heraldic collection in existence. The carving of the stalls, done mainly between 1478 and 1485, deals chiefly with gospel stories, the legend of St. George and the quips and fun of the craftsmen—the cat musician, the monkey medico and the countless troubles of harassed housewives.

To this skilful woodwork must be added the wooden oriel, with delicate traceried panels, built by Henry VIII in the upper chantry of Edward IV so that Catherine of Aragon might watch the Garter services. Either for its elation or dainty protrusion or extraordinary intricacy, it, as Pepys would say, makes one 'mighty merry'.

St. George's has in six hundred years acquired a wealth of memorials ranging in style from plain slabs to ironwork fantasies. For charm, surely the palm goes to the alabaster effigies of Lord Roos (in the Rutland Chapel) and Anne his wife, a comely creature whose mantle is held back by two dogs with collars of bells? For compulsion, one's choice is the flowing marble (in the Urswick Chapel) to Princess Charlotte, only daughter of George IV, who died in childbirth—but what the compulsion is it is hard to say; perhaps the incongruity of the setting or the ambient sadness of it all.

At least two of the chantries deserve long admiration. The one—to William, Lord Hastings, who was beheaded in 1483—has fifteenth-century paintings of the martyrdom of St. Stephen. The pictures are wonderfully intense and the details beautifully coloured. The other—to John Oxenbridge (*ob.* 1522)—is obviously a copy of Lord Hasting's, but hides more obsequiously behind an elaborate stone screen although its painted panels show equally vividly the passion of St. John the Baptist.

The ironwork of St. George's Chapel rivals in intricacy and exceeds in rarity its work in stone and wood. Scrolls bearing leaves and flowers, forged by Gilbertus in the thirteenth century, adorn the door of the ambulatory, while the wrought work of John Tresilian, the King's blacksmith in about 1482, turn the tomb of Edward IV into a wonderment. Its iron gates hang between two open traceried towers, all delicately wrought of superposed strips of metal, pierced and riveted with uncanny cunning. The same craftsman probably made the iron almsbox—a marvel of castellations and offertory slits, now standing near the entrance door.

After the warmth of St. George's, the smooth marble mosaics of the interior of the Albert Memorial Chapel strike chill and unromantic. Of the three splendid tombs which occupy the site once coveted by Henry VII, Wolsey and Henry VIII, the central one—to Prince Albert Victor, Duke of Clarence—has a quite peculiar fascination, a feeling which arises not so much from the beauty of the effigy as from the mysterious qualities of the bronze screen enclosing it. Its sculptor was Sir Alfred Gilbert, who carved the statue of Eros in Piccadilly Circus.

Of the artistic appeal of the furnishings of the State Apartments it would be folly to be wise—to some the furniture, to others the china, to others the robes and insignia. The imagination plays strange tricks as the tour proceeds. Who does not see Henry VIII lifting the visor of that broad suit of armour made for him at Greenwich in 1540, or feel the excitement of the two boys of James I when their armour first arrived, or catch the silence of Westminster Hall as the mounted King's Champion (now dominating the Guard Chamber) rode down to the dais and threw out his challenge from the high table?

Charles II's adornments now meet with widespread approval and the three surviving ceilings by Verrio and that wealth of carving by Grinling Gibbons and Thomas Phillips makes us long for those that are lost. In fact, the three rooms still in the 'wretched style' of France have, right or wrong, an irresistible appeal to our sense of culture.

The State Apartments, however, are probably best loved for the King's pictures. Here is a Rubens Room where 'The Holy Family' stands over the fireplace between two larger canvases: the one of Philip II prancing over a wonderful landscape; the other, by Van Dyck, of St. Martin dividing his cloak with a beggar. Equally famous is the self-portrait of Rubens in the nearby Picture Gallery.

The Queen's Closet provides a feast of Canaletto. Here Rome and Venice shine with the radiance of Mediterranean skies and 'The Horses of St. Mark' prance before the exquisite reflexions of the 'Islands of San Michele and Murano'.

The Picture Gallery pays full homage to Holbein, who is represented by portraits of Derick Born, Sir Henry Guildford, William Reskimer and above all by that of Thomas Howard, Duke of Norfolk. Close by are a notable picture by Jean Clouet, another by Durer, and several by Rembrandt, including a famous picture of his mother. There is too a charming portrait of Elizabeth before she became queen.

The Van Dyck room shows clearly what the great artist made of Charles I. The head of the King in three positions is almost too handsome judging from the homely faces of his children, three of whom occupy one group, and five in another. How much Van Dyck excelled in double-portraits may be seen in the pairings of Thomas Killigrew and Thomas Carew, and of George Villiers and his brother.

The pictures of the Waterloo Chamber have an artistic and historical unity, as here are depicted in thirty portraits by Sir Henry Lawrence, with the aid of a few portraits by other artists, all those who contributed most to the defeat of Napoleon. The result is an array of medals and majesty which if shown to Napoleon when young would have turned his feet into the path of peace. However, judged on the purely artistic response there seems no doubt that Pope Pius VII and the Archduke Charles were the allied towers of strength, with Cardinal Consalvi and the Duke of Wellington as aides-de-camp.

The King's collection of drawings, some of which are exhibited in the Grand Entrance Hall, contains many sketches by Leonardo da Vinci and eighty-seven drawings by Holbein. Many of the Holbein's were preparatory to portraits, some now lost; others probably were intended as studies in a medium in which no artist excelled him. Consequently Henry VIII's good fortune in Holbein, is, like the spiritual debt of Charles I to Van Dyck, for all concerned one of the happiest associations of Windsor.

* * * * *

WINDSOR, OLD AND NEW

Old Windsor and Clewer have an antiquity quite unknown to New Windsor which is a mere youngster only eight hundred years old, a cuckoo in the nest carved from the domains of its two venerable neighbours. At Clewer a church part Norman stands close beside the Thames; at Old Windsor the flat riverside plain had a royal residence long before William built the first palisades on the castle crag. T. E. Harwood has at last given Old Windsor its due. In Saxon times a royal palace stood near the river probably on the site of the present Priory Park, where water-transport and good hunting were available. In 1086 the 'vill' of Old Windsor had more than ninety-five dwellings or closes, and in Berkshire was exceeded in size only by Wallingford and Reading. Between 1095 and 1097 Rufus held at least three regular courts here while Henry I held one or two similar meetings, the last being probably in 1107 about which time work was begun on the new castle two miles to the north-west. In later years Old Windsor slipped into obscurity and much of it was absorbed into the Great Park, but it became fashionable again in the eighteenth century and has expanded rapidly in more recent years. It is now a medley of brick dwellings dispersed about an older nucleus of church and manor near the Thames. The church has Early-English work in the chancel and tower but most of the windows are square-headed, late-Decorated style. Each of the three trefoils of the north-eastern window of the nave contains a pair of purple birds or dragons with necks interlaced.

Old Windsor has a sprinkling of larger houses and of these the most unusual is the present Beaumont School which overlooks the Thames some way to the north. From July 1786 to March 1789, Warren Hastings lived here, and was succeeded by Henry Griffiths, a wealthy Anglo-Indian, who had the two longer sides of the house decorated with the 'sixth order of architecture'—to wit, a series of columns resembling beech trees which bifurcate above capitals representing head-dresses worn by the Knights of the Garter.

This unusual decoration does not seem to have spread even

to New Windsor, the home of its designer. This stripling town had sprung up after 1110 under the skirts of the new stone castle. It soon blossomed exceedingly, for Edward I made it a 'free borough' and it returned two members to Parliament in 1306. By 1686 it was growing rich and then the citizens began a new market-house which was completed by Sir Christopher Wren, who to assuage doubts as to its stability inserted extra pillars—and carefully left a space between them and the upper story. In 1707, the people of Windsor were so delighted at the accession of their old friend Queen Anne that they placed a statue to her on the Town Hall and later the younger Wren gave a companion figure of George of Denmark, her husband.

In 1811 the borough had 5,000 inhabitants of whom nearly half belonged in some way to the Court or the garrison. In 1838 the railway reached Slough and, although no station was allowed, Windsor felt the impact. By 1850, two railways reached the town itself but not before an abortive scheme had been proposed to remove Eton and most other buildings cluttering up the vicinity and to bring the railway underground to the castle. Subsequently, the rise of Slough accentuated Windsor's growth and today its population exceeds 20,000.

A considerable literature has been written on the attractions of Windsor borough. The Garter Inn, the haunt of Sir John Falstaff, was burnt down in 1681 but the house where Nell Gwynn lived for some years still survives. There are, too, many pleasant Georgian dwellings and a great many more Victorian residences, but of Windsor's 5,000 families we are interested only in one. The narrow cobbled Church Street, with its delightful mixture of seventeenth- and eighteenth-century façades, is a mere frame for Henry VIII's gateway and surely the streets leading up to the castle crag were intended to set off its soaring walls and rounded turrets?

But the aurora of royalty has its fascination and sheds on the nearby town its own ineffaceable traits. *Tel maître, tel valet* was never truer than of Windsor castle and Windsor borough. Witness Adelaide Terrace of the 1830's, or Queen's Terrace of 1850, or Osborne Road of about 1860! Or notice the ornamentation of telephone kiosks, or the Tudor-style waiting-room (now put to other uses) at the northern railway-station, or the shop where the King buys his groceries. Statues to sovereigns adorn the cross-roads and who else but Windsorians could have written beneath the statue of Queen Anne

> 'Arte tua, sculptor, non est imitabilis Anna;
> Annae vis similem, sculpere, sculpe deam?'

Moreover, objects less intangible than affections and influences pass through castle walls. The parish church boasts of a chancel decorated in mosaic by Salviati who worked on the Albert Memorial Chapel, of an oak screen by Gibbons which came from the royal chapel, and of a large picture of the Last Supper which in George III's day was the reredos of St. George's. And, it is not altogether impossible that the wardrobe of at least one citizen includes the insignia of a knight of the Garter, for in 1521 when Edward, Duke of Buckingham, was disgraced, his badges of office were 'spurned out' at the west door and kicked over the quadrangle into the castle ditch.

★ ★ ★ ★ ★

WINDSOR FOREST AND PARKS

In early times the Forest of Windsor was wild country in which the game was preserved for the King. It was as Alexander Pope says,

> 'A dreary desert and a gloomy waste
> To savage beasts and savage laws a prey.'

Under Henry I all Berkshire east of the Loddon was permanently afforested and then, or in later years, the Forest proper seems to have extended into all the adjacent counties. It had always been a favourite hunting-ground of English kings, and even our queens excelled themselves here, for Elizabeth rode with rare boldness, and Queen Anne, when too fat for horseback, drove like a Jehu over standing corn and amazing obstacles in a narrow single-seater one-horse chaise. The clayey eastern tracts of the Forest were the earliest tamed while the sterile sands and gravels farther west long remained the haunt of vagabonds, gamesters, robbers and thiefs of the ilk of the ruffianly murderers known as 'The Blacks' in the 1720's.

In the early-nineteenth century the forest covered 59,000 acres and included part or all of seventeen Berkshire parishes. Legally, it disappeared in September 1817 with a complex Inclosure Award and there was no doubt whatsoever of its disappearance when the Royal Horse Guards and Fifth Infantry Regiment drove the deer into the Great Park. Subsequently the old forest was fashioned into three landscapes; the Home Park, with its oak-shaded lawns and farms on London Clay; the Great Park, with its deciduous trees and farmland on the clay and a coniferous fringe on its sandy southern perimeter; and the wide amorphous territory between Ascot and Finchampstead where the sandy gravels now support a vast sea of conifers.

This great stretch of pines and heaths has retreated before the inroads of man. The oldest villages—Finchampstead and Easthampstead—have long lain in semi-cleared country. The former has a church, with some Norman work, which stands on a hill where ancient earthworks are still visible. The latter is visited chiefly for the tomb of Sir William Trumbull, the friend of Pope, and for the Burne-Jones' panels in its windows. Elsewhere hundreds of dwellings nibble into the forest, and near California, Bracknell, Ascot and

Sunningdale threaten to destroy it. Yet it still keeps many square miles of tree-growth broken only by forest rides and the dead-straight Devil's Highway, the line of a Roman road directed on Silchester. Where the soils become clayey, heath and pines give way to a profusion of oak, beech and bracken, but where gravels prevail brambles and bilberry form a desolate waste.

The whole woodland rises southward so as to dominate the Blackwater valley, and here is the fine viewpoint of Finchampstead Ridges, now National Trust property. From the east, the Ridges are reached through a mile-long avenue of Wellingtonia while from the west the route traverses clumps of rhododendrons. The Ridges abound in heather, bracken and birch, and although only 332 feet at their highest look down upon dark pine plantations, broken with smaller expanses of gorse, and with occasional patches of emerald-green sphagnum bogs. To the south, far below, is the Blackwater valley and beyond it Eversley where Charles Kingsley lived, and on the south-eastern horizon the outline of the Hog's Back.

At least two other spots will give much enjoyment. Caesar's Camp—an Iron Age earthwork with a double rampart now smothered in bilberry—surveys the Wokingham country and the chalk hills of Oxfordshire. Deeper in the forest is Lower Star Post where eleven drives converge, each with a coniferous countenance running straight and lonely to haphazard objectives. Here you can take the choice of Wellington or Sandhurst, of a lunatic asylum or Caesar's Camp, of the poverty-stricken Gravel Hill or the shallow waters of Rapley Lake, of crossing Camberley Golf Course or of making acquaintance with The Jolly Farmer at Bagshot Heath. Each is full of surprises—the dainty flowers of the conifers, the golden hue of larch in the fall, the grace of bracken and foxglove, the wealth of butterflies, and the scents and sounds of a myriad trees growing in unison.

The tracts of woodland nearest Bagshot have a martial tinge whereas those nearest Windsor are quite suburban. Here amid pines, birch and larch are houses ranging in type from Victorian fancies to the more utilitarian cottage of inter-war years.

The famous race-meeting was founded on the open heath by Queen Anne on August 11th, 1711, but it was much popularized fifty years later by the Duke of Cumberland. Today the affair is a feast of fashion and of elegant motor-cars, with the good-natured horses forming a diversion at specified moments.

Northward of Ascot all public motor-roads except that direct to Windsor skirt the wooden fence of the Great Park. The southern part of the park consists mainly of a deer enclosure, a large private farm and the Royal Lodge estate but elsewhere it is open to visitors, other than motorists, who find great opportunities within its circumference of fourteen miles.

Charles II began the improvement of the native woodland hereabouts by a warrant of May 12th, 1680, which provided for 'an avenue 240 feet broad in a direct line between the Castle of Windsor and the Great Park'. This, the Long Walk, was completed about 1684, Sir Christopher Wren supervising its final stages. By 1945 so many of the elms were decrepit or diseased that the whole avenue was felled and replanted with alternate chestnut and plane, the weaker species being eventually doomed to removal. Queen Anne in 1703 planted another straight drive of nearly three miles and the great Park then began to look truly civilized. As Pope wrote in 1704:

> 'Here hills and vales, the woodland and the plain,
> Here earth and water seem to strive again;
> Not chaos-like together crush'd and bruis'd,
> But, as the world, harmoniously confus'd:

Where order in variety we see,
And where, tho' all things differ, all agree.
Here waving groves a chequer'd scene display,
And part admit and part exclude the day.'

The next royal beautifier of the park was George II's son, William, Duke of Cumberland, who was the Ranger from 1746 to 1766. He appointed Thomas Sandby as Deputy Ranger, and this fine artist together with his famous brother Paul—both foundation members of the Royal Academy—showed exquisite skill in the arrangement of clumps of beech and oak and in the construction of serpentine stretches of water. The very popular Duke, that 'active and useful man, as John Wesley called him, supplied much of the money needed out of his own pocket with a view to employing demobilized soldiers. The Sandby brothers soon created Virginia Water out of a bog and cunningly made the many-armed lake look enormous.

George III began the extensive agricultural experiments at Norfolk and Flemish farms, for which the Great Park has been noted ever since. But it was left to the Prince Regent, later George IV, to add to the Duke of Cumberland's landscaping. He was responsible for many of the clumps of sweet chestnut, for some of the conifers near Virginia Water, and for the gorgeous rhododendron walk near Bishops Gate. He is, however, better known for the Fishing Temple and Roman ruins on the banks of Virginia Water. The ruins were brought from Leptis Magna in Tripoli in 1817 and re-erected here a few years later. He too was responsible for the great copper statue to George III, erected in 1831 on Snow Hill at the far end of the Long Walk. The gigantic figure broke the truck just before reaching its site and a forge had to be set up on the spot to mend one of the horse's legs. Twelve workmen ate their dinner inside the horse, before finally completing it and its naturalistic platform.

From the 'Copper Horse', the Castle takes on a new loveliness and, whatever may be said of Wyatville's work, there is no denying the grace of the outline as seen from the Park.

In recent years Windsor Great Park has acquired three notable additions. In 1949 a new village was completed near the Prince Consort's workshops. Built around a curving green, in attractive patterns and varied materials, the houses are models of comfort and the whole village sets a standard for estates elsewhere. The two other modern attractions are the Valley Gardens and Woodland Gardens which have arisen under the present Deputy Ranger. The former are laid out with a variety of rhododendrons, azaleas and camelias and a wealth of flowering plants that will entrance all who see them. Nearby, on the north bank of Virginia Water (also unfortunately in Surrey!), several small valleys running down to the lake have been similarly beautified to form the Woodland Gardens. Here rare rhododendrons and exotic azaleas and other flowering shrubs bloom with a tropical brilliance in May and June and keep a cheerful green all the year.

The Great Park is entered daily by hundreds of grateful visitors who even bathe in Virginia Water from The Wheatsheaf on the Staines–Bagshot road. The Home Park, however, is for the most part private, since it forms, as it were, the castle grounds and covers only 400 acres. Yet even here the northern part in the Thames loop between the station and Victoria Bridge is always public as it was exchanged by Queen Victoria for the privacy of roads near Frogmore. And Frogmore itself is open to the public on Whit-Monday afternoon.

The Home Park includes the termination of the Long Walk, the royal gardens, Shaw Farm and Home Farm (where the cowsheds have latticed windows), several lodges, and Frogmore House, a late-seventeenth-century dwelling which was transformed by James Wyatt in 1794 into a stately Grecian mansion with a Doric colonnade facing lawns and a winding lake. On an artificial promontory above this man-made lake is a circular, domed temple that was built in 1861 as the mausoleum of the Duchess of Kent, mother of Queen Victoria. Just to the north-west stands the mausoleum of the Queen herself and the Prince Consort. Designed in the form of a Greek cross, it is enduringly built of granite below with Portland stone above, and dome and roofs of Australian copper, now weathered into a bright green. Black marble steps lead up to a triple-arched porch which frames huge gun-metal doors backed by a grille. The interior is a symphony of great arches and canopied niches, of gilt bronze and mural paintings, of coloured marble and grey polished granite. A granite block, adorned at each corner by bronze angels, encloses the mortal remains of the Queen and the Prince Consort, and is surmounted by their effigies in marble. The mausoleum deeply touches the emotions. It epitomizes sorrow and beatifies grief as only the Victorians could. It is heartbroken loneliness set out in the coldest of stone.

Yet, the Home Park is full of happier memories for it was the scene of many acts of the *Merry Wives of Windsor*. Sir John Falstaff was enticed to 'Go about the fields with me through Frogmore; I will bring thee where Mistress Anne Page is, at a farm-house, a-feasting and thou shalt woo her'. Sir John was eventually carried with the stinking linen to Datchet Mead, then a meadow between the Home Park and the Thames, where the 'shelvy and shallow' shore of a 'muddy-ditch, close by the Thames side' saved him from becoming 'a mountain of a mummy'. Such a ditch, known as Hog Hole, was filled in during the reign of Queen Anne. The tale of Herne the Hunter 'sometime a keeper here in Windsor Forest' told by Mistress Page has led to much seeking after his oak. An old oak said to be Herne's was cut down in 1796—although George III denied it!—and no wise man would look farther. It was in the same 'field in Frogmore' that Evans sang immortally

> 'To shallow rivers, to whose falls
> Melodious birds sing madrigals.'

Here, too, Shakespeare expressed a wish especially dear to all who love the hills and vales of the Berkshire Thames:

> 'About, about;
> Search Windsor Castle, elves, within and out;
> Strew good luck, ouphes, on every room:
> That it may stand till the perpetual doom,
> In state as wholesome as in state 'tis fit,
> Worthy the owner, and the owner it.'

BIBLIOGRAPHY

PERIODICALS

Berks., Bucks. and Oxon. Archaeological Journal
Transactions Newbury District Field Club.

WORKS ON THE COUNTY

Victoria County History of Berkshire, ed. by P. H. Ditchfield and W. Page.
Vol. I (1906) Includes birds, &c.
II (1908) Includes schools.
III (1923) Includes Windsor and Reading.
IV (1924) Includes Abingdon and Newbury.
(1927) Index: General and Domesday Survey.
Berkshire (*Magna Britannia*), D. and S. Lysons, 1813.
Highways and Byways in Berkshire, J. E. Vincent, 1906.
Place-names of Berkshire, F. M. Stenton, 1911.
Berkshire (Cambridge County Geographies), H. W. Monckton, 1911.
Byways in Berkshire and the Cotswolds, P. H. Ditchfield, 1920.
Berkshire Regional Planning Survey, ed. W. R. Davidge, 1930.
Berkshire (Methuen's Little Guide)—F. G. Brabant (revised 1934).
Berkshire Book of Song, Rhyme and Steeple Chime, A. L. Humphreys, 1935.
Kelly's Directory of Berkshire, Kelly's, 1939.
The Oxford Region: A Pictorial Survey (Touches on some Berkshire towns), C. F. W. Gullick, 1939.

AGRICULTURE AND SOILS

General View of Agriculture of Berkshire, W. Mavor, 1809.
Agriculture in Berkshire, J. Orr, 1918.
Soils of Berkshire, N. H. Pizer, 1931.
Soil Survey of the Eastern . . . Vale of White Horse, F. F. Kay, 1934.
Berkshire (The Land of Britain, Part 78), J. Stephenson, 1936.

ARCHAEOLOGY

Archaeology of Berkshire, H. J. Peake, 1931.

ARCHITECTURE AND CHURCH DETAILS

Seats and Mansions of Berkshire, Beard & Co., *c.* 1870.
Monumental Brasses of Berkshire, H. T. Morley, 1924.

Church Plate of Berkshire, J. W. and M. I. Walker, 1927.
Murray's Berkshire Architectural Guide (quite indispensable), J. Betjeman and J. Piper, 1949.

FLORA AND FAUNA

Flora of Berkshire, G. C. Druce, 1897.
Victoria County History of Berkshire, Vol. I, 1906.
Birds of Berkshire and Buckinghamshire, A. Kennedy, 1868.

GEOLOGY AND WATER-SUPPLY

Water-supply of Berkshire, J. H. Blake, 1902.
Geology of Oxford, W. J. Arkell, 1947.
The following Memoirs and Maps of the Geological Survey:
Reading (Map. 1 inch to 1 mile 268), J. H. Blake, 1903.
Hungerford and Newbury (267), H. J. O. White, 1907.
Windsor (269), H. Dewey and C. E. Bromehead, 1915.
Geology of Thames Valley near Goring, A. Strahan, 1924.
Country around Oxford (special sheet), T. I. Pocock, 1926.

POETRY

Robert Bridges, Edward Thompson, 1944.
Studies in Prose and Verse (with essay on Bridges), Arthur Symons, 1904.
The Pleasures of Pope (introd. by P. Quennell), 1949.
New Light on Pope, Norman Ault, 1949.
Ballad of Reading Gaol (by C. 3. 3.), Oscar Wilde, 1898.
The Ballad of the White Horse, G. K. Chesterton, 1911.

A FEW VOLUMES DEALING WITH PARTS OF THE COUNTY

THE CORALLIAN RIDGE

Cumnor Place, A. D. Bartlett, 1850.
Fifty years of S. Peter's College, Radley, T. D. Raikes.
Great Faringdon Past and Present, R. J. Goodrich, 1928.

VALE OF WHITE HORSE AND LAMBOURN DOWNS

Tom Brown's School Days, Thomas Hughes, 1857.
Scouring of the White Horse (new ed. 1949), 1859.
White Horses, Morris Marples, 1949.
History of Lambourn Church, John Footmen, 1894.
Wantage Past and Present, A. Gibbons and E. C. Davey, 1901.
Martin Tupper, Derek Hudson, 1949.
East Hendred . . ., A. L. Humphreys, 1923.

History of Abingdon, James Townsend, 1910.
News of a Country Town, 1914.
Early History of Abbey of Abingdon, F. M. Stenton, 1913.
Anglo-Saxon Cemetery at Abingdon, E. T. Leeds and D. B. Harden, 1936.
Abingdon Abbey—published by Friends of Abingdon, 1948.

THE PANG VALLEY

Yattendon and its Church, Rev. J. E. Smith-Masters, 2 vols., 1929–1934.
Gray of Bradfield, S. Gray, 1931.
Bucklebury (a magnificent volume), A. L. Humphreys, 1932.
The Kenneth Grahame Book (an omnibus volume; Methuen's), 1932.
Kenneth Grahame: Life, Letters, P. R. Chalmers, 1933.

VALES OF KENNET AND LODDON

History of Newbury, Walter Money, 1887.
Swallowfield and its Owners, Lady C. Russell, 1901.
Story of Hungerford . . ., Rev. W. H. Summers (ed. H. J. Peake), 1926.
Kennet Country, F. S. Thacker, 1932.
Our Village, Mary Russell Mitford (Everyman ed.), 1936.
Mary Russell Mitford and her surroundings, C. Hill, 1920.
Mary Russell Mitford, Vera Watson, 1949.
Records of the Church and Parish of Wokingham, B. Long, 1937.

READING

'Reading; Its position and Growth', in *Trans. S. E. Union of Scientific Socs.*, E. W. Gilbert, 1934.
'The Industries of Reading . . .', in *Sociological Review*, W. F. Morris, 1926.
History . . . of Reading, Charles Coates, 1802.
History . . . of Reading, J. Man, 1816.
The Town of Reading during the Early Nineteenth Century, W. M. Childs, 1910.
Reading, Streets and Street lore, A. L. Humphreys, 1926.
Making a University, W. M. Childs, 1933.
Belford Regis, or Sketches of a Country Town, Mary Russell Mitford, 1835. (This long work is a series of imaginary sketches.)

THE THAMES VALLEY

Account of . . . Maidenhead, G. C. Gorham, 1838.
Chronicles of Wallingford Castle, J. H. Crofts, 1870.

Thames Valley Villages, Charles G. Harper (2 vols.), 1910.
The Thames Highway: General History, F. Thacker, 1914; Locks and Weirs, 1920.
History of Wallingford, E. Le Breton Walker, 1928.
History of Maidenhead, J. W. Walker, 1931.
River Thames, F. V. Morley, 1926.
Thames Valley from Cricklade to Staines (C.P.R.E.), 1929.
Guide to the Thames, J. H. and J. A. Salter (45th ed.), 1947.

THE WINDSOR COUNTRY

Annals of Windsor, R. R. Tighe and J. E. Davis (2 vols.), 1858.
Windsor Park and Forest, W. Menzies, 1904.
Windsor Castle (two magnificent volumes), Sir W. St. John Hope, 1913.
Windsor Old and New, T. E. Harwood, 1929.
The Romance of Windsor Castle, Hector Bolitho, 1946.
The Romance of St. George's, H. W. Blackburne and M. F. Bond, 1947.
Official Guide to Windsor Castle (pub. by the Lord Chamberlain), 1949.

A NOTE ON MAPS

The following 1 inch to 1 mile Ordnance Survey Maps deal with Berkshire.

Sheet 158 *Oxford and Newbury* (covers almost all Berkshire).
,, 159 *The Chilterns* (for Thames country between Reading and Windsor).
,, 169 *Aldershot* (for Forest area and Loddon valley).
,, 168 *Winchester* (for Inkpen and hill country south of Newbury and Hungerford).

The 2½ inches to 1 mile maps are excellent for local studies.

GARDENS

Many Berkshire gardens and estates are occasionally opened to the public in aid of the Queen's Institute of District Nursing. The list may be obtained (if 1*d*. stamped envelope enclosed) from Miss Raphael, County Organizer National Gardens Scheme, Kingston House, Kingston Bagpuize, Abingdon.

WINDSOR CASTLE

The precincts are open daily from 10 until sunset. Except on Fridays and when the Court is in residence. The State Apartments are shown from 11 until 3 o'clock in winter and 5 o'clock in summer. Friday is *never* a visiting day. For other details, it is best to obtain the *Official Guide* (price one shilling) and if in doubt to inquire of the Superintendent of the Castle, Windsor Castle. Frogmore Mausoleum is open to the public only on Whit-Monday, 11 to 4 o'clock.

YOUTH HOSTELS

Full information may—on sending stamped-addressed envelope—be obtained from Youth Hostel Association, 22, Gordon Square, London, W.C.1.

INDEX